MY OWN STORY

THE MACMILLAN COMPANY
NEW YORK · BOSTON · CHICAGO · DALLAS
ATLANTA · SAN FRANCISCO

MACMILLAN & CO., LIMITED
LONDON · BOMBAY · CALCUTTA
MELBOURNE

THE MACMILLAN CO. OF CANADA, LTD.
TORONTO

My Own Story

By
FREMONT OLDER
Editor
The San Francisco Call

New York
THE MACMILLAN COMPANY
1926

New Edition Revised and with new material,

Set up and electrotyped.
Published October, 1926.

FOREWORD

For some years I have wanted to write a frank story of my experiences as an editor of a newspaper in San Francisco. But I couldn't. I was not allowed to. Such a story, to have any value, implied a confession, and I was not free to confess.

This I learned when, in an address before the Council of Jewish Women in March, 1914, I approached as near to confession as I dared in a statement of a part of the truth. Guarded as that attempt was, a lifting of the curtain the least little bit, my temerity was bitterly resented. The owners of the paper I served wished to cling to the halo the *Bulletin* had set upon us all in the graft prosecution. No doubt entered our minds. We had performed a high public service. The dark forces of corruption had fought us savagely. We had encountered danger, financial reprisal, and the cold stare of former friends and acquaintances. We had bravely faced it all. Why shouldn't we enjoy the daily thrills, proudly wearing the decoration bestowed upon us by a righteous people? But time and reflection had cooled me until the poor little halo had lost its value. I wanted to strike deeper, to dig at the very roots of the causes of evil which I had become convinced jails would not cure.

I wanted to tell why I was making so hard a fight for the parole of Abraham Ruef. I couldn't. I realized that I was in an utterly false position, and I couldn't say so. Not alone the owners of the paper deterred me from frank expression, but I knew my old associates would resent any word of mine that would taint the glory they felt they had achieved in so hard a struggle. Also, the people who had been sympathetic with the prosecution had a fixed opinion that newspapers that made their kind of fight were incapable of doing wrong. If the end we were striving for was "noble," we also were "noble." Unconsciously, the old idea that the king can do no wrong has been handed down to us, and is made to apply to those who lead and win a popular fight. That is why I based my appeal for Ruef upon sentimental grounds. I could only urge that now, since Ruef had gone to the penitentiary, had been shaved, striped and numbered—one poor, helpless being crushed—why not be merciful? That was what I said in a big, flaring page editorial.

That wasn't the whole truth. Fighters, fanatically sure they are right, are likely to be without the restraint of conscience, and, in battling against evil, become careless of the methods employed, firmly believing that the end justifies the means. Thus we—the reformers and the lawyers, the courts and the law, the detectives and the officers of the court—had to do whatever it seemed necessary to do to win. I realized that we had to get down once or twice to Ruef's level in order to prove him guilty and get him into the penitentiary; where later I hated to see him, knowing what I knew, knowing what I propose now to tell. For with Ruef out of the penitentiary, and I myself out of my prison, I can tell this and all the other stories of my life as an editor.

It is difficult, it is almost impossible, for any one to talk about himself and his actions without unconsciously trying to excuse wrongdoing or to exaggerate his better motives. I may not be able entirely to avoid these errors, but I shall try to avoid them. I shall try to tell, without concealment or evasion, either for myself or others, the whole truth behind the most important chapters in San Francisco's life as a city.

While I call this my own story, it will be the story of many editors, many reformers, many righteous crusaders against graft and crime, vice and bad people. I shall start the story when I became editor of the *Bulletin* in 1895. Worldly success was my only ideal. I knew nothing of life as it is really lived. I saw only shadows of men, believing that the villain, as in the plays of that day and, unfortunately, of this day, was thrown from a bridge, and the hero in evening dress married the perfect lady in the last act. Passionately fighting in many battles what I conceived to be evil, I gradually discovered that it was the evil in me that brought defeat. It was evil fighting evil. This truth took possession of me. I wanted others to know it. I believed it could best be understood by asking bad people who knew they were bad, and good people who thought they were good, to tell their stories.

For some years I devoted much time and energy to this work. The stories took on the character of confessions, and were published as serials in the *Bulletin.* In this confessional have stood Abraham Ruef, political boss; Donald Lowrie, ex-prisoner; Jack Black, ex-prisoner; a Baptist clergyman; Alice Smith, a prostitute; a sure-thing gambler; a bunco man; a prominent physician, and Martin Kelly, political boss.

These confessions were all intended to help other

people to see themselves and to recognize themselves; but there were always some who thought I inspired the confessions, and wondered why I, too, did not confess. I received many letters asking me why I didn't tell my story as fully and frankly as I urged others to do. I invariably replied that I wanted to, but that I couldn't. But now that I am free to write it, I hope my readers will try to find themselves in my story and recognize that it is really the story of all of us.

INTRODUCTION

"My Own Story," by Fremont Older, is the story of a man's faith in humanity. It is an old-fashioned story out of an old-fashioned social background; a story harking back to the time when it was the cult of the hour to believe in the essential nobility of man and the wisdom of God. Upon that thesis the literature, the politics, the business and the moral creeds of the final decade of the last century and the first decade of the new century were built. Books were written about heroes—men who struggled against fate. Sometimes the struggle was against untoward circumstances; sometimes the struggle was an inner struggle, a spiritual struggle. And sometimes even the heroes failed and fell, but one knew that in their hearts a divine fire smoldered which quickened their motor power to struggle on. One knew in that old-fashioned day that in men was some nobility, some deep urge not of the flesh but of an inner spirit which made them fight on and on against odds, whether the odds were of their own flesh or the odds of an outer and perverse world.

Politics, too, in those first decades of this century, was a combat between right and might. The contest to give the average man a broader participation in government, a wider authority in the affairs of his state, was engineered by men who believed that man is decent, that he is better than his environment makes him. The widespread militant belief that government may wisely be used as an agency for human welfare—a belief which prevailed in the days of Bryan, Roosevelt and Wilson—came from that old-fashioned notion that men are good, that they want to be decent, that they would like to be honest, aspiring, neighborly and affectionately helpful; and more than this—that the force that moves the universe, which we call God, is wise.

Mr. Older's "My Own Story" was written under the psychology of those days when even great builders in business pretended to have some aspirations for the common good, though they often violated the common moral amenities to achieve their individual ends. All through his book one sees the author's deep, moving current of faith in the nobility of man, even the most unfortunate man, tethered to the hardest conditions of adversity!

Just now we are moving through another psychological environment. It is the reflex of our dreams come true. A quarter of a century ago we dreamed of a time when "the poor would be filled with good things." And for nearly half a century before that the dream of the world visioned justice as an equitable distribution of the products of our machines. The Populists, Bryan, Roosevelt and Wilson preached a physical millennium. It came. It came with a rush in a decade. Here it is, and we are for the moment stark mad worshippers of Baal—the god of machines. The common belief of humanity is that man is a mechanistic contrivance set in motion by some weird demon whose will has evolved Ruthless Law under which nothing means anything and everything is reached by footless chance. These are days of the knave's paradise. The god of sheer luck, the god of uncontrolled and unsignifying fatality, is the god of the greedy grabber from whose heart consciencc has been wiped out.

The psychology of to-day differs so vitally and fundamentally from the psychology of those days that we left ten years ago that it seems impossible that the same human beings are living in this changed world who lived and strove and loved and failed from Lincoln to Harding.

Of course in another decade or so we shall look back on the materialism of our present psychology aghast, as to-day we look back on the sentimentalism of yesterday with supercilious tolerance. But nevertheless sentiment is the mainspring of spiritual progress. To get a good look back into that old faith in human nature, that old belief in man's nobility which inspired us before the spiritual holocaust of the Great War, one should read Mr. Older's stirring story.

Mr. Older is a San Francisco newspaper man, the managing editor of a powerful daily paper. He rose up in the days following the Civil War, full of ideals, full of aspirations, full of that rampant love of man and belief in man's decency which was the motive of his time. As an editor he assailed the things he felt were wrong. He helped, wherever he could find it, to fan the divine spark in any human heart into a fire which in that halcyon time marked our kinship with God.

Of course humanity has learned something even in its disillusion. We know now that mass humanity for whom the leadership of another day strove so hard, is just common humanity; the oppressed no worse than their oppressors. Indeed, we have drained the dregs of disenchantment in the bitter knowledge that the oppressors of the poor are no worse than their victims! One of the major premises of the political philosophy of the generation that closed with Armageddon of 1912 was the belief that if one changed the environment of the poor the changed environment would produce a changed spirit; that more goods, chattels and impedimenta would mean a broader spiritual outlook, a kindlier attitude of life, a more generous neighborliness. We felt, in those first years of the century, that the first duty of man was to take the heel of the oppressor off the poor because, we reasoned, when the poor had justice they would return justice to society. Those whom we called the poor a generation ago now ride about in motor cars, listen to radios, live in bungalows, may have at their whim music, pictures and scores of the refinements of life. Their environment has changed; somewhat through the endeavors of the reformers, but largely because the mass production of goods has compelled manufacturers to distribute goods equitably with some show of justice. And what has happened? Those who were mean in a mean environment are mean in a better environment. Those who were kindly are kindly; those who were dull are dull. We know that the political power which was handed over to the masses after so much struggle and turmoil has not greatly benefited the masses except to make them responsible for their own mistakes and to lead them into a slow and tortuous course of education. And we can no longer be too sure that they are capable of political education. It is sadly evident now that political education does not come with prosperity to any social group. Political education is possible only when into a social group comes the understanding heart which adversity brings. Prosperity and adversity, adversity and prosperity in procession teach us the vanity of material things and still the fever of greed which to-day is making the new rich world put its trust in the princes of materialism. We know now that much was futile in that early vision which sought to give men freedom while they still carried servile hearts. But none the less we would do it all over again. Still there abides the faith that somehow, somewhere in the heart of man there is the spirit, there is the flame that consecrates him apart from the rest of his fellow travelers on this planet. And those who see or believe they see the flame must follow the light. Older is one of those who still follow the light, even the will-o'-the-wisp of hope for mankind's progress, in a day of disillusion.

He has written a strong story, a beautiful story, a faith-renewing story, to be published for a wicked and stiff-necked generation. Heaven knows we need it! We have gone mad with the belief that man is motor and that there is no wise governance under the stars.

Quite apart from the philosophy of this book it is a stirring story, dramatically told. Every page carries its own healing and triumphant tragedy. Every chapter in itself is a complete narrative and yet until one has read the whole story one does not get the impact of the truth that man is the son of God and in his heart, however lowly he may walk, or however high, for that matter, is a divine fire which makes us all akin and testifies to our divine paternity.

W. A. White.

CONTENTS

MY OWN STORY

MY OWN STORY

CHAPTER I

The Beginning Of The Story. The San Francisco *Bulletin* In 1895. The Process Of Rejuvenating A Newspaper. Sidelights On A Managing Editor's Job In The Nineties. First Essays In Public Reform.

I became managing editor of the *Bulletin* in January, 1895. Before that time I was a reporter on various San Francisco newspapers, and had acquired a local reputation as a young man with a "nose for news." In addition to this news instinct, I had a great deal of enthusiasm for my work, a persistent desire to run down each story until I had exhausted every possible angle. As an alert and enterprising young newspaper man, I had been chosen by R. A. Crothers to be city editor of the *Morning Call.*

At that time the *Call* and the *Bulletin* were both owned by the estate of Loring Pickering, the estate of a man named Simonton, and George K. Fitch, then living. There was a great deal of friction between Fitch and R. A. Crothers, who represented the Pickering estate. Shortly after I went on the *Call* as city editor, Fitch brought proceedings in the Federal Court to have both papers sold at auction, as a means of settling the difficulties.

I had been on the *Call* less than a year when the sale occurred. The *Call* was sold to Charles M. Shortridge for $361,000. A few days later R. A. Crothers bought the *Bulletin* for $35,500.

The paper was at very low ebb, having a circulation of perhaps nine thousand, and advertising insufficient to meet expenses. I think it was losing about $3,000 a month. But Loring Pickering, before his death, had expressed a wish that his widow should hold the *Bulletin* for their son, Loring, then about seven years old. The father's idea was that the *Call* in competition with the *Examiner* would be a difficult property to handle successfully, and he felt that the *Bulletin* could be developed into a paying paper.

Before Loring Pickering died he gave his brother-in-law, Crothers, a very small interest in the *Call*—a twelfth of his one-third interest—which, when the paper was sold, realized a few thousand dollars. This sum, added to Crothers' savings as a lawyer in Canada, was sufficient to enable him to pay one-half of the *Bulletin's* purchase price. The other half was paid by his sister, Mrs. Pickering, who held her share in trust for her son, Loring. The purchase was made in Crothers' name and he became the ostensible owner of the paper.

After the sale he found himself in possession of a property which was losing a large sum monthly. It was necessary to turn this deficit into a profit without loss of time, in order to save the capital invested. Crothers offered me the managing editorship, which I accepted.

As I remember, at that time I had no ideals whatever about life, and no enthusiasm beyond newspaper success. I was proud of my newspaper talent; that is, the ability to get hold of news and special features that would interest the public and increase circulation.

Neither Crothers nor myself had any other view in the beginning than to make the paper succeed financially.

It had to be done quickly, too, because Crothers had no money and the Pickering estate consisted largely of real estate, so that we could get no help from that source.

The office of the *Bulletin* was on Clay street, between Sansome and Montgomery, in a building that was almost on the verge of tumbling down. It had been there for more than thirty years. We had only one old press, and that was wholly inadequate for handling a circulation of any size. Our type was set by hand.

It was almost impossible to make improvements, because we had no money. We were running so close on revenue that Crothers was constantly worried for fear we should encounter losses that would destroy our hopes of success.

I worked desperately hard in the beginning. I had a staff of only five men besides myself, and I acted as managing editor, city editor, book reviewer, dramatic critic and exchange editor, thus doing the work of several men. I lived, breathed, ate, slept and dreamed nothing but the paper. My absorbing thought was the task of making it go.

I was utterly ruthless in my ambition. My one desire was to stimulate the circulation, to develop stories that would catch the attention of readers. The character of the stories did not matter. They might make people suffer, might wound or utterly ruin some one. That made no difference to me; it was not even in my mind. I cared only for results, for success to the paper and to myself.

It was not long before the paper began to respond to the strong pressure I put upon it. We had only two competitors in the evening field, the *Post* and the *Report*, and I had the satisfaction of seeing our circulation slowly creep upward, until we had passed the *Post* and were becoming a serious rival of the *Report*.

Meanwhile, I urged that we move away from the old quarters, get a new press and install linotype machines. Crothers and I decided that five linotypes would do the work of twenty-six compositors, and that the saving made would perhaps help to keep us on the right side of the financial line. Five months after we took charge of the *Bulletin* we moved to Bush street above Kearny and installed the five linotypes and a new press, which was only partly paid for.

In my ceaseless efforts to make the paper attractive and do unusual things, I undertook art work on chalk plates, which was a novelty at the time. A plate of chalk was used, the artist making his drawing upon it with a steel tool. With Will Sparks as artist, we produced some very good effects. This was before we were able to install a photo-engraving plant.

I was working under heavy pressure, trying to overlook nothing that would help the paper. I watched the circulation, the street sales, the art work; I wrote several departments of the paper myself, and I was tireless in my search for news scoops. One of my typical stories, through which ran the same overwrought enthusiasm that characterized the later and more important ones, was the fight against the pastor of the First Congregational Church, Reverend C. O. Brown.

Brown had been accused of having improper relations with a young woman, a member of his church, and we made quite a scandal about it. The preacher, of course, denied the story, but I was able to stir up enough discord in his church to cause some of the members to ask for an investigation. The investigation resulted in a trial of Brown by a jury of preachers from other churches.

I made desperate efforts to get condemning evidence, and succeeded to some extent, running big stories with flaring headlines daily during the trial. During this fight, Brown, in order to frighten me into abandoning the fight against him, caused to be written to me a forged letter signed by John J. Valentine, the manager of the Wells Fargo Express Company and a prominent member of his church. The letter asked me to drop the matter, saying that Brown was a very fine man, and undoubtedly innocent and persecuted.

As soon as I received the letter I immediately rushed down to Valentine with it. He said that it was a forgery, that he had never written it. This made what I considered a great story. I published a facsimile of the letter, with a heading across the page, "Brown, the Penman," and a handwriting expert's testimony added.

Brown was acquitted by the friendly jury of preachers. He resigned and went East, and nothing was heard of him for more than a year. Then he reappeared in San Francisco, hired a hall, and in a public speech admitted his guilt. No one seemed to know why he made the confession.

By this time, however, my work as an editor was beginning to involve me in large questions. I came into direct contact with national politics, and my first experiences were illuminating.

CHAPTER II

A Venture Into Politics. A Brilliant Idea and What Came Of It. Brotherly Love In Public Life. An Interview With McKinley. Mark Hanna "A Baby In Politics." My First Political Mission A Failure.

It was in 1895, during my first year as managing editor of the *Bulletin*, that McKinley opened his campaign for the Presidency. In our harassing need for money to keep the paper going, when we were searching in every possible direction for means of increasing our slender revenues, Crothers insisted that some money ought to be forthcoming from the McKinley forces.

In my endeavor to make this money as legitimately as possible, I hit upon the idea of getting out a special McKinley edition. One hundred thousand extra copies, boosting McKinley, distributed throughout California, should be worth $5,000 to the Republican committee. Crothers had always been a Republican; so far as I had any political convictions they were in harmony with those of the Republican party. The special edition would not only be in line with the *Bulletin's* editorial policy, but with its business needs. I eased my conscience with the thought that we were only asking the normal price, five cents a copy.

Crothers liked the idea and I went to Chicago, where I saw Mark Hanna and urged the plan. He referred the matter to Judge Waymire, who was in charge of the campaign on the Pacific Coast. On my return to San Francisco, Waymire approved it.

Before we could print the edition, however, a tremendous protest went up from other San Francisco papers, led by the *Argonaut*. They were getting no money; they violently opposed our getting any. Senator Proctor of Vermont came West, representing the National Republican Committee, and there was a vigorous controversy which ended in our being paid $2,500, half the sum agreed upon. The other $2,500 was repudiated. But Judge Waymire said he would personally assume the debt. He failed soon after, leaving the balance unpaid.

Dropping into my office one day during the course of these negotiations, Judge Waymire showed me a letter received by him from Mark Hanna, in which the great Republican boss promised Waymire an appointment in McKinley's Cabinet as Secretary of the Interior.

I had a brilliant idea. If the *Bulletin* were to come out editorially urging Waymire's appointment, we would gain immensely in prestige if later he was appointed. It would then appear that we had waged a successful political fight for Waymire. And we risked nothing, because the appointment had already been promised him, behind the scenes.

I set to work on the editorial, was engaged in finishing it, when Senator Perkins came in to bid me good-bye before leaving for the East. I showed him the editorial.

"Fine!" he said. "I love Judge Waymire. He's the dearest friend I have in the world. There's nothing I wouldn't do for him. I'm just on my way East now; I'll stop off at Canton, if you like, see McKinley, and urge him personally to appoint the judge." He was most enthusiastic.

I told him he need not do that. I was gratified to know that he would be strong for Waymire.

Much encouraged by his enthusiasm, I ran the editorial, while Perkins went on to Washington. Immediately upon his arrival there the Associated Press brought back an interview with the Senator in which he declared himself for Horace Davis for the Cabinet position. Davis had been president of the University of California and was a commanding political figure.

This jarred me considerably. I was not yet accustomed to the ways of politics, and I was astounded by Perkins' action. Moreover, the *Bulletin* was committed to Waymire's cause, and I began to be troubled with fears that he would lose the appointment. Rumors came to me that Judge McKenna, then occupying the Federal Bench in San Francisco, was also a candidate for the position and had good hopes of getting it.

I had become very well acquainted with Waymire, and when he learned that Judge McKenna was likely to be appointed to the Cabinet instead of himself, he said that, of course, the Southern Pacific Railroad was the controlling influence.

Waymire told me that when McKenna was first appointed to the Federal Bench he also had been a candidate for the same position. Knowing that Leland Stanford, at that time a United States Senator, would say the ultimate word in the appointment, Waymire called on Stanford and asked him if he would consider him for the place.

"Senator Stanford was very frank," Waymire said. "He told me that he liked me very much indeed, admired me greatly. He also liked and admired McKenna equally with me. The Senator said, 'If all things were equal, I would have difficulty in deciding which one should have this position of Federal judge. But while I like you both, I can't overlook the fact that your mind leans more to the protesting people, the people who have made it difficult for our corporations to be successful here in California.

" 'You tend more to the side of the agitating public than McKenna does,' Stanford said. 'McKenna is equally honest, but his mind naturally tends the other way. He honestly believes that corporate interests should be protected and that the sacred rights of property should be carefully safeguarded. Therefore, between the two, both of you being equally honest, I feel I must decide in favor of McKenna.'

"So," Waymire concluded, "if McKenna is appointed Secretary of the Interior, no doubt it will be for the same reason, because he is friendly to the Southern Pacific organization."

Apart from my personal feeling toward Judge Waymire, I might have wished myself well out of the situation; for the *Bulletin* was in no condition to make a losing political fight. However, we were definitely committed to Waymire's candidacy; friendship and self-interest pulled together. I determined to do my utmost to force his appointment.

Judge Waymire thought McKinley would hesitate to appoint McKenna to a Cabinet position which was connected with the schools, because of his religion. He was a Roman Catholic. McKinley was a devout Methodist, and Waymire sought a prominent local Methodist clergyman and asked him if he would be willing to help. The clergyman at once called on Bishop Newman of the Methodist Church, who was at that time in San Francisco. He was keen to assist and wrote a stinging letter to McKinley, rebuking him for having even entertained the idea of McKenna for such an important position. He even told him that he should not listen to either Archbishop Ireland or C. P. Huntington, both of whom, the bishop said, had called on him in McKenna's behalf.

With Bishcp Newman's letter in hand I telegraphed McKinley, asking for an interview; and, having received a cordial telegram in response, indicating the time at which he would see me, I went East to confer with him in person regarding Waymire's appointment as Secretary of the Interior.

On my arrival at Canton I proceeded to McKinley's home, where he received me in his living room. I had traveled through ice and snow across the continent for this meeting with the future President, and was nervous and keyed up with excitement.

McKinley's face lighted up when I mentioned Judge Waymire.

"Oh, yes, the dear judge!" he said. "How is he? I love Judge Waymire."

I seemed to hear an ominous warning in these words. I had heard them before. Senator Perkins had used them. They had cheered me then, because I believed them, but now I was doubtful.

"Waymire is one of my dearest friends," said McKinley. "How is he getting along? Tell me all about him!"

I approached the question of the appointment to the Cabinet, and McKinley, saying that we could talk better upstairs, led me up to his bedroom and closed the door.

I produced the scorching letter from Bishop Newman, protesting against the appointment of McKenna.

"The dear old bishop!" said McKinley. He read the letter without a change of expression, bland and smiling. "Now he raises here what seems to me a very trivial point," he said. "Of course, I'm a deacon in my church —I love the dear old bishop—but he says here that I should not appoint McKenna because he is a Catholic. Would that make any difference to you, Mr. Older?"

"Not any at all," I said. "But that's because I have no feeling about any church. They all mean the same to me. Of course, I believe in the doctrines of Christ. I consider His message the most beautiful ever given the world. But I have no feeling about sects. However, if I had——"

"Now, the bishop says here that Archbishop Ireland has been to see me—and that Huntington has been to see me. That is true. I have talked with them both. But they have had no influence with me, no influence at all. You know, Mr. Older, a Cabinet is a family matter—one might call the Cabinet a large, harmonious family. In picking a Cabinet you choose men whose work you know—now wouldn't you, Mr. Older?"

"You have McKenna in mind, no doubt," I said.

"Yes," he replied. "When I was chairman of the Ways and Means Committee, McKenna, then in Congress, was on the committee with me. Working with him I came to know him well. If you were going to employ a writer on the *Bulletin,* Mr. Older, wouldn't you pick a man whose work you knew?"

"Probably not," I said, "if there were two men whose work was equally good, and this man had tried to prevent me from holding the position that made it possible for me to give the job."

"What do you mean?"

"McKenna was against you for the nomination," I said. "He openly urged his political friends in California to support Tom Reed."

For just an instant this seemed to disconcert McKinley, but he rallied quickly and said: "No doubt Reed at some time has done McKenna a favor. That should not count against him."

Then I spoke about Waymire and his ability and talents. McKinley agreed to all I said, and repeated that he loved Waymire. He also said that he had not fully decided to give McKenna the place. McKenna would not take it unless the President would promise to put him on the Supreme Bench later. McKenna would not give up a $6,000 a year life job on the Federal Bench for a four-year job at $8,000 a year as Secretary of the Interior. He would not take the Cabinet position unless McKinley would promise him a life job later, which McKinley told me he hesitated to do. However, he would make no promises for Waymire.

McKinley later appointed McKenna Attorney-General, thus avoiding offense to his Methodist friends who didn't want a Roman Catholic in the Department of the Interior, which has something to do with the schools. He subsequently elevated him to the Supreme Bench.

I wired Waymire the result of my interview. He advised me to see Mark Hanna. I went on to Cleveland and called on Hanna. I told him what McKinley had said about McKenna and Waymire.

"Why do you come to me?" he inquired.

"Because," I replied, "you wrote a letter to Waymire before the election saying he would get a Cabinet position, and knowing that you are the politician of the firm, I thought you would decide it."

"So I am the politician of the firm, am I?"

"You are so regarded all over America."

Hanna rose from his chair and came over close to me and said: "Mr. Older, I am a baby in politics compared with our good friend in Canton. He has already decided upon McKenna. If you had understood the language of politics you would have saved yourself this trip. Give my love to Waymire and tell him I am sorry, but it can't be helped."

I returned to California.

CHAPTER III

Planning The Mayoralty Campaign. The Southern Pacific's Powerful Grip On The Golden State. Favors In Exchange For Friendliness. John D. Phelan The *Bulletin's* Choice For Mayor Of San Francisco.

My first plunge into politics had ended disastrously for my hopes; but the local election of 1896 brought me other and more encouraging experiences. It was an important election from my point of view, because from the beginning of the campaign I felt that it would help the *Bulletin* tremendously if I could win a political victory in which a mayor would be elected.

The entire State of California was, at that time, politically controlled by the Southern Pacific Railroad. Not only did this powerful organization dominate the legislature, the courts, the municipal governments, the county governments, which included coroners, sheriffs, boards of supervisors—in fact, all state, county and city officials—but it also had as complete control of the newspapers of the state as was possible, and through them it controlled public opinion.

There was hardly an editor who dared criticize to any extent the railroad domination. Country editors, many of them, were satisfied with an annual pass for the editor and his wife. Some of the more important ones expected and got money for advertisements. Some of the metropolitan papers fared better, and among these was the *Bulletin*.

This use of money and favors was quite open. Few criticized it. At every session of the legislature, in addition to the secret money that was distributed, blue tickets were openly handed about. On Friday or Saturday, when the legislature adjourned until Monday, railroad lobbyists passed these blue tickets around among all the members and all the newspaper men and all the attachés of both houses. These tickets entitled the holder to a free passage to San Francisco and return.

Even Supreme Court judges traveled on annual passes and made no secret of it, and most influential people traveled to and from the East without any cost. I have been on an overland train when there were only three or four people on the entire train that had tickets they had paid for. In the Pullman I was in none had even paid for their berths. One man, a cigar drummer, had a pass for meals at eating stations.

I remember one session of the legislature in the early nineties, when a certain Assemblyman from San Francisco told me that his leading constituents had advised him to get all he could up there. He was quite open in taking money, discussing boodle in committee meetings, and rising to make inquiries as to whether or not there was any money coming up from Fourth and Townsend. The railroad building was located there at that time.

The Southern Pacific Railroad was openly the Republican party. When there was a Republican Governor in Sacramento, the office of the Governor was in the office of William F. Herrin, attorney for the Southern Pacific, in San Francisco. If a group of men wanted anything from the Governor, they did not go to see the Governor; they went to see Herrin. He would put it through for any one whom he liked; that is, for any one who would be useful to him.

The Southern Pacific dominated not only the Republican party, but also, to a large extent, the Democratic organization. Virtually every one of influence supported the railroad, because it was in control—and thus the sole dispenser of political favors.

A man who wanted anything that political power could give went to Bill Higgins, the Republican boss, who responded to William F. Herrin; or to Sam Rainey, the Democratic boss, who also responded to Herrin; or he went to Sacramento to the railroad lobbyists, who were henchmen for Herrin. The rest of the people did not count.

So far as I know, this control of Herrin's was absolute in California except in San Francisco. Here there was a small rebellious group of Democrats, headed at that time by Gavin McNab, a young and ambitious Scotchman, a clerk in the Occidental Hotel, who was studying law in his spare time. He had a great deal of energy and dash and spirit, and was strong against crooked politics. While he was a hotel clerk, with no money except his salary, he already had a small but growing influence, and I took him into account in considering my political plans.

No fight of any consequence had, however, up to that time been made against the conditions I have outlined. Corporations were regarded as legitimate business enterprises, bound up with the welfare of the community. People believed that corporations must have special privileges in order to succeed, and that they must succeed if the community was to be prosperous.

This was the state of affairs when I began casting about

for a suitable candidate for Mayor of San Francisco; a candidate who could be depended upon to make a conspicuous and winning fight, and to reflect credit upon the *Bulletin*. I had sense enough to know that there would be nothing brilliantly conspicuous in getting behind Herrin, the railroad boss, and helping him to put his mayor in. What I wanted was a fight against the machine, but it must be a winning fight.

Earnestly considering the situation, I thought of James D. Phelan. He was a multimillionaire. His wealth gave him leisure and made him independent of money considerations; he was of Irish stock and a Catholic. I thought that if the *Bulletin,* which had been a very solemn, conservative paper under the old management, were to take up and carry to a successful conclusion a political fight for a young, clean and popular rich man, its standing with the public and its interests in general would be tremendously advanced.

Nevertheless, there were many difficult angles to be taken into consideration. Politically, the *Bulletin* had always been Republican. R. A. Crothers had very strong Republican convictions; and, as I have said, so far as I had any political opinions at the time, they were also Republican.

In addition to this, the *Bulletin* was on the payroll of the Southern Pacific Railroad for $125 a month. This was paid not for any definite service, but merely for "friendliness." Being always close to the line of profit and loss, Crothers felt the paper could not afford to forfeit this income. Yet I urged the advantage to our circulation which would come from a startling political fight in which we would be victorious. In order to make such a fight it was necessary to back a candidate outside the Southern Pacific ring.

It was a delicate situation. However, I reasoned that I could count upon a certain indifference to purely local affairs on Herrin's part, and I believed that if I could find the right candidate I could make the fight successfully.

At this time I had never met Phelan, but I knew he took much interest in civic affairs. He had been a director of the World's Fair at Chicago; he had made some contributions of works of art to San Francisco; he was a good public speaker, and a very rich man. I felt that his wealth would prevent him from following the corrupt practices that had always been common in San Francisco, would enable him to make a fight against the Republican machine, and would leave him free, if elected, to give the city an independent government.

With these things in mind, I called upon Phelan at his office and introduced myself. I told him that my name was Older, that I was managing editor of the *Bulletin,* and that I thought he ought to run for mayor.

He looked at me sharply and said, "Why, what put that in your head? What gave you that idea?"

I said that I understood that he was a man of leisure with an interest in civic affairs, that he had ability, that he would give the city a good, clean government. I made a strong plea to him to run for the nomination. I told him that I knew it would be very difficult to persuade the owner of the *Bulletin,* Crothers, to permit the paper to support any one not a Republican, but I thought it could be accomplished if he would ask a friend of his who had great influence with Crothers to talk with him.

Phelan was noncommittal, but I saw that I had made an impression on his mind.

A few days later Phelan's friend called at the *Bulletin* office and talked with Crothers.

After he had come and gone I approached Crothers myself and urged that the paper support Phelan. At first he demurred at leaving the Republican party and supporting a Democrat, but I insisted that the election was only local. We could still be Republican nationally and in state affairs; we could go so far as to be Democratic locally and it would not be held against us. I argued strongly that a successful city campaign would largely increase our circulation and aid in putting the paper on its feet. I minimized the possibility of resentment on the part of the railroad.

Finally he reluctantly consented, and on the following day I published the first article suggesting Phelan for mayor. His being a millionaire, of course, made him popular at once. All the politicians felt it would be a fat campaign and there was much enthusiasm for him.

This feeling permeated Crothers' mind also. He felt that our scant finances would be somewhat improved by our support of Phelan. I feared this thought in Crothers' mind because of the public-spirited attitude I had taken with Phelan. I felt ashamed that Phelan should ever know that we would take money from political candidates, or from any source other than the so-called legitimate sources.

I hoped to convince Charley Fay, Phelan's manager, to accept the same plan in Phelan's fight that I had used in the McKinley campaign; that is, to get Phelan to buy a certain number of extra *Bulletin* editions. I suggested the idea to Fay that if I could be allowed several 10,000 editions of the *Bulletin* in addition to our regular circulation, for each of which we would charge $500, I thought I could hold the paper in line throughout the campaign.

Fay agreed to the plan, and it was understood that a certain number of Saturday nights would be selected for these extra Phelan editions of the *Bulletin.* I promised him that we would have our regular carriers distribute them and the cost to Phelan would only be five cents each, our regular retail price on the streets.

This arrangement seemed to me quite legitimate. I trusted that it might meet Crothers' hope that some money would flow in from Phelan. As the campaign progressed this sum did not entirely satisfy him. It was not the custom at that time to give something for nothing in political affairs, and he felt that the *Bulletin's* support was worth more than an occasional $500.

His pressure upon me for more money finally became so strong that I called on Charley Fay and told him that I would have to get out another extra edition besides the number agreed upon between us. Otherwise I was afraid that Crothers could not be restrained from sending some one from the *Bulletin* office to make a demand upon Phelan personally. Fay agreed to allow me to get out the extra edition, and by this means I prevented Phelan from being directly importuned for money. We got through the campaign with no other contributions from Phelan than the payments for these editions.

For years a great many people believed that Phelan had subsidized the *Bulletin.* Many thought he owned it. These amounts, however, were the only sums paid the

Bulletin by Phelan throughout that campaign. He was elected, and, as I had hoped, the fight gave us some standing in the community and materially increased our circulation. Many of our readers believed that we were a free newspaper; as free, that is, as any newspaper could be.

The campaign had not been so seriously opposed by the Southern Pacific as to disturb our place on its payroll, and up to this time nothing had appeared in the paper to indicate that the railroad was controlling us. I felt that I had handled a difficult situation with a great deal of ability and finesse.

But a situation was approaching that was to prove far more difficult to meet.

CHAPTER IV

Foreshadowings Of The Labor Problem. Objectives Of The Phelan Administration. The Charter Fight; How It Increased My Difficulties. The Teamsters' Strike. "Business Is Business." Eugene E. Schmitz For Mayor. A Three-Cornered Campaign. The *Bulletin* Keen For Tribute. Ruef Comes Into The Picture.

San Francisco was, of course, locally controlled by the corporations, which, while they worked in harmony with the Southern Pacific machine, had their own separate organizations in the city. The labor unions were fairly strong and were gaining in strength; but as yet they had made no determined effort to dispute the power of the corporations.

So far as I had any attitude toward labor unions at that time I was against them, because they annoyed the paper with demands, and, in my narrow view, made our success very difficult. They insisted upon more money than I thought we could possibly afford to pay.

When we put in linotypes the work seemed so simple and easy that Crothers regretted that we were compelled to pay men $4 a day.

"It's a girl's work," he said. "We could get women to sit there and tap those keys for $1.50 a day. That would be ample. Think of those creatures getting $4 a day for that."

I had been a printer in my younger days and had sufficient trade sympathy with the men to resist this suggestion. In the main, however, I held at this time the employer's views on union labor.

Phelan's administration gave me my first social sense.

It was not a conspicuously revolutionary administration, but it was conventionally honest, and Phelan felt a genuine desire to serve the people and safeguard their interests.

A Board of Supervisors had been elected with him, the members of which responded to him and were incorruptible in the sense of not taking bribes, as nearly all boards prior to this time had done. The administration was based on economy, combined with constructive work for the city—improving the streets and public buildings, laying out parks and playgrounds, and putting up fountains. Phelan had a deep love for San Francisco, and dreamed of making it a clean, beautiful city, worthy of its magnificent natural advantages, its hills and its great bay.

Nearly every step brought him into conflict with the old régime. For example, the gas company charged the city excessive rates for lighting the streets; and as the more lights there were the more money flowed in, it had put in as many gas lamps as it could possibly plant. In one stroke, Phelan eliminated six hundred of them, cutting the gas company's revenue in proportion. For this public-spirited act he was ostracized by the fashionable Pacific Union Club, which would not tolerate as a member a man who had torn up six hundred gas lamps to save money for the people at the expense of the gas company.

However, Phelan continued to watch the people's interests, building better streets, better pavements, striking at graft, closely scanning city contracts and keeping the railroad's hands out of the Board of Supervisors as much as possible.

I began greatly to admire his attitude. Up to this time I had concealed from him and his followers the fact that the *Bulletin* was not free, that we were on the payroll not only of the railroad, but of the gas company and the water company. I wanted Phelan to think that I was an honest newspaper man. Of course, I dimly realized that I was not, because part of my salary came from these corporations. However, I had intended to try to eliminate these subsidies if I were able to do so. Meantime, my earnest effort was to keep them from coming to Phelan's knowledge.

Then Phelan began his fight for a new city charter. He had found that the old charter was inadequate for the reforms he contemplated, and he proposed the election of a Board of Freeholders who would draft a new one. His administration was popular with the people, and their support was behind the plan for a new charter.

The railroad immediately came into the fight with a nominated board of freeholders, known as the Martin Kelly board, but in reality controlled by Herrin. The *Bulletin* supported the board nominated by Phelan and it was elected.

The Phelan board drafted the charter, and then came its election. By this time the railroad was really fighting in earnest. The new charter, as drafted, spread political power too much for the Southern Pacific's purposes. It provided for many commissions—the police commission, election commission and others—which would be difficult to control.

The fight had barely been started when Crothers came to me and said that W. H. Mills, who handled the newspapers of California for the railroad company, had agreed to raise the *Bulletin's* pay from $125 to $250 a month if we would make only a weak support of the new charter.

I saw that it would be almost impossible for me to maintain my reputation for honesty with Phelan and his followers and at the same time not offend Mills to the point of his withdrawing his subsidy.

I went ahead desperately, doing my best to satisfy both sides, and daily feeling more self-contempt. Phelan, expecting me to be loyal to the charter, forced me by his very expectation to run several editorials supporting it. I was checked by Crothers, who told me that Mills had complained.

Then I killed several articles favoring the charter that had been prepared by the editorial writer. For several days we were silent.

This brought Charley Fay up to the office. He said:

"What the hell's the matter with the *Bulletin?*"

That frightened me. I went to the editorial writer and told him to write a strong editorial supporting the charter. He looked at me strangely and said:

"What's the use? It will be killed."

"No," I replied. "It will not be killed. This one won't. You write it and I'll publish it to-morrow."

The next day I published it in the *Bulletin* without consulting the owner. The campaign was so nearly over that I was able to finish it without any further complaint from Mills. We won the charter fight, and the paper and I came out of it clean, so far as Phelan's knowledge went.

Phelan's first administration was a huge success. The people greatly appreciated the little he had been able to

do for them, and he became very popular. He was elected a second time under the new charter, to administer it, and then he was elected a third time. It was during these years that Henry T. Gage was picked by Herrin as Republican candidate for Governor.

By this time the *Bulletin* was prospering. The circulation had gone over twenty thousand; we had cut out the losses and were showing a profit every month. So when it came to a question of supporting Gage, although the *Bulletin* was a Republican paper and Gage was the nominee of the Republican party, Crothers felt that the influence of the *Bulletin* was worth more than the Southern Pacific had been paying.

He insisted that I go to Mills and demand $25,000 from the railroad for supporting Gage. I told him that this was ridiculous, that they wouldn't consider such a sum for a minute. He insisted that he would have $25,000 or he wouldn't support Gage, and demanded that I tell Mills that.

I knew Mills very well socially and liked him. In fact, our families were friends. Mills knew how I felt about this sort of thing and he knew Crothers' attitude, so I could be perfectly frank with him. I called on him and said, laughingly: "How much do you think Crothers wants to support Gage?"

He said, "I haven't any idea. Why, how much?"

"Twenty-five thousand," I said.

Mills laughed aloud. He said, "He's joking, isn't he?"

I said, "No, he wants that."

"Well," he said, "he won't get it. You can tell him that from me. I'll see Boyle, the business manager, and fix things up a little better for him."

I learned later that they increased the *Bulletin's* subsidy to $375 a month. The first $125 was for friendliness, the next was to go light on the charter, and the last was for supporting Gage for Governor of California.

Thus matters stood in the *Bulletin* offices—I still maintaining my reputation for honesty with Phelan and his group—when, in 1901, the teamsters' strike occurred, out of which Eugene E. Schmitz emerged as a political figure in San Francisco.

In this strike, Mayor Phelan was put in a very embarrassing position. The Teamsters' Union, striking for better conditions, had tied up all the teams in San Francisco. Business was practically stopped.

The merchants, also strongly organized, found non-union men to put on the wagons, and demanded police protection for them. They insisted that the streets were made for traffic, that the teams should be allowed to move upon them, that no power on earth should be permitted to delay them.

Phelan hesitated, but the pressure upon him from his old friends and associates was strong; they urged their opinion, which to a certain extent was Phelan's also, as a member of his class. In the end he reluctantly yielded, putting policemen on the wagons with orders to protect the drivers and see that the teams were kept moving.

The strikers formed in mobs and attacked both the wagons and the police. Goods were destroyed, there were riots in the streets, men were crippled and killed. There was a miniature reign of terror, and armed conflicts raged daily.

The leading merchants urged the *Bulletin* to stand against the strikers, and for "law and order." It was our inclination to do so anyway, but the merchants held out high hopes for the future of the paper if we would stand "right" in the fight. When the *Examiner* took the side of the strikers our business office had visions of a harvest of advertising contracts.

The merchants immediately undertook to boycott the *Examiner* for its stand. They tentatively organized for the purpose, but one or two of the business houses refused to sign the agreement, and so defeated their purpose. However, the largest advertising firm in town did withdraw its advertisement from the *Examiner* for a short time.

At length the strike ended, with a compromise. The teamsters did not get all they had demanded, but they went back to work after having gained a part of it. Labor was enthusiastic for the *Examiner,* and that paper's circulation was larger than ever. Immediately the largest advertising firm in town went back, increasing its advertising space there and cutting down the space formerly given us.

When our advertising manager remonstrated, he was told, "Business is business. We are advertising strictly on a proposition of circulation, and your circulation has gone down."

This was true. We had come out of the strike boycotted by labor union men. And we had gained nothing from the business men who had promised to support us.

The conflict had stirred workingmen more deeply than any previous labor trouble. They were advised by the Reverend Father Yorke, who had their confidence, that the thing for them to do was to go into politics and elect a mayor. They organized politically, held a convention, and selected as their standard bearer Eugene E. Schmitz.

Schmitz was at that time a member of the Musicians' Union and leader of the Columbia Theater orchestra. He was every inch the right looking man for a candidate. Tall, well formed, handsome, always well dressed and self-possessed, he was a commanding figure of a man, the center of all eyes in a crowd.

The campaign was three-cornered. Asa R. Wells was the Southern Pacific candidate; Schmitz ran as a Labor Party man; Joseph S. Tobin was the Democratic nominee. The Democrats tried to persuade Phelan to run again; but he had already been elected mayor three times, and he refused. The best man that could be selected from his group of reformers was Tobin. He was a supervisor under Phelan, had always fought with the reform element, and had a fine record. He was considered a strong character and a capable, honest man.

Of course, I was very eager that the *Bulletin* should pursue the same course it had followed since Phelan first ran for mayor. I wanted to stand firmly by the group of men who had worked with him through the charter fights and the various reform movements.

I felt that my personal honor—or rather, their belief in my honesty and my efforts to deserve that belief—was involved in my fighting for these men, whom I respected and in whom I believed. But I was afraid that I would not be able to hold the paper for Tobin because of the money question.

I could not go to Phelan and ask him for money, because I had never betrayed to him that the *Bulletin* took money, nor could I go to Tobin, who was close to Phelan. But I knew that I must get some money in order to hold the paper to the Phelan group.

I went to Prince Poniatowski, brother-in-law of Wm. H. Crocker, who was a close friend of Tobin. I told him my predicament in confidence and insisted that he must get some money that I could give to Crothers to hold the paper for Tobin. Otherwise it would go where there was more money for it; that is, to the railroad company. The pretext would be that Wells was a Republican, that the *Bulletin* was a Republican paper, that it had been locally Democratic too long and should now return to its own party. Crothers had already intimated this to me.

Poniatowski said: "I will do all I can, but the best I can do personally is $500 a month for three months through the campaign. I will put up the $1,500 out of my own pocket."

I did not dare to go to any one else, and I hoped, but faintly, that this would be enough. I went to Crothers with the information that I had got $1,500 to support Tobin, and he said, "It isn't enough."

I was in despair. Only one other ruse remained by which I might hold him. I asked former Mayor E. B. Pond, banker and millionaire, James D. Phelan, mayor and millionaire, and Franklin K. Lane, then a rising power in California, to call on Crothers and see if they could not prevail on him to stand by Tobin. Always greatly impressed by wealth, I felt that their prominence and financial standing might hold him.

They called, and did their best, but made no impression. Then I wrote an editorial which committed the paper mildly to Tobin, but I did not dare publish it without Crothers seeing it. He was keen on the money scent by this time. When I showed it to him, he said: "The article commits the paper to Tobin." He took a pencil and marked out certain phrases, so that the editorial left the paper on the fence, in such a position that it could support any of the three candidates. I published the editorial as corrected. It was the best I could do.

A few days later the railroad paid Crothers $7,500. The payment was made through an intermediary—a man not openly connected with the railroad. I learned of it almost instantly. The report was confirmed by Crothers ordering me to support Wells.

Tobin learned of the payment of the money and severely criticized me. Thereupon I went to him and told him frankly what had happened, adding that I had done all in my power to hold the paper for him. He apologized and said that he was very sorry, that he did not blame me.

Thomas Boyle, the business manager of the *Bulletin*, was at that time a strong advocate of Schmitz. I—as I have intimated—was for Tobin. Crothers was for Wells. The *Call* facetiously printed an item to this effect:

"Boyle is out for Schmitz, Older is out for Tobin, and Crothers is out for the stuff."

The facts, of course, became well known to the men on the inside of the political situation; but, equally of course, they were not known to the mass of our readers. Our very action in standing for clean city politics, as we had done for several years, added weight to our new position in support of Wells. To my mind, every article that we printed supporting him was a betrayal of our readers, who, gathering their knowledge of public events from our columns, naturally formed their opinions upon what we gave them.

At the time of Schmitz' appearance in politics, Abraham Ruef was a power in the Republican party ring. After Schmitz' nomination, however, Ruef was shrewd enough to divine that in all likelihood Labor, being indignant over the treatment given it in the teamsters' strike, would rally to Schmitz and elect him in the three-cornered fight. Ruef, therefore, broke from the Republican ring and went over to Schmitz, taking with him many strong political influences. He and his group knew the political game, knew the ropes, controlled the bosses in many districts of the city, and Ruef's support effectually turned the tide in Schmitz' favor.

Schmitz was elected. I was furious. While at that time I was not greatly in sympathy with Labor, I was doubly indignant because I felt that Schmitz did not even represent Labor; that he would not be true even to the men who had elected him. I smarted under the belief that the *Bulletin* had betrayed San Francisco, had helped destroy all that Phelan had done for the city.

I was perfectly sure that if we had supported Tobin he would have beaten Schmitz, and I still believe this. Ruef's going to Schmitz, and the *Bulletin's* going to Wells, undoubtedly defeated Tobin; and we were as much responsible for Schmitz' election in his first campaign as any other force in San Francisco.

My experience in this election enlightened me considerably. I began to feel a disinterested enthusiasm for decent government, and a genuine hatred of graft. I thought I saw a great opportunity for Schmitz, and, sending for Thomas Boyle, business manager of the

Bulletin, who was a great friend of Schmitz, I gave him this message to take to the newly elected mayor:

"Tell Schmitz that while I fought him in the campaign he is not to let that linger in his mind, but to remember this—that he has in his hands the greatest opportunity that any politician has had in America for many a long year. If he will be really true to Labor, to the people that elected him, and not associate himself with the evil forces in San Francisco, there is nothing that he cannot achieve politically in the United States. He can become Governor, he can become Senator, he can have a brilliant political career. Tell him that, and warn him against associating with Abraham Ruef, for Ruef will lead him astray."

Schmitz' reply to this was that he thanked me very much for my advice, but that Ruef was his friend and they were going to stand together.

This was the beginning of the struggle that led into every cross-section of San Francisco life; into the depths of the underworld; to attempted murder; to dynamiting and assassination—the struggle that involved some of the biggest men in the American business world, and wrecked them; that ended by filling San Francisco with armed thugs and overturning the Southern Pacific rule of California.

CHAPTER V

The Graft System Thrives In The Golden Gate City Under Schmitz Rule. I Make A Futile Attempt To "Clean House" In The *Bulletin* Office. Sharp Practice In The Business Department, Followed By A Public Exposé. Our Newsboys Go On Strike.

Immediately after Schmitz' installation as mayor of San Francisco petty graft began to crop up on every side. Scraps of talk, small bits of evidence, little intimations, came in to me at my office. I heard of bootblack stands, houses of prostitution, gambling joints, that were being forced to pay small graft money. Nothing definite; merely hints here and there, a glimpse of something not quite clearly seen, an atmosphere that began to envelop the city. The bigger graft did not develop at once, but the times were ripening for it.

From the hour that Schmitz' message came to me I was doggedly in pursuit of him, doing my utmost to get hold of something he had done or was doing that would uncover the underground of his activities. It was something like playing blindman's buff. Constantly I clutched at something that I could feel, but could not quite get hold of.

The graft within the *Bulletin* office was a different matter. I saw it clearly, and I felt more and more intensely that we must clean our own hands if we were to be consistent in our attitude toward other grafters.

The fact that we were taking money from the railroad, the gas company and other public-looting corporations was known in the business office. As a result, that department had become permeated with an atmosphere of chicanery and dishonesty. There was petty graft in the circulation department as well as in the business office. *Bulletin* men, by various shady pretexts, were getting rugs, pianos, bicycles, furniture, jewelry, everything they could lay hold of, in trade for advertising. The books were juggled.

That this was a more or less common practice at that time made no difference to me. I was intensely desirous of cleaning up the whole office, in all its departments, so that I could go after Schmitz with clean hands.

Every step I took was combated, within our own organization, by Crothers. He took that attitude not from inherent dishonesty, but because, like all men, he wanted money, and because he was by temperament opposed to any change in existing conditions.

He came from the middle class in Canada, of a family that was well enough off to educate him at McGill University. He had graduated from McGill with high honors, excelling in Greek; in fact, he had received a medal for his achievements in Greek, and that helped to hold him to what he considered the aristocratic side of life, which in this country is the wealthy.

He had only disdain for men in his employ who were not university men. He made an exception in my case, overlooking the fact that I had been a printer boy in early life, and had been working ever since I was old enough to work; excusing it on the ground that I was unusually clever in making a paper go, and in making money for him. He forgave me for not being a university man, but he had no great respect for my way of thinking.

The methods to which I was opposed were established methods, and he saw no reason for changing them.

At that time the *Evening Post* was owned by the Southern Pacific Railroad, under cover of an ostensible ownership in the name of Hugh Hume. Hume had bought the paper some years earlier on a very narrow margin of money, and, being unable to swing it financially, he had finally turned it over to the railroad company. W. H. Mills, controller of California's newspapers for the railroads, became absolute director and editor of the *Post*.

One day Mills suggested to the *Bulletin's* manager that there was no sense in a fight between the two papers for the city printing. He offered a plan, which our business manager laid before Crothers. The plan was this: The *Bulletin* should bid for the printing at a higher rate than the *Post,* the *Post* bidding twenty cents a square, and thus getting the city printing. The twenty cents should then be divided between the two papers, the *Bulletin* getting nine cents and the *Post* eleven cents, the *Bulletin* performing no service for the nine cents other than the collusive bidding.

This, I knew, was a felony, and I protested with all the vigor I could summon, using every possible argument against it. I feared that the thing would become known, ruining the paper; and that what little reputation I had acquired as an honest journalist would be destroyed. I argued with Crothers that we would gain very little in money—perhaps a few thousand dollars—and that the risk was too great; but neither Crothers nor the business manager would listen to me. They insisted that it was a perfectly good business venture, and the paper needed the money.

The agreement was entered into. Subsequently Mills died and the *Post* was sold to Thomas Garrett, who promptly discovered the felonious agreement, which appeared in the books. He refused to carry out the contract with us, would pay us no money; so that the dishonest deal had only brought us a few hundred dollars.

Later Garrett put in a good-sized bid for the city printing. The *Bulletin* bid under him; but Garrett produced before the Board of Supervisors the evidence of our collusive bidding with the railroad and insisted that we did not appear before the board with clean hands. Our bid was thrown out; Garrett's was accepted and the *Post* exposed us.

I still hoped and struggled to make the *Bulletin* an honest paper, according to my definition of honesty at that time. It had long been customary for San Francisco newspapers to issue what was called an "annual edition." It was always, and still is, largely a holdup. The corporations and wealthy individuals were always bled for sums as large as they could be induced to give up and they received nothing of value in return, save a vaguely defined "friendliness." We had an annual edition under way at this time and I went personally to the various corporations and urged them not to contribute.

I went to Tirey L. Ford, general counsel for the United Railroads, and asked him if he had promised any sum of money to our special edition. He replied that he had agreed to pay $1,000 for certain publicity.

I asked, "Is there anything you really want to advertise?"

"No," he said, "I am doing it as a favor to the paper."

"Well," I said, "it won't do you any good, Mr. Ford. You'd better save your money, because I shall criticize the United Railroads if I think they deserve it, no matter what you pay. If you do what is right toward the people, you will receive commendation; otherwise you will receive condemnation, and your money will be wasted. I want you to understand that thoroughly."

He smiled and said: "That settles it. I won't pay the thousand dollars." I said, "I'd rather you didn't."

I then called on the manager of the gas company and had the same conversation with him. He had promised our business manager to contribute quite a large sum, but he withdrew the promise. I visited others for the same purpose, so that when I had finished there was little left of our special edition except violent indignation from the men who were working on it.

I was fully awake by this time to the grafting idea and saw the inconsistency of my hammering at Ruef and Schmitz for doing the same thing that we were doing. I wanted to be clean, and I wanted the paper to be clean. I was dimly conscious that I was as bad as Ruef as long as I was taking part of my salary from the same source, and I felt it keenly.

About this time I encountered the coming into San Francisco of the Home Telephone Company. They wanted a franchise and they had millions back of them. One day Mark Gerstle, a prominent local capitalist, called on me in behalf of the Home Telephone Company and said that he had decided to advertise in the *Bulletin* and that he wanted reading matter.

I told him that he could not have an inch of it, not for $200 a line. Our columns were not for sale. If he incorporated we would publish the news of the incorporation, free; we would publish all legitimate news concerning the company, and if they treated the people well we would commend them editorially. But that was all the reading matter he would get from us. If he wanted to advertise with us he could get display advertising.

He said that he had a contract with the business office for reading matter. I told him that if reading matter was sent up to me I would refuse to publish it.

Our talk resulted in his going downstairs and breaking his contract. He did not advertise at all in the *Bulletin*. He did use other papers in the way he had hoped to use us, and later, in the graft fight, the fact came out in his testimony before the Grand Jury that he had done so. The fact also came out, testified to by Gerstle, that the *Bulletin* had refused to take his money for the use of our columns.

If Gerstle's testimony had been otherwise, at that crisis in the graft fight, it would have done us incalculable harm, utterly destroyed our usefulness in the fight. Of course, I had no anticipation of the importance of my attitude at the time I took it. It was merely in line with the policy I was trying to establish.

Meantime, I continued my hammering away at Ruef and Schmitz. Although I accomplished little else, I had succeeded in enraging them. Suddenly, one day our newsboys struck. Without warning, as our papers were coming from the presses, ready to go out on the streets, the waiting crowd of boys turned into a howling mob, storming our windows with sticks and stones.

It transpired later that gangsters in touch with Ruef and Schmitz had organized a Newsboys' Union, and at a rousing meeting had declared a strike against the *Bulletin.*

The excuse for this action was petty enough—merely a subterfuge. Like the other evening papers, we were selling the boys two papers for a nickel. They demanded three. But we did not learn even this until after they had descended on us, a storming mob, breaking our windows, attacking our clerks, besieging the office. Policemen stood idly on the corners and watched this, doing nothing, under orders.

It was impossible to get *Bulletins* on the streets for sale. Gangs cut the harness from the horses on the delivery wagons that we tried to get out. They stormed our drivers. Professional thugs broke the arms of loyal carriers, beat up our solicitors with brass knuckles. Word had come down from above that the *Bulletin* must be forced to stop publication in San Francisco.

It did not take me long to suspect the origin of all this trouble. It lasted, however, for several days before I was able to get hold of the men who could stop it. On those days, coming out of the office, I was met by a storm of stones, bricks, bits of wood, everything that could be found and thrown. Whenever I appeared on the sidewalks I was surrounded by a clamoring mob, and I had the time of my life handling the situation.

Within a few days I was able to put my hand on the leaders of the framed-up strike. They were well-known tenderloin characters, inspired—as I knew—by Ruef and Schmitz. I sent for them to come to my office and said to them:

"Twenty-four hours and a thousand dollars to break the *Bulletin* strike."

Their leader said, "I've got to have more time than that."

"No," I said. "Twenty-four hours."

He thought it over. "A thousand dollars?"

"Yes," I said. "To-morrow at this time, if the strike is over."

He said he would see what could be done, and left. The next night the boys who had been attacking us went in a mob to Ruef's house and threatened him with violence. The strike was over, and its leaders had thrown in that act for good measure. That afternoon our papers were on the streets as usual, and I paid the thousand dollars.

CHAPTER VI

A "Hunch" On The Graft Question Leads To Chinatown. Chan Cheung, A Chinese Who Would Not Squeal. The "Municipal Crib." I Seek The Men Higher Up. Lily, A Girl Of The Underworld.

In the midst of all this disturbance within, I still kept my mind alert to what was going on without. I had a vague intuition that Ruef and Schmitz and the Chief of Police were taking money from the Chinese gamblers. I had no positive proof of this, yet I felt absolutely certain of the fact. I was so angry at the whole situation that I printed, on the first page of the *Bulletin,* pictures of the Chief of Police, Ruef, Schmitz and Police Commissioner Drinkhouse, surrounded by a big frame of hands pointing to them, with a caption saying, "One or more of these men are taking bribes in Chinatown."

There was something of a sensation when this appeared.

Ruef immediately ordered the Police Commission to subpœna me to appear before that body and testify as to my knowledge. I went down, and they demanded that I tell them what information I had as to their taking money. I said:

"I haven't any, except my belief. I am positive that some one of those four is taking money. I am not prepared now to say which one, but I am going to find out."

The situation stood at this deadlock when one day Grant Carpenter, an attorney for the Chinese Six Companies, came to my office and told me that Chan Cheung was the paymaster of the police department. Carpenter said that Chan was responsible for several murders, that he knew the highbinders hired by Chan to commit these murders, and that, by putting pressure on Chan with this knowledge, we could make the Chinese reveal what he knew of the police graft.

This sounded good. I was delighted. However, before putting the screws on Chan Cheung I determined to work on Sergeant Tom Ellis, who was in charge of the police squad in Chinatown. I believed that with this information as to Chan we might be able to induce Tom Ellis to confess.

I sent for Captain John Seymour, who had been at one time chief of police, but who was now working for the Fair estate, and asked him to tell Tom Ellis that if he would confess to having been bribed, and would tell us where the money came from, I would put him on the *Bulletin* payroll for two years at $125 a month. It was understood that if he confessed he would lose his job, and this salary from me would protect him against loss.

Seymour undertook to do this, and succeeded in getting a statement from Ellis that he had been paid by Chan $200 a week for seven weeks prior to this time; that he did not know who paid other policemen or whether or not Ruef or Schmitz was paid. He understood that ordinary patrolman got $40 a week, but he did not know whether Schmitz or Ruef or Chief Whitman was getting money, although naturally he assumed they were. He said he was willing to go before the Grand Jury and make this statement.

Accordingly, one afternoon at two o'clock, when the

Grand Jury was in session, Ellis walked into the room, laid $1,400 in bills on the table and said, "I received that from Chan in Chinatown. That's seven weeks' pay to ignore Chinese gambling. I don't know about the others. I only know about myself. There's the money." Then he walked out.

That was the end of that. I had done nothing except put Tom Ellis on my payroll for two years. I had not got Schmitz nor Ruef nor Whitman nor any one of the commissioners. I had simply landed $125 a month on the *Bulletin* payroll.

I determined to get the truth out of Chan. There was a man on the Grand Jury, Ed Bowes, who was a good fighter and a loyal friend of mine. I sent for Grant Carpenter and arranged with him to program the highbinders, the murderers, to testify against Chan before the Grand Jury. Then Carpenter and Ed Bowes and I planned a Belasco drama.

I decided that we would take Chan down to the Grand Jury room, in impressive silence, and at the proper moment the District Attorney, who was friendly to us, should walk in solemnly and say:

"Chan Cheung! You think that you are going home to China to spend the rest of your days in ease and comfort, with your family and your children, but you are not. You are going to be hanged."

Then he would turn toward the door, and through it would come the highbinders, one by one.

"Is this the man that hired you to kill so-and-so?" the District Attorney would ask each highbinder as he faced Chan.

"Yes, that is the man."

Several times this would be done, one after the other, and when it was finished the District Attorney would turn to Chan and say:

"We don't want to hurt you. We don't want to harm you at all. All we want to know is the amount of the money that you pay the police department and public officials, and to whom you pay it. Then you can go free, go back to China and spend your old age in comfort and plenty."

This was the plan, the stage was set, the District Attorney and the highbinders coached and rehearsed. Everything was ready.

Then I found that Chan Cheung knew that I was trying to get him. The trap was all set and baited; the trap that we hoped would catch Ruef and Schmitz and Whitman—or at least one of the three. And Chan Cheung, in his room in Chinatown, lay low and refused to come out!

For several days we had a man watching and waiting for him, with no result. Then one Sunday afternoon I got Ed Bowes up in my room at the Palace Hotel and said to him:

"Something must be done. Now, Ed, we've got to have a friend of Chan ring him up on the telephone and tell him to come downstairs to meet him. Can you arrange it?"

"Yes, I'll do that," he said.

"I want you to be waiting with a hack. The minute Chan appears throw him into the hack and drive off. Tell him you are an officer of the Grand Jury. Carry him to the Occidental Hotel, put him in a room, and stay there with him. See that he doesn't have any opium, and don't give him the slightest hint of what is going to happen to him. To-morrow morning take him to the Mills Building and up to the Grand Jury room, and we'll do the rest."

Ed Bowes carried this plan through without a slip. Sixteen hours after he had kidnaped Chan he brought him into the Grand Jury room. The old Chinese was shaking, nervous and excited, not knowing what would be done to him, and suffering from having no opium for sixteen hours. The District Attorney came in solemnly, and our whole program was carried out as completely as a play on the stage.

"Chan Cheung," said the District Attorney, "you think that you are going back to China, to live the rest of your days in comfort and prosperity, with your children around you. This will never happen. You will be hanged."

Chan did not say a word.

One by one the highbinders slid in like ghosts, without a sound, and to each as he came in the District Attorney said: "Is this the man that hired you to kill so-and-so?" Each highbinder looked at Chan for a long moment, then bowed his head and said: "That is the man."

When the murderers had come and gone the District Attorney made his solemn speech: "Chan Cheung, we don't want to hang you. We don't want you to die in prison, on a scaffold, with a rope around your neck. Tell us who takes the money from you for protecting the gamblers, and we will let you go. You can go back to China and live in peace and comfort and plenty all your days, and die at last in your own country with your children around you."

Chan listened to this in silence, without moving a muscle. Then he said, looking around the room:

"Where your nineteen men? One, two, three, four—Grand Jury nineteen men. I no sabe."

He shut up and would not say another word. He had met only the police committee of the Grand Jury.

This was reported to me, in another room, and I was savage.

"Well, put him back in the room at the hotel. We'll give him nineteen men," I said. "Put him back. And give him no opium."

On Tuesday morning I got permission to use a courtroom, a Superior Courtroom, with the big mahogany desk and the trappings and properties of the courtroom all there, rich and impressive. The Grand Jury was there, in the jury seats; nineteen men, all looking very solemn. The foreman sat in state on the Judge's bench.

Chan Cheung was brought from the Occidental Hotel, and marched in silence through the big room to a place before the Judge's bench.

"Now," the foreman said severely, "tell us. Give us this information about paying money to the police, Chief Whitman, and so on."

Chan would not speak.

"All right. You don't tell us, we will indict you for those murders and hang you."

"No sabe," Chan said. It was impossible to get another word from him.

The handcuffs were clapped on him, he was indicted for the murders, and still he would not talk.

"No sabe," he repeated.

Then he was thrown into a patrol wagon and taken

away to the county jail. Locked up in a small cell, he was given the worst kind of treatment, of course; but never a word.

He had come from China to learn some of the white man's ways, but he had not learned all of them.

And all the while Chief Whitman and Ruef and Schmitz were smiling around the streets of San Francisco. They knew the Oriental. They knew we could boil him in oil and he would not talk. They knew the Oriental, and I didn't; but I found him out then.

The thing ended with nothing accomplished, except Tom Ellis on the *Bulletin* payroll for $125 a month. Chan was released on a writ of habeas corpus and has since died. By that time the matter had dragged on and on until every one was tired of it, and finally Tom Ellis went to the Grand Jury, demanded the return of his $1,400 bribe money, and got it.

However, I did not give up the fight. I had to abandon the Chinese gamblers; but I immediately turned my activities in another direction.

One of the notorious houses in the San Francisco of that day was at 620 Jackson street. I called it "the municipal crib." It had been built by Schmitz contractors, Schmitz had been interested in the construction of it, and there were earmarks about the whole affair that would indicate that the administration had knowledge of the use of the place, and would also have some control over the revenue. There were sixty or seventy women in the house. I was positive they were all paying money to Schmitz. I thought if I could only link up the administration with taking money from these women, I would at last have something that would wake up the people of San Francisco. They surely would not stand for a mayor who took money from prostitutes.

But all my efforts at getting the conclusive evidence I needed were fruitless. I had the Grand Jury raid the place two or three times, take the women and question them. I exhausted every expedient I could think of, without result.

One morning, when I had practically given the matter up, an attractive young girl came into my office at the *Bulletin* and said:

"I'm from 620 Jackson street, Mr. Older, 'the municipal crib,' and I want to help you. I haven't very much information, but I have a little I'll gladly give you, if you will see that I'm protected. Of course, they will be very angry when they find out that I have come to you, and I don't know what may happen. If you will hide me somewhere until it's over, and then give me money to leave town, that's all I want."

I agreed to this, and the girl—whose name, she said, was Lily—then told me what she knew; enough to confirm my suspicions, but hardly enough to take into court. She saw herself that she did not have very definite legal evidence, and said:

"I have a very dear friend over there—Clara—who knows more than I do. She is quite intimate with one of the men who collect for the higher-ups, and she could tell you something worth while."

That evening she brought Clara up to my office. Clara—a startling-looking girl, black-haired, black-eyed and dressed in black velvet—flashed up and down the office, panting with indignation, furiously abusing me for even thinking that she would turn on the people who ran the place. Lily tried to calm her, but she raged on, calling us both every vile name she could think of.

At last we quieted her and prevailed upon her to promise to go before the Grand Jury the following day. She told me enough to convince me that I had conclusive evidence against men who were directly responsible to Schmitz.

Those immediately interested in the "municipal crib" quickly learned that Lily had come to my office. They hunted the town over until they found the hotel in which I had placed her, registered under an assumed name. When she came out of this hotel at ten o'clock the next morning, hurrying to keep her appointment with me, a coupé was waiting at the curb before the door. Within it was a former landlady of Lily's, who had once been kind to the girl when she was ill. The "unseen forces" had taken the trouble to search for this landlady, and, having found her, to send her to use her influence with Lily.

As Lily came out of the hotel, this woman called to her, urging her to get into the coupé and drive with her. She promised the girl that she should be given ample money, be sent anywhere in the world that she wanted to go, and otherwise provided for.

"You can go to China, Japan, or wherever you like, and live like a lady," she said.

"No; I've got to keep my appointment with Mr. Older," Lily replied.

"But he's the very man we don't want you to see!"

"I've got to go. I told him I would," Lily insisted. She refused to get into the carriage, and hurried on to my office.

She and Clara went before the Grand Jury, and Lily told all she knew, simply and directly. But Clara had turned on us again, and would tell nothing of any value. Lily's testimony alone was not sufficient to warrant issuing an indictment, and so that hope was destroyed, as so many others had been.

According to my promise, I gave Lily a small amount of money, enough to take her to some town in Nevada, to which she wished to go, and she dropped out of sight. Many years later, when I had long forgotten the incident, I received a frantic telephone message asking me to come at once to an address far out on Mission street.

I went, and found Clara—very much changed; pale and quietly dressed—in a comfortable, plainly furnished flat. She told me that Lily was dead; shot by a drunken man in a house in the interior of the state.

"I'm sending her body back to her people," Clara said. "They don't know that she's been on the town; she's kept them thinking that she's been working. I don't know what to tell them. I wrote a letter to her mother, saying that she had died of typhoid fever. Then I was afraid they would see the bullet holes, so I wrote another, and said she had been shot by accident, on the street. I don't know which one to send."

I told her to send the second one.

I asked Clara for the details of Lily's death. She told me that a wealthy oil man had shot her and then killed himself. "He wanted Lily to marry him," Clara said, "and he killed her because she wouldn't."

"Why wouldn't she marry him?" I inquired.

"Because he drank terribly," Clara replied, "and Lily didn't respect him."

We talked for a few minutes, and she said:

"Do you notice how much I've changed? I'm married now, to a man I knew when I was a little girl."

She seemed very contented and happy; untroubled by shadows of the past.

CHAPTER VII

Gavin McNab's Quarrel With The *Examiner.* Plot And Counterplot. Bribery At Work In The State Senate. McNab Turns A Clever Trick. The Senatorial Boodlers Walk Into A Trap. The *Bulletin's* Sensational "Extra." Planning to Defeat The Schmitz Machine In The Approaching Municipal Election.

After the failure of this second attempt to produce evidence for the Grand Jury, my struggle with Schmitz assumed, for the time, a purely political aspect. The campaign of 1905 was approaching, the legislature was in session in Sacramento, and local politics promised keenly interesting events to come.

Gavin McNab—who had long since become a full-fledged attorney—had been having a violent quarrel with the San Francisco *Examiner.* This newspaper was strongly opposed to McNab's domination of politics in San Francisco; and in the course of the investigation it was making of his affairs it was discovered that the manager of one of McNab's building and loan associations was an embezzler and had done many dishonest things. The *Examiner* was making a vigorous fight against this man as a means of attacking McNab, who kept him in his position. In an effort to discredit McNab by bringing out the full story of this man's dishonesty, the *Examiner* was working through the Building and Loan Committee in the senate.

McNab was attorney not only for this particular building and loan association, but also for the Phœnix, which was under fire. The man in charge of this second company was Clarence Grange. By forcing an investigation of these companies through the Building and Loan Committee of the senate, then in session, the *Examiner* hoped to bring out the facts behind McNab's control of the two associations.

Grange had not been personally attacked, but he feared that any hostile investigation of the two companies might result in harm to them, and McNab shared his apprehensions.

While the companies were under investigation by the committee, a newspaper man named Joseph Jordan, who had become a lobbyist in Sacramento, came down to San Francisco one Sunday morning and called on Grange. He told Grange that for $1,650 he would guarantee that Senators Emmons, Bunkers, French and Wright, members of the committee, would vote to whitewash the companies. He had to pay each of them $350, and he wanted $250 for himself.

Grange agreed to give him the money, but, before doing so, sent for Gavin McNab. McNab had a brilliant idea, but, saying nothing of it to Grange, he agreed to the plan.

That evening he telephoned me that he had something of importance to tell me, and wanted me to come immediately to my room in the Palace Hotel. When I reached the hotel I found him walking up and down in the corridor, and we went into my room, where he told me what had occurred.

"Now," he said, "I've got this thing all figured out. To-morrow a man will come up to your office with a package. You have $1,650 ready in greenbacks, before he comes, and you mark them yourself. When this man comes with the package, you take it from him, step into the next room and take his money out of the package. Put your marked bills inside, give him the package, then put your money back into the bank and leave the rest to me. I'll see that each of those committee members gets his money and I'll have them watched so we can prove that they received it."

I said: "But—but Grange thinks he's bribing them, doesn't he?"

And McNab gave a step or two of the "Highland fling," crying: "Yes! That's the beauty of it. He does think so. Isn't it great?"

The next day, as agreed, I procured the money and marked it, taking photographs of the marked bills. The man arrived, I took the package from him, changed the money, returned the package to him, and he went out. Then I set to work to prepare the story.

I made a four-page display of it, with pictures of the marked money, pictures of the four senators, flaring headlines, and every detail of the story. I was obliged to trust thirty men in the *Bulletin* office with the story, and not one of them let out a word of it to the other papers. We worked all one Sunday, printing 20,000 copies of this extra, and I hired a special train on the Southern Pacific Railroad, placed the papers in the car, and held it for orders.

Meantime, McNab had the money paid, covering every move in the transaction by witnesses. He employed Frank Nicol, a prominent attorney of Stockton, to prepare a statement disclosing the bribery, and arranged that he should rise to a question of privilege in the senate and read this document on the floor. The four senators who had received the money would be at their desks, and this would be their first knowledge that they had been caught.

Everything was arranged when I left for Sacramento. Franklin K. Lane happened to be here in San Francisco, and Arthur McEwen, a well-known writer. I told them about it, and they went with me to see the fun.

On Monday, when the senate opened, McEwen, Lane and myself were sitting in the senate chamber, well up in front, so that we could watch the expressions of the four senators when the story of the bribery was read. I had a reporter at my side, and as soon as the senate convened, he opened a telephone line to the *Bulletin* office in San Francisco, and kept it open.

The senate opened with the usual solemnity and prayer. At the first opportunity Nicol rose to a question of privilege, spread open his document, and began to read. I whispered to the reporter to telephone to San Francisco, and the special train started, bringing the *Bulletin* extras.

The four senators went white when they realized the meaning of Nicol's statement. Lane, McEwen and I watched their changing expressions. When Nicol had finished each one of them rose, pale and trembling, and stammered a feeble and blundering reply. Then uproar broke loose in the senate.

Stormy speeches were made. An investigation was demanded, a committee was appointed. By the time the senate adjourned, newsboys were swarming into the lobby with the *Bulletins,* carrying the story.

Joe Jordan was there. He rushed to the telephone

and called up Grange in his office in the Mills Building, where he had been sitting all day unconscious that he had not committed a felony.

"Have you seen the *Bulletin?*" Jordan demanded, wildly excited.

Grange said, "No. Why?"

"Go out and get one!"

Grange did so and discovered that he was a hero, a social reformer, a public-spirited citizen.

He was subpœnaed to appear before the investigating committee of the senate, and at the hearing he said that he felt that the corruption of the senatorial body of California was an outrage; that it was an offense to every honest citizen; that he had felt it his duty to his state to devise this method of disclosing the corruptibility of the elected representatives of the people.

Of course, I knew the truth. I knew that he had intended to bribe those senators, that he had been surprised and confounded by the discovery that he had not done so. But it was not my play to disclose that knowledge at that time, nor have I ever done so until now.

All four of the senators were indicted. Bunkers went to San Quentin for a term of years. Emmons also became a convict. Wright fled to Mexico, and French was acquitted. Afterward, French ran again for the senate, getting 3,000 votes in his district.

My knowledge of the truth of this matter was of great value to me later, resulting, indeed, in the nomination of a candidate for mayor against Schmitz in the approaching election.

Herrin had become fearful of Ruef's growing power in San Francisco. He saw in Ruef a rival who was becoming dangerously strong, so he agreed with us, the reformers, that the Schmitz machine must be defeated in the coming primaries.

At about that time Fairfax Wheelan, a prominent merchant here, became imbued with the idea that he should take a hand in reforming San Francisco, and the first move that he made was to organize the San Francisco Republican League. The purpose of this organization was to bring about a coalition of the Democrats and Republicans in the mayoralty election, so that there would not occur again a three-cornered fight during which Schmitz could slip into office.

Wheelan appointed on this league a number of well-known men. He gave me one man, Ed Bowes; he appointed one for DeYoung of the *Chronicle,* one for Herrin, and the rest of the league was made up of well-known politicians.

This group agreed to give me the power of bringing together the two groups, the McNab group and the Fairfax Wheelan group. They also agreed that if Herrin would play fair and join them in the fight to beat Ruef in the primaries they would work harmoniously with the railroad organization. I was friendly to all the factions and undertook the task of unifying them in the approaching fight.

The railroad people—Jerry Burke, Arthur Fiske and George Hatton, representing Herrin—told me that I should have the negative power on the candidate for mayor; that is, they would not insist on any candidate whom I opposed.

All three groups agreed that the Republicans should

have the mayor, and the Democrats should have the other offices.

The first name that Burke and Hatton presented to me was that of Judge Sloss, who afterward had an honorable career on the Supreme Bench. I told them that I did not think he could be elected. He was a good man, but he was not a good mixer, not a good campaigner, not the kind of man who could beat Schmitz. While I thought that he would make a good mayor, I did not believe that we could win with him.

I then suggested Colonel Kirkpatrick, manager of the Palace Hotel. I knew he was a Herrin man, but I also knew he was financially incorruptible. He was a good mixer, fond of horses, a good story-teller; a man about town who drank a little, had a lot of magnetism, possessed all the qualities that I thought a candidate must have in order to be elected. Burke and Hatton were glad to accept him.

Before presenting the name of Kirkpatrick to McNab, I went down to his office with Thomas Hickey and said: "Mr. McNab, very soon I am going to bring you a name from the Republicans for you to indorse in your Democratic caucus, and I want you to accept it."

"You mean on sight, and unseen?"

I said, "Yes."

"You mean that you will put the name in an envelope, seal the envelope and give it to me, and that whatever name I find I'll accept it?"

I said: "Yes, if you want to put it that way."

He said, "All right, I'll do it."

The next day I brought him the name of Kirkpatrick.

He flew into a violent rage and said that Kirkpatrick was a Herrin man. I admitted that he was, but pointed out my reasons for urging him as a candidate. "I want you to accept him. I want you to do it," I said.

I left with no definite assurance from him, and I was suspicious from that moment that McNab had some candidate of his own that he was planning to nominate in conjunction with Fairfax Wheelan of the Republican League. In fact, I had heard rumors to that effect, and the man had been mentioned—Harry Baer, who was at that time the Republican Auditor of San Francisco.

However, the good faith of McNab and Wheelan was pledged to the agreement with the railroad people, and I decided to make another effort.

CHAPTER VIII

A Coalition Fight The Only Hope For A Reform Administration. The Reform Party Fails To Keep Faith. Breakers Ahead. Forcing A Candidate's Nomination By Both Parties.

I felt that our hope of preventing Schmitz from again becoming mayor lay in combining all the Republican and Democratic forces behind one man, this man to be the opposition candidate.

It seemed to me that success was almost in my hand. Wheelan, of the Republican League, McNab, controlling the Democratic strength, and Herrin, dictator of the Southern Pacific machine, all agreed to back the man I chose. When I saw that McNab and Wheelan were conspiring to defeat that agreement I was in a cold, fighting rage.

I went to the railroad people and suggested, since McNab objected to Kirkpatrick, that we substitute John Lachmann. He had been supervisor and sheriff, and, justly or unjustly, he had been given the title of "Honest" John Lachmann. I knew that he was a railroad man, but I thought he was as good as anybody we could get for mayor.

When I suggested "Honest" John to Jerry Burke and Hatton, they said, "Surely. He is all right. We will stand for him."

I telephoned to San Anselmo, where Lachmann was staying, and asked him to come over at once, without a moment's delay. He hastened to Hatton's office in the

Crocker Building, and I explained the situation to him, saying that we would run him for mayor, with both the Democratic and Republican nominations.

He agreed to run, and Jerry Burke said to him, "All we ask of you, John, speaking for the Republican party, is that when you are elected you give us an even break."

Lachmann replied, "Why, certainly I will do that. It's a fair request."

I hurried from Hatton's office to McNab and told him that I had hit upon John Lachmann for the coalition candidate. He considered the suggestion for a moment and said, "I think maybe something can be done with Lachmann. We'll all meet you in your office to-morrow morning at ten o'clock and talk it over."

The next morning at ten o'clock Wheelan, McNab and one or two others came to my office. Wheelan began the conversation by laying on my desk a typewritten sheet containing the names of every office in the mayor's power to fill, with the name of a man for each. He asked me whether or not Lachmann would appoint those men if he were elected.

When I had read the paper I leaned across my desk and looked at him.

"That's a felony!" I said. "Isn't it? You're a lawyer, Mr. McNab. Isn't that a felony?" McNab hesitated. Then he said, "Yes, Older is right. It is a felony. A pre-election bargain is a felony."

Wheelan was momentarily staggered by the situation. He said that perhaps we had better wait a while and discuss the matter later.

They left my office and went to see Lachmann. They told him that I had suggested him as coalition candidate for the nomination. Then, pulling out this list of offices, they asked him if he would appoint the men whose names they had chosen.

He said, "I certainly will not. The railroad people haven't asked anything of me but a square deal, and I'm going to give it to them, and to you, and to all the others. I promise that, and that's all I promise. This thing you're talking about is against the law."

They came back to me that afternoon and refused to accept him as their candidate.

The Republican League was to meet next morning, and by this time I had learned definitely that McNab, in league with Wheelan, had decided to nominate Harry Baer, breaking their agreement with the railroad people. I spent the night thinking it over.

Early next morning I sent for John S. Partridge, a young and promising lawyer, fairly well known in politics, and a member of the Republican League. He was an upright, upstanding young fellow, known to have lived a clean life and to be thoroughly reliable. I invited him into my office and said to him, "John, it's you for mayor. Don't say a word about it to any one."

He was stunned. He said: "You don't mean it. You are joking. Why—how could it be done?"

"Never mind how it can be done. You go up to the meeting and sit in there. Don't say a word, just watch it work out."

When he had gone I got in touch with the railroad people again and asked them if they were satisfied with Partridge. They immediately said that Partridge was all right. Then I sat down and wrote an editorial.

In it I revealed every detail of the attempted felony

of Wheelan and McNab, denounced them for it, washed my hands of the entire crowd, and cast them to the wolves. With this editorial in proof I sent for Ed Bowes, my man in the Republican League, and one other member of the League.

"I want Partridge nominated by two o'clock to-day. If he is not indorsed at two o'clock, this editorial will be published. Read it."

They read it. They were very much excited and rushed out of the office with hardly a word. At one o'clock Bowes came back, perspiring, and asked me if I would make it two-thirty.

"No. Two o'clock, or the editorial goes. That is our press time."

At two o'clock Bowes rang me up and told me that Partridge had been selected by the Republican League.

McNab had felt that some embarrassing situation might arise during the day, so he had told his friends that he was going to Sacramento to try a case in the Supreme Court. Then he remained all day buried in his San Francisco office, thinking that the Harry Baer scheme was going through as programmed, without a hitch. Early in the day Hugh Burk, a reporter for the *Call,* called at his office and McNab saw him, knowing that Burk was not in on the fact that he was supposed to be in Sacramento.

Burk asked, "Who's the man for mayor, Mac?"

"Baer," said McNab.

Burk said, "What about Older?"

"Oh, to hell with Older!"

At three o'clock, after Partridge had been nominated, Burk dropped into McNab's office again and, supposing that McNab knew what had happened, remarked, "Well, I see it's Partridge."

McNab, startled, said, "Partridge? Oh, yes, you mean for chairman of the Republican convention."

"No!—mayor," said Burk. "He has been indorsed by the Republican League."

McNab, wholly unprepared, leaped from his chair and exploded.

When I came into his office at five o'clock the "old guard" was all lined up against the wall in a row. McNab was purple in the face. He said to me:

"So it's that foul bird, Partridge, is it?"

"Yes, it's Partridge," I said.

"Well, let's see you nominate him. Let's see you get him through the conventions."

"But," I said, "he's my man, and you agreed to nominate the man that I brought you."

"Just let's see you put that bird in."

That frightened me. The Republican convention met that evening and I feared McNab might have sufficient influence in the convention to defeat Partridge. I hunted up Partridge and told him that he must nominate himself as soon as the convention opened. He must give McNab not a moment to start anything.

The convention met in old Pioneer Hall. When it assembled I was walking up and down in a dark alley beside the building. Through the window I saw hats going up in the air and heard a roar of cheers, and I knew that Partridge was in.

I walked out onto Market street and found McNab standing there with his sub-bosses, Fay and Braunhart.

"Partridge is nominated," I said.

"You aren't going to get him through the Democratic convention," McNab said. "If you put him over on us it will be over my dead body."

I said "Good night" and walked away.

I was considerably disturbed by McNab's threat concerning the Democratic nomination. With Partridge nominated by the Republicans, it needed only the nomination of another man by the Democrats to kill absolutely our hopes of defeating Schmitz. Another three-cornered fight would inevitably put him back in office.

Now, McNab and Wheelan were not a whit less sincere than I in a desire to thrust Schmitz out of the mayor's chair. Whatever motives actuated them—and we were all impelled by desire for power, prestige, success—they were earnest and sincere reformers in politics. They wanted to clean the grafters out of San Francisco.

But when they went into politics they went into a dirty game, and they found it must be played in a dirty way. They did not trust a railroad man to play fair with them, so they did not play fair with the railroad. They did not know that nowhere in the world is honesty more necessary than among thieves.

The railroad did know this, and never, in my relations with them, did the Southern Pacific politicians break a promise. The reformers did. Wheelan and McNab broke their agreement with me; they broke their agreement with the railroad. The only hope of defeating Schmitz lay in standing shoulder to shoulder with the railroad in this fight.

I was in despair. If McNab, furious at my putting Partridge over on the Republican convention, nominated another man for the Democrats, the fight was lost before it began. I did not believe there was any possible way in which I could nominate Partridge in the Democratic convention.

In this mood, I received a subpœna from the Superior Court in Sacramento citing me to appear the following day as a witness in the Emmons case. Emmons was on trial for accepting bribe money from Grange in that affair of the building and loan committee.

The subpœna reached me late in the afternoon, and that night the Democratic caucus met to nominate its candidate for mayor.

That evening my wife and I were at the Palace Hotel. I asked Dr. Washington Dodge to come up to my room. He came. I said:

"Doctor, I hate to ask you to do this, but I'm desperate. It's the last shot in my locker. The Democratic caucus meets to-night at eight o'clock. I want you to go over and see McNab. I want you to tell him that unless Partridge is nominated at eight o'clock to-night I will go to Grove L. Johnson, attorney for Emmons, and I will tell him to ask me, when I am on the stand as a witness, whether or not Grange intended to bribe the Senate Committee."

"My God! That's an awful thing to ask me to do," Dodge replied.

"I know it. But you must do it, doctor. I'm desperate. I must have Partridge nominated. I tell you we've got to beat Schmitz."

"All right," he said. "I'll do it."

He went away, and shortly afterward Mrs. Older and I went down to dinner. We were sitting at our table, in the old palm court of the Palace, when I happened to look up. Through the glass that surrounded the court I saw the white face of Dr. Dodge. I rose and went out to him.

He was much agitated. He said: "I gave the Scotchman your message." I waited, and he went on. "His reply was: 'Tell that long-legged blank blank blank that if I am alive at eight o'clock to-night Partridge will be nominated.' "

At eight o'clock, with wild enthusiasm, Partridge was indorsed by the Democrats as the Reform candidate for mayor.

That was a jubilant night for me. The *Bulletin* next day was full of rejoicing in the prospective victory of right over all the powers of graft and corruption. And this attitude was sincere on my part, for I honestly believed that Ruef and Schmitz were the bad forces in San Francisco, and that when they were eliminated we could have a clean city.

CHAPTER IX

My Bitter Campaign Against Schmitz And Ruef. I Get New Light On The Graft Operations, And Make Use Of It. Election Day Finds Me Confident of Success. An Incredible Defeat. Planning The Graft Prosecution. I Visit Washington And Interview President Roosevelt.

I plunged immediately into a most vicious campaign against Schmitz. The *Bulletin* was filled with cartoons showing Schmitz and Ruef in stripes. Our editorials declared that these men should be in the penitentiary and would be put there eventually. I spared no effort in running down and printing news stories to their discredit.

At this time I used to dine frequently at Marchand's, a famous restaurant in San Francisco, controlled by Pierre. One evening when I entered the Frenchman met me with a face of despair and said:

"Mr. Older, I'm a ruined man. They're going to put me out on the sidewalk after all these years building up this business."

"Why, Pierre, what is the trouble?"

He told me that the French restaurants were threatened with loss of their licenses. I said, laughingly:

"Why don't you see Ruef?"

But he was utterly hopeless. He said that nothing could save him.

A few days later a friend telephoned my office. He told me that the French restaurants had paid $10,000 for protection, and that they would not lose their licenses. I rushed over to Marchand's.

Pierre was seated at a side table, his spectacles on his nose, contentedly reading his *Chronicle* and sipping black coffee, apparently at peace with the world. I said to him:

"You look happy, Pierre."

He replied:

"Yes, Mr. Older. My troubles are over. You know, when you are seek, send for the doctor. Well, and I send for the doctor—Dr. Ruef—and everything is all right."

This confirmed the information I had received over the telephone, and that afternoon the *Bulletin* printed the story with a flaring headline across the front page. My recollection is that all the other papers permitted me to have this scoop without protest, and made no effort to follow up the story in their own columns.

My old hope of basing some criminal charge against Ruef and Schmitz flamed again and I interested the foreman of the Grand Jury in it. He employed a well-known lawyer and paid him a fee to look up the law and see if there was basis for criminal prosecution in the French restaurant story. The lawyer put in two weeks on the case, wrote a report and sent it in with a bill to the Grand Jury, advising that nothing could be done.

Meanwhile, the Partridge campaign was being waged with great enthusiasm on my part. I did not for a moment believe that the candidate could be defeated. I was so wrought up that I could not believe that Labor would stand by men so discredited as Schmitz and Ruef. It was far out of the range of my thought to imagine that any great number of the business men would vote for them.

McNab and Wheelan were deeply angered by the enforced nomination of Partridge, and there were rumors that secretly they were working against him; but I had no direct evidence that they were. However, they certainly did nothing for him.

I made what I considered at the time a very strong and effective fight. Partridge campaigned the city, speaking in all the districts. The burden of his talks was the shameless graft that was going on. The billboards were covered with his utterances, headed always with a big, attractive line, "Partridge says—"* The *Bulletin* hammered ceaselessly at Schmitz.

Even on the day of election I could not be convinced that Schmitz would win. Many people came to me and told me they heard nothing but Schmitz sentiment, but I simply would not listen to them. It was impossible for me to realize it.

Even one who was deaf and dumb and blind should have known the truth, but I didn't. I went to my office on election night confident that we would win.

At seven o'clock that night I sat in my office watching the news of our defeat flashing on the bulletin boards. Schmitz was elected.

It was incredible to me. I could not believe it, though I knew it was true. I could not believe that the people of San Francisco had again chosen the Schmitz-Ruef crowd to rule the city. But they had. The fight was over, and we were overwhelmingly defeated.

* John Partridge was appointed by President Coolidge to the post of Federal Judge in San Francisco. He died in 1926.

Crowds of Schmitz-Ruef enthusiasts were marching up and down the streets beneath the windows, yelling, half mad with excitement. Rockets were going up, whistles were shrieking. It seemed that all the powers of bedlam had broken loose.

Out in the local room the reporters were working at fever heat, checking up the returns and writing bulletins, in a confusion of noise and hurry and excitement. In the earlier part of the evening various men who had been in the fight dropped into my office to say a word or two: "Well, we're beaten." After a while they stopped coming.

Mrs. Older was with me, and Arthur McEwen, the writer, who had been helping the *Bulletin* make the fight. We did not say much. We just sat silent in despair. McEwen said he was through. He would not remain in the rotten town. He was going back to New York the next day. I could not do that. I had to stay.

About ten o'clock the mob outside, going mad with victory, attacked our office and smashed the windows. They screamed and jeered, howling insults while the glass crashed. When Mrs. Older and I came out of the office we were assailed with yells and hooted all the way down Market street to the door of our hotel.

I went to bed feeling that the world, so far as we were concerned, was a hopeless place to live in. At a late hour I fell asleep, only to be awakened almost immediately by the shouts of bellboys in the corridors. They were calling that the *Chronicle* building was burning—that all the guests must rise and dress; the fire might extend to the Palace.

We hurriedly threw some things into a dress suit case and rushed out into the hall. Others were doing the same. With other hastily dressed, excited, half delirious persons we rushed to the Market street side of the hotel and watched the tower of the *Chronicle* building burn, a blazing caldron of flames.

A victorious skyrocket had been shot up into the sky and descending upon the *Chronicle* tower had set it on fire. But against the blackness and the excitement of that night it seemed more like the breaking loose of malignant fiends; as though the powers of darkness had clutched the city and were destroying it; as though the end of the world was upon us. Overwrought as I was from the long fight and our defeat, nothing was too wild for me to imagine.

When, after some weeks, my mind returned sanely to the fight that I had lost, I reasoned this way about it: The people of San Francisco did not believe me. They thought I had some ulterior political motive in fighting Ruef and Schmitz so desperately. And only in one way could I convince them that I was telling the truth. I must prove my charges in court.

I recalled a speech Francis J. Heney had made one night during the election fight in the Mechanics' Pavilion. He had said:

"If the people of San Francisco ever want me to come back here and put Abe Ruef in the penitentiary, I'll come."

My mind dwelt on that. I thought, "If only I could get Heney—" He was at that time a conspicuous prosecutor of land frauds in Oregon, and had acquired a national reputation in this work. If only I could get him! There was the French restaurant case. Something surely could be done with that!

In my desire to "get" Schmitz and Ruef I conceived the idea of going to Washington and asking Heney to come to San Francisco to start a case in the courts. I knew, of course, that he was working for President Roosevelt at that time in the Oregon land fraud cases; but my obsession was so great that I believed I could convince Roosevelt that the graft in San Francisco was far more important than the land fraud cases in Oregon.

At any rate, I told Mrs. Older and Crothers that I was going. They both said, of course, that it was a crazy thing for me to do, but as I was so much disturbed and excited the trip would perhaps be good for me. They both believed nothing could come from my idle dream. But I would rest and become calm, maybe, and the journey could do no harm.

So, without letting any one know besides Crothers, Mrs. Older and Eustace Cullinan, who at that time was editorial writer on the *Bulletin,* I departed for Washington.

By appointment I met Heney at luncheon at the Willard Hotel and told him my mission. I also told him that I thought I had one definite case that he could make good on in the courts—the French restaurant case. Heney said he would be glad to come, but he would want William J. Burns, who was working with him as a detective in the land fraud cases. They were both employed by the Government.

He asked me to meet Burns in his rooms that afternoon. I did so and we had a long talk. Burns was eager to come, and so was Heney, but Heney said:

"We'll need some money."

"How much?" I asked.

Heney thought about a hundred thousand dollars would be as little as we could afford to begin work with. In my desperate frame of mind I said: "Well, I'll take care of that. I'll arrange it."

The following morning I saw President Roosevelt, who said that he was in sympathy with what I was trying to do and would do all in his power to help, but that he could not see his way clear to releasing Heney and Burns. Perhaps, he said, something could be done later.

With these half-satisfying assurances I returned to San Francisco.

Immediately upon my arrival I had a visitor who gave me the first ray of hope that had shone for me since the election. This visitor was Langdon, the newly elected District Attorney.

The Ruef ticket had been made up rather loosely, with a number of men more or less connected with Labor as supervisors, and Langdon for District Attorney. Langdon up to that time had been Superintendent of Schools.

His opponent was Henry Brandenstein, one of the strongest figures, from our point of view, in San Francisco. He had rendered excellent service as a supervisor and as chairman of the Finance Committee, and had stood for all the reform measures we were interested in. Under the old system of voting, I think undoubtedly he would have defeated Langdon. But, for the first time, in this election voting machines were used, and no one understood them very well. In order to scratch a ticket one had to understand these machines better than most voters could understand them, so, rather than not vote for Schmitz, the voter banged one key and voted the whole ticket in. This was the reason for Langdon's election.

I had not thought much about Langdon, assuming, in general, that he would stand with the people with whom he was more or less loosely allied politically.

Shortly after I returned from Washington, however, I called upon him at his office. We talked for a moment or two and he said:

"Mr. Older, I think perhaps you misunderstood me because of my affiliations in the election. I want you to know that I am the District Attorney of San Francisco. My duty is to enforce the law."

He picked up a copy of the penal code that lay on his desk and, holding it in his hand and looking me in the eye, he said: "My job is to enforce all of the laws in that book. I mean to prosecute any man, whoever he may be, who breaks one of those laws. Any man. No matter what happens. Do you understand me?"

I said that I understood and that I congratulated him. From that moment I knew that at heart Langdon was with us. Ruef soon learned that he was.

Meantime, I set to work to get the money that I had promised for financing the prosecution of Ruef and Schmitz.

CHAPTER X

Wanted: A Hundred Thousand Dollars. I Seek Aid From Phelan And Spreckels, Both Of Whom Stand On The Side Of Clean Government. Rudolph Spreckels' Interesting Career. The Great Fire. Newspaper Publication Under Difficulties. Heney Visits Our Stricken City. We Get Under Way.

When I had so rashly promised to raise a hundred thousand dollars for the graft prosecution I had in mind James D. Phelan and Rudolph Spreckels as possible resources. I had come back from Washington revolving in my thoughts, all the way across the continent, the probabilities of obtaining from them such a huge sum for this purpose.

Phelan, as I have already stated, was a rich man. He had been born and brought up in an atmosphere of wealth and refinement. He had toward the city somewhat the attitude of a rich man toward a great business in which he is interested. His life had always been identified with that of San Francisco. He loved the city, and wished to see it clean and well ordered, with an upright government efficiently administered. I knew that he was eager to see the graft faction driven out of the city administration, and I believed that he would gladly contribute toward that end.

Rudolph Spreckels also came of a wealthy family, but he had quarreled with his father when he was seventeen years old. The quarrel was caused by Rudolph's standing by his brother, Gus, when their father had quarreled with him and had cast him out. Rudolph said to his father: "Even though this causes a break between us, I am going to stand with Gus. I think Gus is right. Father, I am always going to stand for the right all my life."

His father ordered him out of the house, and he went. From that time, with scarcely any one to help him, Rudolph made his own way, finally accumulating a fortune. His father, in his old age, relented, forgave him, and left him a large share of his estate. But Rudolph Spreckels was a big man without his father.

His actual contact with political affairs had been very slight, and, such as it was, it had grown out of his efforts to improve the Sutter street car line, some time prior to my trip to Washington.

The Sutter street line was an old, ramshackle cable system, owned by the United Railroads. It not only ran out on Sutter street, passing some of Rudolph Spreckels' property there, but it turned up Polk street and rounded on Pacific avenue, where it passed his residence. The line was so dilapidated and out of date that the United Railroads was considering changing it into an overhead trolley system.

To this, naturally, Rudolph Spreckels was opposed. He thought that if a change was to be made, the new system should be the most modern that any city had. He had in mind the underground conduit system used in Washington, D. C., and in New York City; a system which conserves the beauty of the streets and increases rather than diminishes the adjacent property values. Nothing short of that admirable system would satisfy Rudolph Spreckels.

In order to force the installation of this system, he formed an organization of property owners and made a very intelligent campaign in favor of the underground conduits. But Patrick Calhoun, president of the United Railroads, considered the improvement too expensive. He declared it to be impossible because of the grades. Spreckles met all the objections intelligently, offering to pay out of his own pocket for any work required on the grades in order to make the system practical. Calhoun refused to listen or to have anything to do with the conduit system. He insisted on the overhead trolley, which would cost less.

Then Spreckels conceived the scheme of organizing a separate street car company. He planned to obtain franchises on certain streets having no car lines, and to build up a system operating with the underground conduit; the idea being that such a system would compete with the United Railroads, compelling it to abandon the outgrown cheaper system and install the underground conduit.

This struggle gave Rudolph Spreckels his first practical experience of politics. He organized the company with his father and, I think, James D. Phelan. Rudolph and his father called on Mayor Schmitz in regard to the proposed franchises. Schmitz would not listen to any such proposition. He was definitely tied up with the Calhoun interests and the United Railroads, although at this time Calhoun had not yet bribed him to grant the overhead trolley franchise.

Rudolph Spreckels retired from this attempt with increased knowledge of underground conditions in San Francisco.

I knew this, and I felt that his public spirit had been awakened to such an extent that he would, perhaps, go further and back a big fight against graft in San Francisco. I did not have Calhoun in mind, because at that time I did not know that he had done anything unlawful. However, I felt that Spreckels was a man upon whom I could call for help.

I first visited Phelan and told him what I had done. I informed him that I had seen Heney and Burns and Roosevelt, and I felt that if I could raise a hundred thousand dollars to meet expenses Heney and Burns could be induced to come to San Francisco to investigate graft and punish those guilty of it.

Phelan was very much in favor of the attempt, and said he would help to raise the money. Then I called on Rudolph Spreckels and told him how matters stood. He was most enthusiastic. He rose from his chair, walked over to me and said:

"Older, I'll go into this! I'll put my money in this and back it to the limit. But I want one understanding —that our investigation must lead to Herrin. Herrin is the man who has corrupted our state. He has broken down the morals of thousands of our young men. He has corrupted our legislatures and our courts. He has corrupted supervisors of counties, and coroners and sheriffs and judges. He is the worst influence in California. If we go into this fight, we've got to stay in till we get him."

Later, when the fight was on, it was charged that Spreckels' motive for going into it was his antagonism to the United Railroads, because he had organized a rival company. This was wholly untrue. He had organized a railway company for the reasons I have stated; but it had nothing to do with his going into the graft prosecution, because at that time none of us knew of anything that Calhoun had done unlawfully. As a matter of fact, at that time—December, 1905—Calhoun had not yet bribed the supervisors. That occurred later.

Assured of Phelan's and Spreckels' support, I got into communication again with Heney, and in the following February he came to San Francisco. I had him meet Phelan and Spreckels at luncheon at the University Club, and there we had a preliminary talk. I had nothing definite to offer as an entering wedge beyond the fragments of evidence in the French restaurant case, but we were all confident that if this were followed up it would lead to deeper disclosures; perhaps in the end even to Herrin himself.

Heney said that he had to go on with his Government work for the present, but as soon as there was a lull in it he would make the investigations and the prosecutions, if there were any to be made. We parted with this understanding.

Three weeks later came the great fire. San Francisco was destroyed. I was in the midst of the cataclysm, working desperately—as all men did in those feverish days and nights; first to save what I might of the *Bulletin*, and later to help others needing help. But my mind was so filled with one idea that, even in the midst of fire and smoke and heaps of ruins, I thought continually of our plans to get Ruef and Schmitz, and lamented the delay I feared the fire would bring about. I worked frantically, realizing that this overwhelming disaster must be met and handled in order that we might go on with our hunt of the grafters.

The *Bulletin* staff was assembled in Oakland, and there we managed to get out the paper, printing it in the plant of the Oakland *Herald*. Many of our files had been destroyed; our papers were scattered; of course, our advertising had been wiped out. We struggled with innumerable difficulties.

As soon as conditions permitted we returned to San Francisco. We found temporary quarters on the roof of the Merchants' Ice Company, in the northern end of Sansome street, at the foot of the Telegraph Hill cliffs. And here, on the roof, we built temporary editorial and linotype rooms. The pressroom was in a shack on the ground below. With these makeshift expedients we resumed publication in the city. All around us San Francisco was a heap of blackened ruins.

Walking on Fillmore street one day, I met Heney, who had come from Washington on a flying visit. We shook hands and I said: "I'd like to have a talk with you."

"Where can we talk?" he said. I took him into a tent on Fillmore street, and we each got a cracker box, turned it on end and sat down. "How about the graft prosecution?" I asked.

"I'm ready to go ahead," he replied, "any time you people are. Let's go down to see Spreckels."

Together we made our way through the mass of wreckage in search of Rudolph Spreckels.

We found him in the little temporary office, roughly made of boards, which he had built amid the ruins of his bank on Sansome street, surrounded by miles of burned brick and tangled steel girders.

At once we plunged into discussion of our plans. It had already been agreed that we should borrow Burns from the United States Secret Service. Spreckels undertook to raise the necessary money to finance the investigations. He had already procured thirty or forty thousand dollars for the fund. Spreckels said:

"Now that we have made terms about Burns, what is your fee to be, Heney?"

Heney said: "Well, I was born in San Francisco and raised here. I have always felt that it was my city. I have a little money, enough so that I am not going to need money very soon. I am willing to put my time and services against your money. I'll do it for nothing."

"That's very fine of you," Spreckels answered, "but it's more than we should ask."

Heney looked out at the ruins of the city and said: "No, I think I ought to do it, for San Francisco. It's my town."

From that day to this Heney has never received one cent for his work in the graft prosecution. Even when he was appointed Deputy District Attorney in order to operate in the courts, he paid the salary of $250 a month to the man displaced by him in order to allow him to take the office and conduct the prosecution.

We ended the interview with Heney's promise to bring Burns to San Francisco and begin definite work as soon as possible. I returned to the office on the roof of the ice plant, a happy man. After five years of hard work on the trail of Ruef and Schmitz I felt that at last the real fight was beginning.

Shortly afterward, Heney and Burns arrived in town, ready for business. They established themselves in what was later known as "The Red House," on Franklin street, between Post and Geary. Heney took Charles W. Cobb, a brilliant San Jose lawyer, into partnership with him, and he also engaged the services of Joseph J. Dwyer. Burns had brought with him a small number of assistant detectives, and later added others to this nucleus of a strong detective force.

The first move had to be the appointment of Heney as Deputy District Attorney. At that time the giving of such an appointment was in the hands of District Attorney Langdon, who was stumping the state as candidate for Governor. After some difficulty, we persuaded him to appoint Heney. He was very fond of Hiram W. Johnson, and would have preferred to appoint him, but he finally yielded to our arguments and agreed to give us Heney.

Before this became public I made a move in the direction of getting rid of what I considered a crooked Grand Jury. I told Judge Graham that I was associated with a group of men who meant business in their fight on the grafters. I went into the matter so forcefully that the judge finally consented to dismiss the Grand Jury.

Two days later I got information of a definite case of bribing Ruef. Four prize fight promoters had raised $20,000 and it was given by an emissary to Ruef for prize fight permits. This was the first definite information we had received. Heney had meanwhile been working on the French restaurant story. He decided that he could make a case out of it. This was encouraging. But of all the big briberies that we suspected, there was as yet not a shred of evidence.

CHAPTER XI

Events Begin To Crowd. Ruef Makes A Daring Move. The Mass Meeting At The Synagogue. San Francisco's Black Friday. Schmitz And Ruef Are Indicted. We Fall Foul Of The "Big Interests." Calhoun Engineers The Carmen's Strike. I Deplore The Strike, But Lend A Hand To The Strikers. By Devious Pathways We Reach Calhoun At Last.

When Heney's appointment as Deputy District Attorney became public, things began to happen.

At that time I was living in San Rafael. Late one night, after I had gone to bed, I was called to the long distance telephone. Rudolph Spreckels was speaking from San Mateo.

"Ruef has removed Langdon and appointed himself District Attorney," he said.

"What!" I cried, astounded. "This is incredible!"

Spreckels insisted that it was true. At the alarm, the acting mayor, doubtless at Ruef's command, had removed Langdon from his place as District Attorney and put Ruef himself into it. The brazen effrontery of this staggered us. Immediately, however, we perceived the danger in which we stood.

Graham had discharged the old Grand Jury. We insisted upon the drawing of a new one. With Ruef as District Attorney, our chance of getting a friendly Grand Jury was removed from the realm of the possible into that of the fantastic.

I took the first boat for the city in the morning, in a

desperate frame of mind. The morning papers carried the story of Ruef's appointment. Crossing the bay on the deck of the ferryboat, I made up my mind that there was only one thing to do.

At two o'clock Judge Graham was to decide whether he would recognize Ruef or Langdon as District Attorney. By eleven o'clock that morning I had twenty thousand extras on the streets stating the facts and calling on all good citizens to rally to the synagogue on the corner of California and Webster streets, where Judge Graham was holding court, and help uphold his hands in giving us justice. Hundreds of newsboys rushed all over the city, giving away these extras.

Long before two o'clock thousands of people were congregated around the synagogue. The streets were jammed with them, traffic was at a standstill. Indignation was running high against Ruef and Schmitz.

At that time even our so-called "best people" were with us in the fight. On a bit of lawn, outside the windows of Judge Graham's chambers, a large group of influential persons gathered, silently glaring through the windows, just steadily glaring, without a sound, as though to warn: "Don't dare!" Some of these were the people who, later when we touched Calhoun, fought us so desperately; but at that time they were with us, and that bit of lawn looked like a first night at the opera.

On the street sides of the synagogue there was pandemonium. The crowds surged this way and that, cheering, hooting and yelling; dangerous, in a mood for anything. Ruef not only controlled the city government, but the sheriff as well. The sheriff's deputies were there in full force, but they could not control the crowd. They could only center upon certain men, throwing us about. They handled me as roughly as they dared.

Heney and Langdon appeared on the steps and were wildly cheered. Ruef came out and was roughly treated by the mob. He bravely held his ground, protecting himself as best he could, never losing his nerve nor showing fear for an instant, though he was in danger of his life. He was rescued by the deputies, and the roars of the crowd subsided into mutterings.

Then Judge Graham arrived. He passed through the black mass of people, heard their mutterings and disappeared into the courtroom.

That day was long known in San Francisco as Black Friday; the day when, in the silence of the courtroom, besieged by the aroused crowds outside, Judge Graham recognized William H. Langdon * as District Attorney of San Francisco.

Whatever the thoughts of any man present in that courtroom, they were overshadowed by the knowledge of the mob outside, waiting to see that Ruef was dethroned, that Langdon was recognized. The days of the Vigilantes, of riots and lynchings, were not so long past that any one could fail to recall them, and the temper of the crowd around the synagogue was unmistakable.

Every one in the courtroom sensed the temper of that stormy crowd. Excitement was at fever heat. The *Bulletin* had two men there through all the proceedings,

* William H. Langdon has for some years been a member of the Appellate Court of California.

trained newspaper reporters, and neither of them telephoned a line to the paper. They decided that the situation was too big, too overwhelming, to be reported at all. They must have felt that they were at the center of the universe, that all the people in the world had gathered there, that every one knew what was happening.

After Judge Graham had recognized Langdon there came the drawing of the Grand Jury. Old machine methods were, of course, employed. The names in the box had been prepared for the drawing. Bits of paper bearing the chosen names were folded together, so that the searching hand of the clerk could feel a thick bunch and draw from that.

Knowing this, I managed to force my way into the courtroom, in spite of the efforts of a big fat "push" bailiff, who tried to throw me out. When the drawing of names was about to begin I rushed up to the judge's bench and loudly demanded that the names be emptied out of the box and separated.

This was done. The carefully prepared bunches of paper were broken up and scattered through the others. Then the Oliver Grand Jury was drawn.

This was a triumph for us, for with Langdon as District Attorney, and an honest Grand Jury, we had in hand all the weapons we needed. All that was necessary was to furnish legal evidence of the crimes that we knew had been committed, and we would be able to go on and punish the men who had committed them.

After I furnished Heney with the evidence of the bribery of Ruef in the matter of the prize fight permits, there was a long interval of searching and investigation without results. Spreckels was somewhat discouraged.

At length, however, the evidence secured by Burns was presented to the Oliver Grand Jury, and early in the fall of 1906 Schmitz and Ruef were both indicted for extortion in the French restaurant cases.

We all felt these cases to be a side issue. We had already suspected the bribery of the supervisors for the overhead trolley franchise, and our principal efforts were spent in trying to get at those facts.

Up to that time there is no question that public opinion was with us. Public opinion was with us until we began to touch the big fellows. We could have gone on uncovering petty graft, saloon graft, tenderloin graft, convicting and punishing men, even to the extent of exposing the police department, and the city—that is, the powerful men of the city—would have been with us. But the moment the big men were in danger their support was withdrawn.

Black Friday had alarmed Calhoun. The indictment of Ruef and Schmitz were ominous danger signals to him. He was a very brilliant man, clever, resourceful, daring, ruthless; of a temper that stopped at nothing. He knew what we did not know at that time. He knew that he had paid $200,000 to Abraham Ruef through his attorney, Tirey L. Ford, for the purpose of bribing the supervisors to give the United Railroads the overhead trolley franchise. He knew, when Heney was appointed and upheld by Judge Graham, that he stood in danger of being exposed. Sooner or later, the trail we were following would lead to him.

His first move was characteristically adroit and unscrupulous. He precipitated a street car strike.

Some time previous to Heney's opening headquarters

in San Francisco in commencing operations against the grafters, the United Railroads carmen had made a demand for an increase in pay. The United Railroads prevailed upon them to submit their grievances to arbitrators. Probably suspecting that Heney in his investigation might uncover the United Railroads bribery, Calhoun offered to make Francis J. Heney one of the arbitrators. Heney might have accepted the position. He had it under consideration when Burns came excitedly into his office and told him not to accept it, because he had just learned, through an employé of the mint, that Calhoun had transmitted $200,000 through the mint in San Francisco to Tirey L. Ford to be used to secure the overhead trolley permit. When Heney declined the position the labor men agreed to accept Chief Justice Beatty of the Supreme Court.

There was a long investigation of the claims of the carmen for more pay, a lot of testimony was taken, and some time passed before the matter was adjusted. The men were not satisfied with the terms that the United Railroads offered them. Calhoun seized upon the situation to bring on a strike among the carmen. The deal was made in Mayor Schmitz' house, with Bowling, secretary-treasurer of the Carmen's Union, acting with Calhoun and Schmitz.

Cornelius, the president of the Carmen's Union; Michael Casey, Andrew Furuseth and other labor men were anxious to prevent the carmen from striking, fearing they would lose and hoping that Heney's investigation would lead to the discovery of the bribing of the supervisors by Calhoun.

In this situation, Cornelius stood against the strike

and Bowling for it. Our plan was to try to bring about a secret ballot, reasoning that if the men voted secretly they would vote against the strike. Bowling was advocating an open ballot, counting on the men's fear to vote openly against the strike. Bowling won out.

We so nearly succeeded that I still believe that if we had been able to get a secret ballot in the meeting which declared the strike, we could have averted it. But Bowling's influence and strategy were too much for us. He succeeded in putting the question to a *viva voce* vote.

The question of striking was trembling in the balance. But many men were not brave enough to rise and openly vote "no" against a strike for higher wages. Bowling, working with Calhoun and Schmitz, had so inflamed certain elements in the union that others did not dare openly to stand against them. The men rose, one by one, and voted "yes."

Immediately the street cars were tied up. This second calamity, following hard upon the disaster of the fire, and halting the city's attempt at rebuilding, infuriated the business men and property owners of San Francisco. Calhoun knew the city; he knew what would influence the powerful men of the city. He knew that San Francisco was in ruins and that the business men above all things wanted the street cars to run; otherwise they would be utterly ruined.

With the entire approval of the business men of San Francisco, he imported professional gangs of strike-breakers, headed by Farley, and attempted to run the cars. The strikers attacked these strike-breakers viciously. Rioting broke out on the streets, men were beaten, crippled, killed. The city was in a turmoil. In the midst of it, in the most picturesque way, Calhoun rode up and down Market street in his automobile, winning tremendous admiration from the business people and property owners.

"There's a man who isn't afraid of anything! He's for San Francisco and the rebuilding of San Francisco. He'll break this strike, and save us, if any man can," they said on every hand. Calhoun could not have made a better move than secretly to force this strike, and then boldly and openly to break it, by force.

It was a spectacular move, cleverly planned; endearing him to the powerful people of San Francisco, who hated labor unions anyway, and particularly at this time, when the hard work of rehabilitation and the desperate task of keeping business going depended on the street cars moving.

While the strike was in progress the men received $5 a week each in benefits. One week the money did not come—$5,000 for a thousand men. The international president, McMahon, was away from his home office and had failed to send it. The Labor men who had been with me in the fight to prevent the strike came to me and said: "If we don't have $5,000 by one o'clock to-day, the strike will be broken. If the men don't get their $5 apiece at one o'clock they'll give in and go back to work, and all their efforts and suffering will come to nothing."

I had exerted every effort of which I was capable in trying to prevent the calling of the street car strike, but I did not want to see the strike lost now and the men who already had been led into so much suffering forced to lose their chance of getting something out of it all. Therefore, since it was necessary to have the $5,000 by one o'clock that afternoon if these men were to get their strike benefits and be held in line, I determined to do my utmost to provide the $5,000.

I found two friends who were willing to lend me $2,500 each. I had the money changed into $5 gold pieces, put it in a sack, and sent it out to the headquarters of the Carmen's Union. Bowling, the traitor secretary-treasurer, who had planned the strike with Calhoun, was there. The sack was given to him and he was told to distribute the money among the men. He was obliged to do so, but he kept the sack and carried it to Calhoun as evidence that I had saved the men from losing the strike at that time.

Eventually Calhoun, through his force of imported strike-breakers, succeeded in crushing the strike he had begun, and the men went back to work—beaten; and Calhoun became the hero of the hour. Before that time came, however, we struck a trail that led us hot on his track. We were getting closer to him every day.

While we were in the midst of our investigations, Schmitz suddenly set out for Europe. The day after he left it was announced in the newspapers that he had dismissed the president of the Board of Works, Frank Maestretti. The news came as a thunderbolt.

Could it be possible that Ruef and Schmitz dared to dismiss Frank Maestretti, a man who, we felt convinced, was in on all the city graft, or at least knew of it?

I was very much excited, and sent for Maestretti and Golden M. Roy. I knew Roy to be a close friend of Maestretti, the two men being partners in the Pavilion Skating Rink. They came to my office, and I talked with them about the removal of Maestretti. They still hoped he would be reinstated by wire from Schmitz.

I said: "Well, if he is not, perhaps you will be willing to talk with me." After some discussion, they left, saying they would know about it next day, and asking me to call on them then.

On the following day I met them in their office at Pavilion Rink. I told them that I represented powerful interests in San Francisco who were going to get the facts of the graft, and that I thought they would do well to get in on the ground floor with me. They admitted that they could tell me some very interesting things, but they put me off, saying they would see me again.

Maestretti followed me out of the office and warned me against Roy, saying he was a Ruef man and could not be trusted. When I reported this to Burns he very cleverly analyzed it as meaning that Maestretti wanted the whole thing to himself and wanted Roy shut out.

I carried to Rudolph Spreckels the news of the possibilities that I thought lay in Roy and Maestretti, and Spreckels said: "Can you trust them?"

"Well," I answered, "unfortunately, Rudolph, the crimes that were committed here were not known to respectable people like Bishop Nichols or our leading prelates. If we are going to get anywhere, we've got to get our information from crooks."

Burns had many meetings with Maestretti, and he soon discovered that Roy was the man who knew all the facts, and that unless we could get Roy we could get nowhere.

"Work on Roy," he said.

In my eagerness to get information from Roy my

mind went back to the days before the fire. At that time Roy owned a jewelry store on Kearny street, near the *Bulletin* office. A friend of his called on me and said that Schmitz had offered Roy a position as police commissioner. Having a wife and family whom he dearly loved, Roy did not want to take the place if I was going to attack him.

I said: "Well, tell him to come up and see me."

Roy called and I told him that if they offered him this position, they expected him to take their program, and that if he took their program it would be a crooked program, and, therefore, it would come under my criticism. It was impossible, in my judgment, that they would appoint him with any other idea than that he would stand in with their graft.

He insisted that he could be honest, even though a Schmitz police commissioner. But I remained unconvinced, and in the end he did not accept the position.

Later, in the Schmitz campaign, Roy organized what he called the "Schmitz Business Men's League." I published an article that was really gentle, coming from me at that time. I reproved Roy for having anything to do with Schmitz. I said that he was a man of family, that he ought not to risk his reputation by affiliating with such men as Ruef and Schmitz. Afterward I learned that this mild criticism worried him tremendously.

Recalling this episode gave me an idea. I had a very violent personal attack written on Roy. It was a page article, embellished with pictures. I raked up everything in Roy's activities that could place him in a discreditable light before the community. Then I had a page proof of this article printed secretly in the *Bulletin* office. When it was ready I laid it face down on my desk and sent for Roy. Burns waited in an adjoining room.

Roy came into my office. He said: "Well, what can I do for you, Mr. Older?" in what I thought was a patronizing tone.

I was very much excited. "You can't do anything for me," I said, "but I'm going to put you in the penitentiary." I picked up the page and handed it to him to read.

He began to read it, turned pale, and reeled on his feet. "Read it all," I said.

"I'm reading it all."

He finished, laid it down and said: "What do you want me to do?"

"I want you to tell the truth."

"All right," he said. "I'm willing to tell you the truth—everything." I pressed a button and Burns came in. I turned Roy over to Burns and left the room.

In a little while Burns called me and said: "Roy wants to see his friends before he talks."

I said: "I don't think we ought to let him see his friends. It's a friend; it isn't friends. It's Ruef he wants to see." Roy sat there without saying a word.

"No," Burns said. "I think it best to let him see his friends."

I said nothing more. After a moment Roy got up and walked out. He was shadowed, of course. He went directly to his home, where his wife and children were, and stayed there, sending no messages and telephoning nobody till midnight. Then he telephoned Burns and asked to see him. When they met he told Burns much that he knew about the Ruef briberies. This interview led directly to the confessions of the eighteen supervisors who had taken money in the overhead trolley franchise deal. We had reached Calhoun at last.

CHAPTER XII

Calhoun's Grand-Stand Play. Ruef, Out On Bail, Endeavors To Intimidate Our Star Witness. Roy's Ingenious Scheme. We Set The Stage For A New Act. The Suspected Supervisors Confess. We Make A Deal With Ruef, As A Result Of Which Calhoun Is Indicted. Calhoun Becomes The People's Hero. My Pursuit Of Him.

All this time the street car strike was going on, with almost daily violence and bloodshed. Calhoun still rode up and down Market street, to the admiration of all who saw him. His ruthlessness in dealing with the strikers and his terrific efforts to quell the storm he had raised were having exactly the effect he had desired when he plotted the strike. He was daily becoming more of a hero to the big men of San Francisco who controlled public opinion.

Meantime it became known to Ruef that Roy had come over to our side. In order to frighten him into silence Ruef had introduced into the Board of Supervisors an ordinance making it illegal for any girl under eighteen years of age to visit a skating rink without her mother. If this became a law, Roy's and Maestretti's business, Dreamland Rink, was doomed.

Roy, far from being intimidated, responded to this threat with an ingenious scheme. He suggested to us that by means of this proposed ordinance we could trap the supervisors. His plan was to bribe them to kill the ordinance, have them caught taking the money, and terrorize them into confessing the overhead trolley briberies.

We rehearsed for the plan in Roy's office at Pavilion Rink. There was another room next to his office, in which we planned to hide and watch the bribery. Burns borrowed a gimlet from a near-by grocery store and we bored three holes through the door so that three people could look into Roy's office.

After this was done Burns and I stood on the other side of the door and looked through the holes, while Roy rehearsed the coming scene.

Roy sat at his table with imaginary bills in his hand and the chairs placed in such a position that we could see him. Then, leaning toward the empty chair in which the unsuspecting supervisor was to be placed, Roy began, pretending that Supervisor Tom Lonergan was present.

"Tom, I want that skating rink bill killed. If it goes through——"

We would interrupt, "A little louder, Roy—move to the right. Now go ahead."

"Tom, I want that skating rink bill killed. I'm willing to pay $500 for it, and here's the money. The bill's coming up to-night and I want you to go against it."

The rehearsal was perfect. It was beyond my imagination to conceive of anything like that being fulfilled and I said to Roy: "It's too much of a melodrama for me. I don't believe it's possible that anything like this will ever happen."

Roy replied: "Don't worry. It will happen exactly as we have planned it."

And it did.

Two days later Supervisor Tom Lonergan came into the office, while Burns and two other witnesses stood behind the door. He took the chair that had been placed in position, listened to Roy's talk pitched in a key that the witnesses could overhear, took the money and pocketed it. After him came two others, one at a time. I have forgotten which two they were. We were elated, and were arranging to trap the others speedily when the *Chronicle* got a tip that something was happening and ran a story which scared them all.

So we worked on the three. And finding that we had the goods on them, they confessed everything, including the overhead trolley deal. And their confessions involved the others, and the others were scared and got into line. The whole eighteen made their confessions as quickly as they possibly could, one after the other scurrying to safety, with the promise given them by Heney and Burns and Langdon that they would not be prosecuted if they testified.

We had in our hands all the evidence that I had been combing the town for during many years.

Burns later got the whole credit for obtaining these confessions. He soon became nationally famous and amassed a great fortune. But the trap which caught them was entirely Roy's idea, planned by Roy and carried through by Roy.

While these confessions were being taken down, Ruef hid himself away in a roadhouse at Trocadero. He was out on bail, under indictment in the French restaurant case. Burns was searching for him. He finally found him, brought him back into custody and put him into the Little St. Francis Hotel, a temporary structure put up after the fire in Union Square. Here Ruef learned for the first time of the supervisors' confessions, and

Burns believed that he could be induced to make one himself. But Burns said that Heney was so exalted over his success with the supervisors that he would not listen to any confession from Ruef.

"Let the blankety-blank go over the bay! We won't allow him to confess and have immunity. We've given the eighteen supervisors immunity and we'll make him sweat!"

Burns shook his head and said to me: "That's the way it always is when you haven't got complete control. They don't know now that in less than two weeks they'll be pleading with me to get Ruef to do the very thing I can easily get him to do now. He won't think of doing it when he gets his second wind and has a chance to connect up with his powerful friends. They'll order me to get his confession in two weeks. Remember. And it'll be hard to do."

Sure enough, in less than two weeks Burns was hard at work trying to get a confession from Ruef.

By connecting up with Rabbi Kaplan and Rabbi Nieto, he managed to secure a confession from Ruef in the overhead trolley bribery. There was an understanding with Ruef that he was not to be prosecuted at all, not even in the French restaurant case, which was then pending. Burns told me little, almost nothing, about the details of his arrangement with Ruef. It was not until much later that I learned the facts. At that time I knew only that Burns was well along toward pulling Ruef through.

One day Burns came to me and asked me to go with him to Judge Lawlor and try to convince Lawlor that if Ruef was a good witness in all the big bribery cases he should be allowed to go free in the French restaurant case.

We found Lawlor in his room at the Family Club. Burns presented the case to him. Lawlor flatly refused to have anything to do with any such program. He said that the city would not stand for Ruef's not going to the penitentiary; that Ruef must be put in stripes. Anything less than that would mean the failure of the graft prosecution.

"We've already given immunity to eighteen supervisors," said Lawlor. "Now to give full immunity to Ruef would mean our ruin. This must be done: Let him be a witness in all the big bribery cases. Let the French restaurant case be pending the while, and then, when he has made a good witness, let him come into court and plead guilty in the French restaurant case. Let the District Attorney state to the judge that Ruef has been a good witness for the state and ask leniency for him, and then the judge will let him off with a year.

"But one year at least he must serve in the penitentiary, to save our reputations."

I agreed with Lawlor. Burns went away much disappointed. Later Heney met with the rabbis, Nieto and Kaplan. It was a secret meeting, held at midnight. The result of it was an agreement that Ruef would testify before the Grand Jury, fully and truthfully, in all the important cases. If he did this he would be allowed to plead guilty in the French restaurant case. Heney assured the rabbis that the judge would let Ruef off with a year.

Ruef then appeared before the Grand Jury and gave evidence necessary for the indictments of himself,

Schmitz, John Martin, De Sabla, Frank Drum, Patrick Calhoun, and some others, on the big bribery charges. That day the foreman of the Grand Jury telephoned Cornelius, president of the Carmen's Union, and asked him to be very careful to prevent any disorder among the strikers. We knew from this that the Grand Jury was about to indict Calhoun.

It was after his indictment that Calhoun crushed the strike. The men went back to work, the street cars began running again, and Calhoun at once became a great, public-spirited figure in the eyes of the people. He loomed up as the savior of the city, once ruined by fire and again threatened by labor unionism. His indictment made no dent at all in his popularity. The prominent men of San Francisco stood before him and said: "Let's see you convict him!"

"But don't you want him convicted if he is guilty?"

"No!" one of them said. "If I were on the jury I'd vote to acquit him if he were guilty as hell! He's the man that saved San Francisco!"

After the street car strike had been successfully engineered, Bowling, the secretary-treasurer of the Carmen's Union, was placed on the payroll of the United Railroads. However, after Calhoun's indictment, Bowling became dissatisfied with the amount of money he was getting. He must have felt that he had been unfairly treated by Calhoun, or, perhaps, he endeavored to get more than Calhoun was willing to pay. At any rate he finally came to Burns and offered, for $10,000, to give us the evidence that Calhoun, Schmitz and he had planned the street car strike.

Burns, being employed by the District Attorney, was

not in a position to negotiate with him directly, and sent him to me. He sketched roughly this story of the making and breaking of the carmen's strike, and offered to put himself on record, to make an affidavit of it, for $10,000. Burns finally got him to agree to $6,000. I consented to this and arranged to meet him the following day.

Next day I met Bowling in an office in the Spreckels Building, with a stenographer. I had arranged for the $6,000. With Bowling was a man who had shared in the deal with Calhoun. The stenographer was ready, waiting. I said, "Go ahead. Everything is arranged. Tell your story."

He said: "Well, we met at Calhoun's house."

I said: "Go on. Who was present? Calhoun? Schmitz?"

There was a long silence. He turned white. Finally he stammered that he couldn't go on.

"Why? Don't you want the money?"

"Yes," he said. Then he said, desperately: "But they—they'll kill me!" He meant the carmen he had betrayed.

I said: "All right. Good day." Bowling left the room.

Burns bitterly reproached me for this action later. He said I should have coaxed him along, given him a little money, played him from day to day until he was ready to talk. But I was not experienced in such matters.

Next morning there appeared in one of the morning papers a story, backed by an affidavit by Bowling, charging me with attempting to bribe him with a sum of money to tell a lie against Calhoun. Then he proceeded to tell the story of the sack of money I had taken to union headquarters to support the strike. Thereupon the whole powerful part of the town became violently prejudiced against me because I had helped to uphold the strike, and because I was attacking Calhoun, who in their opinion had crushed the strike and saved San Francisco from ruin.

I had in fact first attempted to prevent the strike that Calhoun had ordered. Then I helped hold the men steady by paying their benefit money, which was afterward repaid to me, in the hope that if they held together they could save something from the ruin in which Calhoun had involved them.

But in the eyes of the powerful people of the city I was branded as a dangerous agitator, plotting against the city's peace, while Calhoun was given a halo. I had no recourse except to continue to help in uncovering the truth in the courts.

Tirey L. Ford had been indicted with Calhoun. He was chief counsel for the United Railroads and was the man who had passed the $200,000 from Calhoun to Ruef for bribing the supervisors. He was placed on the calendar for trial before Calhoun, in the hope that if he were convicted he might come through with a confession involving Calhoun, in return for leniency in his sentence.

While these cases were pending, and San Francisco people in general were absorbed with their own personal affairs, the city became filled with armed detectives, employed either by Burns or by Calhoun. To one who knew the inside facts, the very air of the streets became tense. Every few feet one met a man who was working for one side or the other. Many men of prominence were constantly shadowed by both sides, and even the men who were following them were also followed and watched.

Shortly after Calhoun's indictment, he sent a mutual friend to ask me to name my price for quitting the fight. I replied: "Tell Mr. Calhoun that I have no price, that nothing will stop me until he has been convicted and sent to the penitentiary."

In my relentless pursuit of him I stopped at nothing. I learned of a suit that a maiden sister had brought against him for having fleeced her out of $60,000. Calhoun settled the case quickly when he found that Heney was working in San Francisco, but there was a court record in Atlanta, Georgia. I went back to Atlanta personally to get it.

On this trip I spent my own money, $700, saved out of my salary. I had a transcript made of the case and certified to by the county clerk in Atlanta. When the county clerk handed it to me and I paid his fee, he said:

"I don't know what you are going to do with this, but I imagine you are going to take it to San Francisco to use against Patrick Calhoun. Let me tell you something. He's a desperate man. He's a man who would not hesitate to blow up a whole theater full of people to get just one man that he hated."

CHAPTER XIII

I Am Constantly Shadowed, And Many Traps Are Set For Me. I Find Myself Ostracized. Mrs. Older My One Staunch Champion. A Significant Warning. Dangers Threaten On Every Hand. Calhoun Asks Roy To "Name His Price." His Proffered Munificence Halted Halfway.

From the time I returned to San Francisco I was never without a shadow. I never left my office that one or two men did not follow me to my hotel, which was the Fairmont. All sorts of traps were set to catch me. Women would call me upon the telephone and tell me that if I would come to such and such a room, in such and such an apartment house, I could get some very valuable information.

I avoided all these traps. The stress was very great and I was living under great excitement and worry. In the midst of this, Mrs. Older and I were ostracized by many who had formerly been our friends.

After the indictment of Calhoun—a relation of John C. Calhoun; a Southern gentleman with a great deal of social prestige in the East, and necessarily in San Francisco as well; pampered in our best clubs, entertained by our "best people"; a man, moreover, who had "saved" San Francisco's business interests when they were endangered by the car strike—local sentiment toward the graft prosecution changed overnight.

People who had known me quite intimately stopped speaking to me. Labor fell away from us because Eugene E. Schmitz was Labor's mayor and they did not like to see him discredited by a group of men whom they considered to be hostile to Labor. The wealthy people fell away from us because we were attacking one of their own class, Calhoun. So we were stranded between the two.

Up to this time I had been a fairly popular member of the Bohemian Club and used greatly to enjoy going there; but after we touched Calhoun there was hardly any one in the club who would speak to me. The ostracism became so acute that I finally resigned.

Mrs. Older and I had known and liked some members of what is known as "society" in San Francisco, and they, of course, dropped us. One of the women called on Mrs. Older and told her that many of her friends liked her very much and would like to continue their friendship, but that they could not stand for the attitude of her husband.

Mrs. Older replied that she did not care for their friendship in that case; that she was perfectly willing to be ostracized with me; that she believed me to be right, and that was the only thing to be considered.

In the stress and strain of those days Mrs. Older and I tried to escape from it all every evening by going to the beach, where we had a tiny car-house attached to a restaurant managed by Mrs. Gunn. It was our one pleasure, just about sunset, to go for a swim in the ocean, return to our car-house and then dine with Mrs. Gunn.

One evening, as I came from the office and crossed the sidewalk to the automobile in which Mrs. Older was waiting, a very good friend of mine, who had deep connections in the underworld, passed by me, and said warningly: "Keep away from the beach."

He did not stop to be questioned, but went quickly past me, as though he had not spoken to me.

This warning disturbed me. I knew it to be important. The man who had given it to me was my friend, and a man not given to false alarms.

I was very angry at the thought of giving up my one pleasure, that daily swim in the surf with Mrs. Older, and our quiet little dinner later in Mrs. Gunn's small restaurant. I determined that I would continue to have it.

So I secured two plain clothes men from the police department and went to the beach as usual, leaving the two officers sitting in the machine on the beach, watching. Nothing happened. Still I knew that the warning was not without significance, and so each day I took the plain clothes men with me, and never while we were at the beach allowed them to get out of sight.

Later I learned that Calhoun's men had employed a half-breed Mexican gun fighter to come from Arizona to San Francisco to "get" me. The day before my friend warned me, this Mexican was standing opposite the *Bulletin* office in front of the Phelan Building, which was then in course of construction, when another well-known gun fighter, who knew him very well, came along. He asked: "What are you doing here?"

The Mexican answered: "I'm waiting to see Older when he comes down."

"What's the idea?"

"Well, I'm supposed to 'get him.' They want me to go up into the Phelan Building and shoot him through his window in the *Bulletin* office. They told me the noise of the steam riveters would sound so much like a rifle shot that it wouldn't be distinguished, but I'm leary of that. If it didn't, I wouldn't have any chance to get away. So I'm going out to get him at the beach, where he dines every night with his wife."

"What are you staying here for, then?"

"Well, I don't know him. I am waiting here till he comes down. A fellow over there will lift his hat when Older comes through the door. That will give me the signal who he is."

The man to whom the Mexican gave this confidence was a friend of the man who warned me. I had done favors for both of them and they didn't want any harm to come to me. So the warning was given me. That plan was thwarted by the two plain clothes men who guarded us when we were at the beach.

Some years later I heard from Peter Claudianos, then doing life in San Quentin for dynamiting the house of one of our star witnesses, Gallagher, of another plan which was spoiled by the plain clothes men. He told me that when plans were made for dynamiting Gallagher in Oakland they thought they might as well dynamite me at the same time. So Felix Padauveris, who was in charge of the job, rented the cottage just below mine at the beach, and stored in its basement fifteen pounds of dynamite.

He and Claudianos visited the beach, breakfasted in Mrs. Gunn's restaurant, looked the situation over, and made all their plans for placing the dynamite. But the presence of the two plain clothes men frightened them and they abandoned the idea.

These things seem so melodramatic that it is almost incredible that they could have occurred in a peaceful city, where most people were going about their ordinary routine affairs, and, when they read of the graft prosecution, saw only the surface facts that were published and were probably bored by them long before the fight ended. But the plots and counterplots of that time were innumerable.

Calhoun's detectives filled the city. Calhoun was desperate. He saw the penitentiary doors opening before him, in spite of his utmost efforts. He stopped at nothing to save himself or to get revenge upon his implacable enemies.

After Roy became friendly with me we all felt very grateful to him and used to dine or lunch in his restaurant as often as we could. The restaurant was on Van Ness avenue near Sutter street, Van Ness avenue being at that time the center of the city, since downtown San Francisco was not yet rebuilt.

One morning about eleven o'clock I dropped into Roy's restaurant for breakfast. I always chatted with him, and, not seeing him, I asked the waiter where he was. The waiter said: "He's over there in the corner. Don't you see him?"

Roy was sitting with his back to me, talking with a strange man. After a moment he rose, and, coming over to me with an affable smile, handed me an envelope, saying:

"Look at this. Pretend. As soon as that man goes out I have something to tell you."

He went back. When the man went out Roy came over and told me that he was Luther Brown, whom Calhoun had brought from Los Angeles to head his force of detectives. He had come to Roy and said:

"Roy, we want you with us, and we want you to name your price."

Roy asked: "What do you want me to do?"

"We want you to be with us."

"Well, in that case I want to see Calhoun. I want to talk to him."

"All right. I'll see him to-morrow and make the appointment."

Roy reported this to Burns, as well as to me, and Burns suggested that he keep the appointment, which he did. He called at Calhoun's house and found Calhoun out in his garden, picking roses. He met Roy very cordially and asked him into the house, where he took him into a room and closed the doors.

Roy said: "Well, what is it?"

"Roy, I want you to ship with me for the whole voyage."

"Well, what do you want me to do?"

"I want you to name your price for testifying that Spreckels is to pay Older $15,000 and Heney $15,000 the day that I am convicted; that Spreckels also offered you $15,000 and $10,000 each to Gallagher and one or two of the other supervisors for testifying that I had bribed them."

Roy said: "What about my friends?"

Calhoun replied: "I'll take care of your friends. You mean Dr. Poheim and Frank Maestretti. I'll take care of Poheim, and Maestretti is all right because Herrin is handling him. At any rate, I want to see you to-morrow. If you will take a certain boat, go to Oakland, you will find an automobile waiting at a certain place. Get in that automobile, and you will be driven out to where I am. I am going to handle this thing, Roy. I don't want any more Fords handling my affairs. From now on I'm going to handle this case myself."

Roy was by this time sincerely devoted to the graft prosecution and in entire sympathy with our purposes. If coercion had been necessary at first to bring him into line—and I do not know that it was necessary; I only know that I used it—persuasion of that kind was no longer necessary to keep him with us.

He reported to us his conversation with Calhoun, and with Burns' advice he followed the instructions that had been given him.

Next morning, with Dr. Poheim, he took the ferry Calhoun had suggested, found an automobile waiting for them in Oakland, and got into it.

The machine took them to Luther Brown's father-in-law's house, near San Leandro. In the yard were Calhoun, with several of his attorneys, Luther Brown and some of Brown's detectives. Roy said:

"Well, Calhoun, I am not going to allow any Tirey L. Ford to handle my affairs, either. I'm not going to talk before all these people."

Calhoun answered: "Come upstairs and we will talk alone." He took Roy into an upstairs bedroom, and they sat down on the edge of the bed. Calhoun said, quietly:

"Roy, what do you want?"

"Well," Roy said, "I've got to be made whole on my investments in San Francisco. I'm connected with some pretty big people, and if I throw them down San Francisco will be no place for me. I'll have to leave town."

"All right. What are your investments?"

"Well, there's my restaurant."

"What does that stand you?"

"Thirty-two thousand," said Roy.

"I'll take care of that," said Calhoun. "What else have you got?"

"A skating rink."

"What does that amount to?"

"Twenty thousand."

"I'll take care of that. Anything else?"

Roy enumerated various interests that had to be covered. In all, they amounted to $80,000. Calhoun agreed to pay him that amount. In return Roy was to go on the stand and testify that Rudolph Spreckels had promised to pay me $15,000, Henry $15,000 and Gallagher $10,000 on the day that Calhoun was convicted. Calhoun's purpose was to make it appear that he was being persecuted by Spreckels because they were financial rivals.

"Well," said Calhoun, "we've got to arrange this thing in some way so that it won't be subornation of perjury. But that can be arranged. That's only a matter of detail. Now as to Poheim."

It was agreed that Poheim was to have $25,000. Poheim had been a member of the Schmitz police commission and knew of the graft.

All this Roy immediately reported to us. But a few days later he met Calhoun, and Calhoun said:

"There's a little hitch in this plan of mine. I told it to John Garber, and he told me we were all heading for the penitentiary on this stuff. What he said rattled me a little. Still, I'm convinced that I'm right, and I'm going ahead with it. But I want a little time to think it over."

John Garber was a very famous lawyer in San Francisco. His advice undoubtedly disturbed Calhoun. Later, Roy learned that he had acquainted other of his attorneys with the negotiations, and they had told him it was undoubtedly a Burns trap. So the matter hung fire for some time before Calhoun reopened it.

CHAPTER XIV

The Fight Still On. The *Bulletin* Prints All That It Dares. Public Opinion Divided. Schmitz Having Been Convicted, We Search For An Honest Mayor. I Escape A Criminal Act By A Narrow Margin. Calhoun Still After Roy. A Web Of Plots And Cross-Plots. A Mysterious Telephone Call.

Meanwhile, we were hammering at Ruef and Schmitz in the courts. The *Bulletin* was printing all that it dared to print of the truth. San Francisco was divided into two violently opposing camps. One believed that we were pure white crusaders, endeavoring to rid the city of evil men. The other declared that we were henchmen of Spreckels, persecuting the man who had saved the city from ruin at the hands of the unions.

We had brought Schmitz back from Europe, arrested him and tried him, while he was still Mayor of San Francisco. He stood in the dock as Mayor of San Francisco, and he went out from the dock to the Mayor's office and conducted the affairs of the city as a suspected criminal. He was found guilty of bribery in the French restaurant cases and sentenced to San Quentin for five years. The Supreme Court subsequently set the sentence aside on a technicality. After his conviction he was taken to the Ingleside jail, and proceedings were brought to remove him from the Mayor's chair.

The city was then without a Mayor. It fell to us to choose one, because the man to fill the empty place was to be chosen by the Board of Supervisors. We held eighteen of them in the hollow of our hands on account of their confessions.

The matter hung fire for some time while we tried to decide who should be Mayor of San Francisco. Spreckels, Heney, Langdon and I were busy trying to find a suitable man, one who would satisfy the city and be sympathetic with our fight against the grafters.

The first name suggested was that of Dr. Gallwey, a very popular physician in San Francisco. Some one went down to Santa Barbara, where he was staying, to ask him if he would be Mayor. He refused.

Other names were mentioned, but we could not all agree upon one. E. J. Livernash was at that time working with me. He was a writer on the *Bulletin,* and I had him as my adviser in all my activities in the graft prosecution. One day he said to me that Phelan ought to be appointed. I agreed. Livernash said: "Of course, Labor has been against him, but that can be arranged. I think we can induce Labor to accept him."

With this idea in mind, we drove out to Phelan's residence, where Rudolph Spreckels was dining. Just as we stopped in front of the house, Phelan and Spreckels came out together and walked toward our automobile. Livernash said: "We have decided that Phelan is the man for Mayor."

Spreckels said instantly: "I won't stand for him." That angered us both. I said: "Why not?"

Spreckels replied: "Because he is too close to me." He meant, of course, that Phelan was so closely associated with him that his appointment would make it appear that Spreckels was choosing the Mayor.

Livernash became very angry and said: "Well, then, I'm done with the whole thing. I'll have nothing more to do with it."

We drove away in a huff. We were both so angry that it looked as though there was to be a split between the few men in whose hands the selection of a Mayor lay! But San Francisco was without a Mayor, and something had to be done.

On the following morning Livernash and I met as usual. A night's sleep had cooled us both. Livernash said it was a pity to quarrel with Spreckels at such a critical time. I agreed with him and hastened away to find Spreckels. I met him at Heney's office and assured him that we would continue to co-operate with him and try to find a suitable man for Mayor. All along Livernash had been strong for Michael Casey, president of the Teamsters' Union.

At that time Casey was a big figure with the Labor men. He and Andrew Furuseth had fought Bowling's crowd in the Carmen's Union, trying to defeat Calhoun's movement to bring on a strike. They knew that Calhoun had his strike-breakers here ready to break the strike, so that Calhoun might gain the applause of the powerful people of the city. But Spreckels would not stand for Casey. He did not share the confidence that Furuseth, Livernash and I had in him. And we were compelled to abandon him.

After leaving Spreckels I returned to Livernash's office and together we searched our minds for the name of a man that the people would accept. I remembered the old Board of Freeholders that had framed the Phelan charter, and it occurred to me that perhaps some of those names would do. I asked Livernash if he had a copy of the charter which contained the names of the Board of Freeholders, most of whom we had forgotten.

He said he didn't know. He had moved to temporary quarters after the fire, his books were disturbed, and if he had one he didn't know where it was. He went over to a corner of his office, where a lot of pamphlets and odds and ends of papers had been dumped, and pawed them over. He finally found a ragged copy of the charter, knocked the dust from it against a corner of his desk and handed it to me.

I looked over the names of the freeholders, and when I came to E. R. Taylor I said: "Dr. Taylor is the man."

"Wonderful," said Livernash. "But he's dead."

I said: "No! Is he? He can't be! I saw him in a Sutter street car not over a month ago."

"Then," said Livernash, "he's the man, by all means."

We both reasoned that Dr. Taylor was eminently respectable. He was a lawyer and a physician and a poet, and, so far as we knew, he had never done anything that could be held against him by any one. He was just the man for the situation. I went hurriedly up to the Red House. Spreckels was there.

I said: "Dr. Taylor is the man."

"Just the man!" he said.

He called Langdon on the telephone within a minute and said: "Dr. Taylor!"

Langdon said: "Just the man!" Every one agreed.

That night the puppet board of supervisors met and Dr. Taylor was made Mayor of San Francisco. He was an admirable Mayor for our purposes, eminently just and inoffensive to every one. The city seemed fairly well pleased with the selection. He took office immediately.

Meanwhile, we continued our fight against the grafters. We had the confessions of the eighteen supervisors, and of Ruef. We had promised the supervisors immunity, because we knew that behind them were Ruef and Schmitz and Ford. We had promised to let Ruef off with one year's sentence, because we knew that behind him were men still higher up, Calhoun and others, more influential and thus infinitely more dangerous. These were the men we wanted to get.

But while we were engaged in tracking down Calhoun, Calhoun and his hired force of detectives were not idle.

One day a man called at my office and told me that he had been in the employ of the Pinkertons, but had been dismissed. The reason he gave was that a number of Pinkerton detectives had organized, demanded more money, and struck. The local manager, in retaliation, had reported these men to the Eastern headquarters as having falsified their reports, and the men were dismissed.

My informant said that he had then gone to work as a Pullman conductor on the Southern Pacific. Knowing that the Pinkertons were doing work for the Southern Pacific, he had put in a knock against them with the superintendent in San Francisco, and this had resulted in his being discharged by the railroad company.

"Those Pinkertons have got me fired twice," he said bitterly. "Now, Mr. Older, I don't want any money for the service that I can render you. I just want to get evened up with the Pinkertons.

"There is a prominent labor leader, affiliated with the Water Front Federation of Labor, who is a Pinkerton spy, employed by Pinkerton to betray Labor. He makes it a business to keep watch on the docks, and whenever he hears any one advocating higher wages or shorter hours, or in any way objecting to the present condition of affairs, he reports that man to the Pinkerton agency, which reports him to his employers.

"Now, I can get the originals of those reports, and I'll be glad to do it for you. I want to show those Pinkertons that they can't ruin a man like me without any comeback."

His statement was so startling that I wanted time to think it over. If it were true, and he could obtain those reports for me, it would be one of the biggest Labor stories that had ever been published in San Francisco. All my newspaper instincts were aroused. I asked the man to call again next day at twelve o'clock.

The next day the Pinkerton man called, bringing another man with him. I had also asked a man, a friend of mine, to be present during the interview.

The detective introduced the man he brought as "Mr. So-and-So, who is still employed by Pinkerton. But he is as sore at them as I am." He added: "This man can get those reports for you."

They both went over the statement he had made to me the day before. A prominent Labor leader was betraying his followers to the Pinkertons, his reports were obtainable, and these men could get them for me, and would.

I said: "How?"

He replied: "By opening the safe after office hours and taking them."

I said: "Do you know the combination of the safe? Are you sure you can get them?" I knew this would be a tremendous story for the *Bulletin*.

The two men explained how they would get the reports,

the original reports, signed by this man who was betraying Labor. But while they talked, the friend that I had asked into the room looked at me, caught my eye, and I saw in his face that he suspected a trap. I got the two men out of my office as best I could, saying as little as possible.

After they had gone, I sent for Detective Burns and told him what had happened. He said:

"My God, you had a narrow escape. Were you thinking of taking those documents and printing them?"

"I had in mind that he had a big newspaper story in his possession," I replied, "and I hadn't stopped to consider any further than that."

He said: "Well, this is what would have happened if you had gone on with it. The safe in the Pinkerton office would have been blown. You wouldn't have known that until after you had printed the documents. Then you would have been arrested for burglary. The two men who called on you would testify that you had employed them to burglarize the safe in the Pinkerton office. They would testify that they had only carried out your orders. They would have turned state's evidence on you, and you would have gone to San Quentin."

It was the narrowest escape from the penitentiary that I ever had.

Ruef had been tried, the jury had disagreed, and we were holding him for his second trial. Calhoun's turn was approaching. Again he sent for Roy.

Luther Brown came to see Roy, and took him to Calhoun.

"Now, Roy," said Calhoun, "I want you with me in

this trial. I can make you a rich man without leaving this chair. I can manipulate common stock of the United Railroads so that you can make $150,000 easily. I will fix up Poheim, too. Now I want an affidavit from you, testifying to the bribery of Older, Burns and Heney by Spreckels."

Roy pretended to agree, and as he was going out of the room Luther Brown handed him $3,000, carelessly, as a sort of token of good will. Roy brought this money to Burns, and Burns told him to go on with the negotiations.

A few days later Brown sent for Roy. When Roy entered Brown had just finished an affidavit on the typewriter. This affidavit implicated Burns, Heney, Gallagher and myself as having been bribed by Spreckels.

To gain time, Roy said:

"This is an affidavit, a pretty serious thing. I'm liable to be caught up for perjury in an affidavit. Make it in the form of a statement. Give me a copy of it and let me think it over."

Brown gave him a copy, and Roy brought it to me. I made a copy of it instantly and put it in Phelan's safe. It is still there. I did this to protect myself.

Roy went back, under instructions from Burns, and put over a very clever move. He said:

"Now this is not to be used unless I give my consent. Is that right?"

Brown replied: "Yes, I'll agree to that."

"Very well, then, just write that down on the bottom there and sign it," said Roy, and Brown wrote it in his own handwriting and signed his name to it. Roy carried this away with him and we put it in Heney's safe.

A little later Brown said to Roy: "Some one has peached on us."

Roy said: "I don't think so. What do you mean?"

"Well," replied Brown, "Calhoun said to me: 'Some one is leaking in your camp.' I asked him what he meant. He said: 'Well, now here's something. You haven't told anybody that you signed your name to a statement of Roy's, have you?' I told him no. He said: 'Well, you did, didn't you?' I said yes. Calhoun came back at me: 'Well, you see, I know it. How do I know if somebody hasn't leaked?"

"That stumped me," added Brown. "Somebody is leaking. Who do you suppose it is?"

Roy said: "I can't imagine."

Brown was furious, because this leak had destroyed the whole scheme. He had arranged to get $150,000 from Calhoun for Roy and $50,000 for Poheim. Brown was to have half of these sums, or $100,000 for himself, out of the deal. He had counted on making a clean-up. Now this leak had wrecked the whole thing.

Roy came to Burns and me about this. Burns immediately said: "Didn't you show that affidavit to your lawyer?" Roy said that he had. "Well," said Burns, "he's the one that told Calhoun."

According to Roy, Brown attributed his failure to one of Calhoun's attorneys. "He's got a nerve," Roy quoted Brown as saying, "to queer my name, when he came near putting ropes around all our necks." Roy assumed that Brown was referring to the dynamiting of Gallagher's house.

This will give an idea of the web of plot and counterplot in which we were struggling. In spite of our efforts to keep the one issue clear before the people, they were confused by the multitude of persons involved, the innumerable conflicting stories set afloat.

The prominent people of San Francisco had deserted us when we attacked their savior, Calhoun. Now, through the long delays of the courts, and the confusion, a general weariness was beginning to spread through the city. People were tired of hearing about the graft prosecution. We encountered apathy on one hand, and on the other the relentless determination of powerful men who were fighting for their lives.

The United Railroads people had tried innumerable plans to get me out of their way. By this time they had become desperate. We were trying Ford, and Calhoun's turn was approaching. At this juncture, inadvertently, I turned Luther Brown's hatred of me into a murderous rage.

The United Railroads were making an attempt to involve Supervisor Tom Lonergan with a woman, in order to break him down as a witness in the Ford trial. In uncovering the story, one of the *Bulletin* reporters in writing it made the mistake of using Luther Brown's name instead of that of another Brown, who was also a detective in the employ of Calhoun. The following day I corrected the error and forgot the incident.

A few days later I was waiting for Rudolph Spreckels in Heney's office. I was talkng with Charley Cobb, Heney's partner, when the telephone rang. I lifted the receiver. A voice said: "Is Mr. Older there?"

"I am Mr. Older."

"I am Mr. Stapleton, Mr. Older. If you'll come to

the Savoy Hotel on Van Ness avenue I will give you some very important information."

I asked him if he could not come to Heney's office. He said it was impossible. He was being watched, and it would not be safe.

I said: "Very well. I'll come to the Savoy Hotel."

The voice insisted that I come immediately, and I agreed.

Before leaving the office I turned to Charley Cobb and said: "This may be a trap. If I am not back in half an hour, you may be sure that it is. Tell this to Spreckels."

Then I went out and started toward Van Ness avenue.

CHAPTER XV

Calhoun's Octopus Clutch Closes On Me At Last. A Motor Trip To Be Remembered. My Captors Take Me On Board The *Los Angeles Lark.* One Of Them Relents. I Find Friends At Santa Barbara, And Am Released. I Owe My Rescue To An Unnamed Friend—And My Life To A Gunman Who Lost His Nerve. An "Amazing Story" That Traveled 'Round The World.

I walked direct down to Van Ness avenue from Franklin street and turned down Van Ness.

As I turned I noticed an automobile containing four men who looked to me like pretty tough characters. They were all eyeing me. The machine seemed to be hovering along close to the sidewalk as I walked. Suddenly it stopped and two men jumped out.

One of them stepped up to me. He was very pale and nervous; his hands trembled as he pulled out of his pocket a paper which he said was a warrant for my arrest on a charge of criminal libel. He said the warrant was issued in Los Angeles. He then showed me a constable's star and told me to get into the machine and go with him.

I told him I wanted to see my lawyer and arrange bail.

He said: "We will go to Judge Cook's chambers. Judge Cook has viséd this warrant, and you can get an order for bail through him."

I said: "Very well, I'll go." But I was very apprehensive.

As I stepped into the machine, one of the men that

was on the sidewalk passed his hand over my hips, obviously to see whether I was carrying firearms. This made me still more suspicious.

I sat in the machine on the right hand side of the tonneau. Next to me was a young man who had not got out of the car when it stopped. Next to him on the left sat one of the men who had got out. The constable sat in the front seat with the chauffeur. The car started down Van Ness at great speed.

This was after the fire, when the various departments of the Superior Court were scattered, and I had no accurate knowledge of the location of Judge Cook's court. When the car swung out Golden Gate avenue I noticed Luther Brown, Calhoun's chief detective, and Porter Ashe, one of Calhoun's lawyers, in a car, leading the way. They were looking back.

I became greatly excited. When we got to Fillmore street, I said: "Where are Judge Cook's chambers?"

The man in the front seat turned and said: "We are not going to his chambers. We are going to his residence."

Then I knew that it was a trap. The car was speeding faster and faster out Golden Gate avenue toward the park. I started to rise, looking sharply up and down the street to catch the eye of some one I knew or to attract the attention of a policeman.

As I arose the man next to me pressed against my side a pistol that he had in his right hand coat pocket. He said:

"If you make any attempt to escape I'll shoot you."

I could not possibly have been more frightened than I was then. I felt quite sure that they were going to take me out to some lonely spot on the beach or in the San Bruno hills and murder me. The car kept on, following the Luther Brown car. I knew that Brown had planned the expedition and that he was capable of almost anything.

I began trying to summon what philosophy I could. I felt that I was going to die very soon. My only hope was that death would be quick. I feared, however, that they might torture me, in order to get some kind of statement from me before killing me.

However, being an inveterate cigar smoker, I took a cigar out of my pocket and lighted it. My lips were dry, my tongue was parched; but I made a fairly good effort at a careless air, and said to the dark man on the front seat:

"This is a job put up by the United Railroads. I don't blame them for fighting me. It is quite natural that they should. I have been fighting them pretty hard. But this kind of deal isn't fair. It isn't sportsmanlike. They are dealing the cards from under the table."

I noticed a curious expression in the eyes of the dark man as he turned to look at me. This gave me a little hope. He looked like a sport. I thought perhaps my appeal had struck home.

On we went down the road, past San Bruno, past the Fourteen-Mile House, on down through Burlingame and San Mateo, at fully forty miles an hour. After we had passed Belmont it grew too dark to travel without lights. Both cars stopped, Luther Brown's car perhaps two hundred feet in advance. The chauffeur got out and lighted the headlamps, and we went on to Redwood City.

Both cars stopped a little distance from the station, in the shadow of the freight shed, and waited. When the *Los Angeles Lark* stopped I was asked to get out, and was taken into the train and into a stateroom that had been previously provided in San Francisco. Only the two constables accompanied me. The chauffeur and the gunman did not join us.

Dinner was being served. After an interval they took me to the diner. We three sat at one table. During the dinner I thought I would follow up what I deemed to be the slight impression I had made upon the dark man. I said:

"I don't care a damn about myself. I am quite well along in years and have lived a pretty full life. But I am concerned about Mrs. Older. She will be in a terrible state of mind over my disappearance. She undoubtedly is in that condition now, because this is just about the time we were to be together at a little dinner party at the San Francisco Café on Van Ness avenue. By this time the news of my disappearance has spread and no doubt the police department is looking for me. She will think I have been murdered. I don't ask any mercy from the United Railroads for myself, but I don't think it is quite fair to make her suffer, too."

The dark man said: "By God, you write a telegram to her or to any one you like, and I'll file it at San Jose. I won't stand for this thing unless you are allowed to communicate with your friends!"

He pushed a telegraph blank over to me, and sitting at the table in the diner I wrote a telegram to Rudolph Spreckels to this effect:

"I'm being spirited away on a southbound coast train. I don't know where I am going or what is going to happen. It is a United Railroad's job."

The dark man said he would file this dispatch at San Jose.

He got off the train at San Jose, was gone two or three minutes and came back, saying the telegram would go within an hour. There was a telegraphers' strike on, and there might be some delay.

I did not know whether or not to believe him. It was not until later that I learned that Luther Brown had taken the message from him, read it, and torn it up.

After dinner we returned to the stateroom, talked until midnight and went to bed, the two constables in the lower berth and I in the upper.

The train was nearing Santa Barbara when the constables rose in the morning. We went into the diner for breakfast and returned to the stateroom. A little later the train stopped at Santa Barbara. Looking out of the window I thought all of the town was at the station.

There were many automobiles filled with people; ladies with parasols, chauffeurs, boys and men crowding the platform. It was a gay-looking party. I thought they must be seeing a wedding party off to Los Angeles. I did not relate the crowd to myself at all.

Suddenly there was a loud rap on the stateroom door. The constable opened it. A man appeared and served them both with subpœnas and told me to go with him. The dark man accompanied us. The other man disappeared.

We were driven to the sheriff's office in the courthouse and I learned that a writ of habeas corpus had been issued by the judge of the Superior Court in Santa Barbara, upon the telephonic request of Rudolph Spreckels and Francis J. Heney. The legal point was that I had asked for bail in San Francisco and had not been given a chance to obtain it, and the taking me out of the city and county of San Francisco was a felony. Spreckels had employed a Santa Barbara lawyer to look after my interests.

The case was called immediately upon the arrival of the judge. I took the witness stand and told my story. The United Railroads had employed a lawyer and the legal point was threshed out by the two attorneys. During my testimony I saw the United Railroads lawyer talking to the dark man and saw him shaking his head. The judge saw this, too. He looked at the attorney and said:

"I see in the courtroom the constable who accompanied Mr. Older, who has not been called to testify. Unless he takes the stand and denies that Mr. Older asked for bail in San Francisco I shall release Mr. Older on bail."

There was another whispered conversation between the attorney and the dark man and another shaking of the dark man's head. The attorney said:

"There is no evidence. We have no witnesses."

The judge thereupon released me on bail. There were a number of men present ready to provide the bail, among them Franklin K. Lane, who happened to be in Santa Barbara at the time.

After being released I joined the dark man and walked out of the courtroom with him and he said: "You remember the remark you made in the automobile, that it wasn't sportsmanlike?"

I said: "Yes."

"Well, that kind of got me, and so when it came to the point of testifying to a lie, to have you held, I refused to do it."

I thanked him very cordially for what he had done.

I did not realize till later in the day what a shock it had all been to me. Lane and I went out to the beach and had a swim and everything around me seemed queer. I couldn't realize anything very definitely. I was stunned, and I must have been very much more alarmed than I had seemed to be when I was in the greatest danger.

I learned later that the only reason for my being now alive to tell my story was the lack of nerve of the man who sat next to me with the gun. He was told, so he has since informed the chauffeur of the car, that he would be paid $10,000 if he killed me on the trip. The plan was that I should be taken from the train at San Luis Obispo, rushed through the mountains in an automobile and killed there.

They were relying on the evidence of the constables, the gunman and the chauffeur that I tried to escape while under arrest, and was killed in an attempt to prevent my succeeding. Luther Brown was from Los Angeles. He had got a friendly justice of the peace to issue a secret warrant for me, so that they would have acted under color of law. But the gunman said that he lost his nerve.

I was still in the dark as to how the warning had been given my friends. After I returned to San Francisco I learned that a young lawyer was in the diner when I was sitting there, next to the table where Porter Ashe and Luther Brown were. He overheard Porter Ashe's conversation, and it led him to believe that something unusual was happening; that they had some one on the train who was important and whom they were spiriting away.

He followed Ashe outside the diner and asked, "Who have you got?" Ashe said: "We've got Fremont Older."

This young man had overhead in the diner something about taking me from the train at San Luis Obispo and giving me a run through the mountains. He surmised that if that happened I would probably never be seen alive again. He was very much alarmed and, though he had intended to go on to Los Angeles, he got off the train at Salinas at one o'clock in the morning, rang up the San Francisco *Call* and told them what he feared.

This was the first news my friends had of what was happening. They busied themselves preparing the writ of habeas corpus which was telephoned to Santa Barbara. The Santa Barbara morning papers had the story and that was why the crowd had assembled at the station. All the trainmen were placed under arrest and the train searched for me.

The young lawyer who gave the information would not let his name appear in the affair, neither then nor later.

The two constables turned state's evidence before the Grand Jury and the Grand Jury indicted both Ashe and Brown for felony. Both of the chauffeurs disappeared and also the man with the gun. Luther Brown was tried in Judge Dunne's court—not by Dunne, but by a visiting country judge—and was acquitted; which was in itself an indication of how unpopular the graft prosecution had become.

The story of this affair spread around the world and

the London *Times* printed a two-column article about it. Some time later I met a member of the English Parliament. I asked him if he had ever been in San Francisco before.

He said: "No. It's a very interesting city. I've read some very strange stories about you people, but the incredible one I read in the London *Times,* a paper that I had always regarded as a truthful journal."

"What was the story?"

"It was an amazing story," he said. "It was a story of the kidnaping in broad daylight of an editor. He was carried away in an automobile at the point of a pistol."

And I said: "Why, that's a true story. I'm the editor."

CHAPTER XVI

Ford's Trial Approaching, I Am Asked To Aid Him. Byington's Unbelievable Story. I Find Many Things To Wonder At. Ford's Acquittal. The Jury Disagreeing In The Ruef Case, A New Trial Is Ordered. Heney Shot By Haas, Ex-Convict. The City In Uproar. Ruef Convicted And Sentenced.

As I have said, Tirey L. Ford, chief attorney for the United Railroads, who passed the bribery money from Calhoun to Ruef, was indicted with Calhoun. He was put on the calendar for trial before Calhoun because we hoped after convicting him to make him confess and testify against Calhoun.

A short time before his case was to be called in Lawlor's court an old friend of mine called on me at the *Bulletin* office and asked if I was still as friendly to Ford as I used to be. Suspecting that something was about to develop that would be helpful, I dodged the direct answer and said that I was sorry for him.

"Why?" I asked.

My friend said: "Well, I thought if you were still friendly with him you might be willing to sit down with him and talk this thing over."

I told him I would be very glad to talk with Ford, and I would go still further. If Ford was willing to make an affidavit that he had received money from Calhoun for the purpose of bribing the supervisors through Ruef for the overhead trolley franchise, I would guarantee that he would never be tried at all.

I said that I was strong enough with the other members of the graft prosecution to promise this without consulting them. My friend replied that he would arrange a meeting between Ford and me very soon.

A few days later my friend returned, and said:

"We have decided that it is dangerous for you and Ford to meet. Ford is being shadowed by Calhoun. Calhoun is fearful that Ford is about to make some statement. We have decided that a very close relative of Ford will call on you. He has full authority from Ford; anything he says will be just the same as though Ford said it."

"All right, have him call," I said.

The close relative and friend of Ford was Louis F. Byington, a well-known attorney of San Francisco. He came into my office not long afterward, and asked me what I wanted from Ford.

I said I wanted the truth about Ford's connection with the bribery of Ruef and the supervisors for Calhoun. Byington said:

"Ford is perfectly willing to give you that. He will make an affidavit that he employed Ruef as an attorney and paid him a fee of $200,000. Ruef's employment was to secure an overhead trolley franchise for the United Railroads. That is the truth," Byington concluded.

I was very indignant.

"No one could possibly believe such a story as that," I said. "Every one knew Calhoun intended to bribe the supervisors; that he paid the $200,000 to Ford knowing that it was bribe money; that Ford paid it to Ruef knowing it; that Ruef paid it to the supervisors knowing it.

"Now Ford comes forward with this story of Ruef being employed as an attorney, and being paid an attorney's fee. Even if I were willing to accept a statement like that, none of my colleagues would consider it for an instant."

"It is the truth," Byington insisted.

I told him the story was useless to us. We might as well stop negotiations right there, if they began that way. I promised him, however, that I would not publicly use the statement he had made to me, and I never did.

After Judge Lawlor refused to agree to Burns' plan to let Ruef go free on the French restaurant cases. Burns had gone ahead; and with the help of Dr. Nieto and Dr. Kaplan, the two Jewish rabbis, he succeeded in obtaining a statement from Ruef which involved the big magnates of San Francisco.

I knew nothing of the details of obtaining this statement, and nothing of the inducements held out to Ruef, until during the Schmitz trial.

One day while Schmitz was being tried, Burns and I were sitting in an automobile in front of the courtroom. Ruef was on the witness stand, and Burns was uneasy, nervous and absent-minded. At last he said: "I hope to God they don't ask Ruef anything about what he has been offered in this case."

I said: "What has he been offered?"

Burns replied: "He has an immunity contract in all the big cases."

"You don't mean that he has in his possession a written and signed contract giving him immunity on all the big cases?"

"Yes," said Burns. "That's the truth. I am afraid they will bring it out in court. If they do, we're done."

But they did not bring it out, and Schmitz was convicted and sentenced to five years in the penitentiary.

After this it was Heney's intention to use Ruef as a witness against Ford, but suddenly, without explanation to me, he changed his mind. All that he told me was that he had a new plan for trying Ford. I said: "In what way?"

"I'm not going to use Ruef as a witness," Heney said. "I have worked out a scheme by which I can convict Ford without using Ruef."

I wondered at this. It seemed to me strange that Heney should cut Ruef's evidence. I asked Burns why Heney was doing this.

Burns said that Ruef had fallen down, had broken his agreement with us. Jim Gallagher had taken a letter to Ruef from Ford, advising Ruef of the possibility of a Grand Jury investigation of the United Railroads, and warning him to be on his guard. Ruef had testified to this letter before the Grand Jury; but when the evidence was being worked up against Ford, Ruef said he couldn't recall the letter.

This was Burns' story to me, and I accepted it without question. I felt that Ruef had played us false, and I was in favor of prosecuting him most bitterly, giving him as long a sentence as possible.

Ford was tried without Ruef's evidence, and was acquitted. Ruef was tried, the jury disagreed and he was held for a second trial.

It was in this second trial that the greatest sensation of the graft prosecution occurred. We had received several intimations that men on the jury panel had been approached and bribed to vote for Ruef's acquittal; but we were unable to get hold of facts that would definitely prove this, until we came to a man named Haas.

This man was an ex-convict, and the lover of a married woman. One day he boasted to her that he was to be on the Ruef jury, and that he was to get several thousand dollars out of it. She repeated this to her husband; and he, furious with rage and jealous of Haas, sent the information to District Attorney Langdon.

When Haas was placed in the jury box for examination, Judge Lawlor called him up and asked him if there was any reason why he should not serve as a juror. Haas replied that there was not.

Heney did not want to waste a peremptory challenge. He saw that Haas would not take advantage of the loophole given him. Heney then exposed the fact that Haas had "done time" in the penitentiary, and Haas was dismissed.

He was shamed and humiliated by this exposure. The United Railroads detectives seized on this fact, taunted and laughed at him for lying down under such an injury, and at last worked him into a desperate frame of mind. He became obsessed with the idea that he could wipe out the injury only by killing Heney. Just before the court was called to order after recess, he walked up behind Heney and shot him through the head.

The town went wild with excitement at the news. Haas was carried off by policemen and thrown into jail. Heney was placed in an ambulance, supposed to be dying, and was heard to say in the ambulance, "I'll get him yet."

I was, of course, pretty nearly insane. I followed the ambulance to the hospital and got such news as I could of Heney's condition. The surgeons could not say whether or not he would live. I rushed back to the hall that was being used by Judge Lawlor as a courtroom, crying out for Ruef, trying in my half-mad condition to further infuriate the already infuriated crowd there into taking some violent action.

The streets were flooded with extras, and the city was for once thoroughly aroused. Crowds gathered on the streets and in the hotels, the air was electric. Phelan hurried up from San Jose, found me in my office, and wanted to know what should be done. Hiram Johnson appeared, pale, trembling, earnest, and said:

"I'm ready for anything we decide is the thing to do. If it's the rope, I'm for that."

San Francisco's mood was dangerous that night, and the slightest impetus would have precipitated the crowds into mobs, ready for lynching. A wildly excited mass meeting was held. However, cooler counsels prevailed, and nothing was done.

We made every effort to get a statement from Haas as to who had inspired him to do what he had done, but a few days later he was found shot in his cell in the city prison. Obtaining a pistol from some unknown source, he had committed suicide.

The town was still aroused to a point where it seemed we could go ahead with the trial of Ruef and convict him. Hiram Johnson and Matt I. Sullivan volunteered their services in Heney's place, and the trial went on, while Heney lay on his back at the Lane Hospital.

Burns reported that four of the jurors had been fixed,

and gave us their names. Hiram Johnson made most effective use of this information in his dramatic talk to the jury. He called each of these men by name, pointing at him, and said,

"YOU, you DARE NOT acquit this man!"

We hoped to get a quick verdict, but we didn't. The jury retired to a room over the courtroom in Carpenters' Hall, and were out all night. There was a meeting that night and all sorts of wild plans were discussed, but nothing came of it. None of us slept.

The next morning the jury was still out. After a sleepless night I went to the courtroom in a very overwrought condition of mind, and insisted upon making an outcry in the court in case the jury came in to ask for instructions. I would demand that justice be done, and the crowded courtroom should let the jury see its temper.

I was talked out of this foolish idea by another man no less overwrought than myself, who ended by saying that he would make the outcry himself. But the jury was not brought in.

The day dragged on. The jury was still out in the afternoon. At about two o'clock Heney telephoned me that he was well enough to come down to the courtroom and pay his respects to Judge Lawlor. I thought I saw in this a chance to get a verdict.

I telephoned Heney to wait until I came for him. Then I telephoned the League of Justice, a group of people organized to support the graft prosecution. They had a number of men, called "minutemen," whom they could get at a minute's notice. I asked for as many as could be mustered to come at once to Carpenters' Hall.

Fifty, or perhaps a hundred, came immediately, and I told them to jam the courtroom, which was immediately under the jury room, remain there until I arrived with Heney, and as we appeared in the hall to shout as loudly as they could.

I reasoned that while the shout could be considered merely a welcome to Heney, it would have the effect of so thoroughly scaring the jury that it would bring in a verdict.

Heney came. I walked in with him, and I have never heard such a roar as went up. It lasted for five minutes. Twenty minutes later the jury came in, some of them white, shaking and with tears on their cheeks, and returned a verdict of guilty.

This was our first big victory. We had convicted Ruef. Judge Lawlor gave him fourteen years at San Quentin, the utmost penalty the law allowed.

Ford had been acquitted of the charge of giving the bribe money to Ruef, but Ruef had been convicted of taking it. It remained only to try Calhoun. This was to be our big star performance.

CHAPTER XVII

We Are Jubilant Over Ruef's Conviction. His Appeal To The Higher Court Not Sustained. Legal Quibbling And Hair-Splitting. The Situation Is Saved By A Technicality, And Ruef Finally Goes To The Penitentiary. More Intimidation As The Calhoun Trial Approaches. Fighting Crookedness With Its Own Weapons. Disagreement Of The Calhoun Jury Virtually Ends The Graft Prosecution.

The conviction of Ruef was our first great definite triumph. It exalted us. For days I refused to entertain any misgivings or allow anxiety to dilute the unrestrained pleasure I felt. Soon, however, came the worry about the upper courts. Would the Appellate or Supreme Court dare to upset our work of years and save Ruef from the penitentiary? We hoped not, but we feared. Their previous rulings had all been against us.

Henry Ach was Ruef's leading attorney, and we knew his remarkable ability and resourcefulness. He prepared the appeal to the Appellate Court, working on it for months. It was said to contain more than a million words. It had the record for size and hair-splitting technicalities.

To our astonishment and satisfaction, the Appellate Court made short work of it. In an amazingly brief space of time after the case was submitted, a decision came down upholding the verdict in the lower court. This lessened our fear of the Supreme Court. We reasoned that it would not have the courage to interfere.

In time Ach petitioned the Supreme Court for a rehearing, and to our horror it was granted, four of the seven justices voting for it. Were we to be cheated of our prey? Enraged, I assigned several men to the work of attacking the decision, the justices, the lawyers, and every one remotely connected with it. I realized that it would accomplish nothing in legally altering the status of the case, but perhaps I could arouse public indignation, and failing in that at least I could have revenge. The article that I prepared covered every possible angle of the case, including interviews with attorneys favorable to our side, and vicious attacks upon the justices.

At an early hour on the morning following this publication, Charles S. Wheeler, the well-known attorney, called on me.

He said, "I read the article in the *Bulletin* last evening, and I have come to you because you are the only member of the graft prosecution in the city. Spreckels and Heney are in the East. Do you want to send Ruef to the penitentiary on a technicality?"

"Yes, I do," I replied.

"I think myself that it is only poetic justice that he should go over on a technicality," he said. "He has used so many of them himself. Now is the time to decide. If you would rather not, say so now and we will let the matter drop."

"I think he ought to go," I said.

"Very well, then," said Wheeler. "Make an appointment for me with Governor Johnson in Sacramento for this evening and have Attorney-General Webb present, and I will explain how it can be done. In your paper last night you had a story that after Justice Henshaw signed the order granting a rehearing, he left for the East, and when the decision was rendered he was not in the state. You probably are ignorant of the legal significance of that fact, but it means that when Henshaw left the state, he was legally dead. Therefore, only three members of a court of seven justices affirmed the decision. It required four. I will explain it all to the Governor and the Attorney-General this evening."

At that time the legislature was in session and John Francis Neylan was the *Bulletin's* legislative correspondent. I telephoned him to make the appointment.

Wheeler and I took the five o'clock train, and we were in the Governor's office a little after eight. The Governor and the Attorney-General were waiting for us.

I was, of course, in a great state of excitement. In a few words I explained the reason for our visit and asked Wheeler to state the case. He was very cool, calm and brilliant. In the fewest words possible, he explained the significance of the absence of Henshaw from the state and made it quite clear to Governor Johnson that the decision of the Supreme Court was worthless, and that if the Attorney-General would follow his instructions, it would be upset.

The Governor and I were enthusiastic. The Attorney-General was not. He raised many objections. This aroused the Governor, and in one of his characteristic speeches he pointed out to Webb just what his duty was in the matter, and that this was not the time to quibble or hesitate. When the Governor finished, I broke into the discussion with a violent tirade about the enormity of Ruef's crimes, and, being very angry at Webb's apparent hesitancy, said many foolish things which later I regretted.

The meeting ended, however, by Webb agreeing to

do what Wheeler said could be legally done, which was to appear before the Supreme Court and point out to that body that Henshaw's signature to the order was non-existent after he left the state.

The Attorney-General carried out the program to the letter; and the Court, with Henshaw acting, reversed itself.

All obstacles were thus cleared away, and Ruef entered the penitentiary under a fourteen-year sentence.

In the trial of Calhoun, which came next on our docket, Jim Gallagher was our big witness. Shortly before the case came to trial Gallagher's house was dynamited, when he and seven other people were in it. No one was killed, although the building was wrecked. Almost immediately afterward some flats he owned in Oakland were dynamited.

Gallagher began to waver. There was no question that he stood in hourly danger of death because of his value to us in the Calhoun case. He was badly frightened.

We were doing our best to hold him in line, but this was naturally somewhat difficult. Burns said that if something was not done to satisfy him, Gallagher would go away and leave us in the lurch, and we would fail in the Calhoun trial, our biggest case. I asked what I could do, and Burns said that Gallagher felt he should at least be reimbursed for the destruction of his flats.

He wanted me to promise that after the Calhoun case was finished, Calhoun either convicted or acquitted or dismissed, that I would pay Gallagher $4,500 for the destroyed flats. Neither the district attorney, nor Heney, nor Burns, nor any one officially connected with the prosecution, could offer Gallagher that money, but as a free lance I could do so.

I asked Burns if Gallagher would take my word for it. Burns said he would. So I sent for Gallagher and promised him the $4,500 definitely, and he said, "I'll take your word, Mr. Older. I'll remain and testify."

In doing this, I was not troubled by any finely construed point of law. We knew that Calhoun was guilty, we felt that he ought to be punished. If we could have convicted him without using any questionable methods, openly and above board, of course we would have preferred to do it that way. But we could not, and since we had to fight fire with fire, and meet crookedness with devious methods, we did that. The big thing, the only important thing, was to convict. Everything else was lost sight of in that one intense desire, born of the long, hard fight.

When Calhoun came up for trial, Gallagher stayed with us, and testified. The case dragged on through all the delays and vexations and squabbles of such a case.

I was very anxious that Roy tell on the stand the story of Calhoun's many efforts to bribe him, of the trip to the home of Luther Brown's father-in-law near San Leandro, of the promised $150,000, and of the affidavit signed by Brown at the bottom. But Roy was reluctant.

He said: "If they bring it out in questioning me, I'll tell the whole story; but if they don't I'd rather not."

They didn't, of course. Calhoun's lawyers treated him very gingerly. His examination was continued from one day to another, and before he was to go on the stand the second day I talked with him very earnestly. I urged him to blurt out the whole affair. I thought I had got him to the point where he would do it.

I went with him into the courtroom. When Calhoun's attorneys saw me in the court, they felt sure that I had persuaded Roy to tell the story, and they did not call him to the stand at all.

The jury finally came in with no verdict. They stood ten to two for acquittal, and were unable to reach a nearer agreement.

It is hard to say why juries do these things. The long, tiresome delays and arguments over minor and confusing points of law, the innumerable wearisome details, questions of exact time, of the character of witnesses, of precedents and procedures, undoubtedly wear out a juror's patience and exhaust him mentally. But in this case there was no doubt money was used.

In addition to this, the excitement over Heney's shooting, and over the dynamiting of Gallagher's house, had long died down when at last the Calhoun case went to the jury. The graft prosecution had been fought for three long years. People had tired of it. They wanted it ended, no matter how.

The property owners of the city still regarded Calhoun as something of a hero for ending the street car strike, and also they felt that all this agitation about graft was not good for San Francisco's reputation. Public opinion was setting hard against us. The Calhoun disagreement really ended the graft prosecution, although we did not know it.

CHAPTER XVIII

A Sharp Political Fight Impending. I Am Haunted By An Old Ghost. Fidelity To My Early Promise To Spreckels Brings Me To Grips With Crothers. I Determine To Leave The *Bulletin,* But Am Persuaded To Reconsider. The United Railroads' Great Campaign. Fickert's Election Blasts Our Hopes. Failure Of The Graft Prosecution A Bitter Disappointment To Me. Burns Gives Me Something To Think About.

It was the fall of 1909. The city elections were coming on, and again the fight became a political one.

The Calhoun people brought Charley Fickert into the fight as a candidate for district attorney, obviously with the understanding that if he were elected he would dismiss the charges against Calhoun and all the other defendants. Francis J. Heney ran against him.

For mayor, those favoring the grafters put up William Crocker, a planing-mill man. He was a Republican and it was thought by the powerful people in San Francisco that he would be a safe man, and if elected would assist in stopping any further prosecution of the big malefactors.

Crocker's candidacy brought the fight into my own office. I found myself beset from both sides, trying to contend against enemies outside and inside the *Bulletin*.

The trouble ran directly back to the old Tobin-Wells fight for the mayoralty. During the entire progress of the fight against graft the ghost of that old Tobin-Wells fight had haunted me.

In my early arrangements with Rudolph Spreckels,

before he agreed to help finance the graft fight, he had insisted that he would not go into it unless it led to Herrin.

"Herrin is the man behind the corruption of our whole state," he said. "Herrin is the man who has broken down the morals of thousands of our young men, debauched cities, towns and villages, and corrupted legislatures and courts. I will not go into this thing unless it is understood that it doesn't stop short of dethroning Herrin." *

I had promised that the trails should be followed clear to their center in the Southern Pacific ring. From that

* Mr. Spreckels' desire was amply fulfilled. The graft investigation began in 1906. In 1910, under the direct primary, Hiram W. Johnson—one of the attorneys who prosecuted Ruef—was induced to run for Governor of California against Alden Anderson, the Southern Pacific Railroad candidate, and was elected by a large majority. This ended the railroad control of the State, which had lasted uninterruptedly for nearly forty years.

It was a memorable campaign. A small group of progressives organized the Lincoln-Roosevelt League, selecting Johnson for its leader; and, with a modest sum of money made up of small contributions from thousands of citizens in all parts of the State, Johnson set out to defeat the Railroad machine; traveling about in his own automobile, with one of his sons for chauffeur, and visiting every city, town and village in California. It was one of the most picturesque campaigns ever made in America.

Johnson, who is an effective orator, with a great deal of personal charm, succeeded in driving home to the mind of the people the point that the office of Governor was not, as it ought to be, at the State Capitol in Sacramento, but in Herrin's office in the Southern Pacific Railroad Building in San Francisco. As the fight progressed, his meetings increased in volume. The State was at last aroused; and during the closing days of the campaign there was no hall in California large enough to hold the crowds who were eager to attend. Public sentiment became so strong that a progressive Legislature was elected, and at its first session Johnson was enabled to put on the statutes many of the progressive measures contained in his platform; while those not passed at the first session were successfully put through at the second.

California was at last free of Railroad rule.

it naturally ensued that the *Bulletin* must make a vigorous campaign against the head of the law department of the Southern Pacific.

Crothers became very nervous about it and suggested several times to me that he didn't want Herrin attacked. I felt then that he feared Herrin would expose the Wells monetary arrangement with the *Bulletin;* but in spite of that power which Herrin held over us, I continued to go on with the campaign against him.

Frequently Crothers would go into the printing office and look over the headlines himself. If he discovered Herrin's name he would insist on its being lifted out of the paper, but even with this interference I managed to keep up the fight.

Finally, he told me flatly that he wanted the attacks on Herrin stopped, the criticism of Herrin to cease. I replied frankly that it was impossible for me to do this; the entire reportorial force was under full headway in the fight, and they were writing, all of them, from the angle of the paper's policy as it appeared to them. I could not go to each man and tell him he must not criticize Herrin.

"I can't do it, Mr. Crothers, because I am ashamed for you. If it's to be done, you'll have to do it yourself. I cannot."

He did not have the courage to do it, and it was never done. However, all the time our opponents were trying to reach into the office. They succeeded in getting the business manager at that time to undertake to break me down, but I resisted all his efforts. The fight became more burdensome, because it extended into the very building in which I worked.

After the friends of the big grafters put up Crocker for Mayor I heard that some of them were working on Crothers to get him to support Crocker. Again I found myself in the same position I was in when I opposed the *Bulletin's* supporting Wells. I was quite sure Crothers would not switch the course of the paper in the midst of a big fight, such as we were waging, for any other reason than the old reason.

However, as he said nothing to me about it, I hoped for the best. One day he told me he thought we ought to support Crocker. To do it meant to go over to the enemies of the graft prosecution, to support men who were pledged to dismiss our indictments and destroy the result of all our labor. I told Crothers that I would not do it.

He replied that he owned the *Bulletin,* and that it would support whomever he chose. I grew very angry and excited and replied:

"Yes, what you say is perfectly true. You do own the *Bulletin,* but you don't own me, and I won't stand for Crocker."

I walked out of the room, very angry, determined never to return. I went to my wife and told her that I was through with the *Bulletin.* She wanted to know the reason, and I told her Crothers had gone back to his old methods. He was determined to get behind the candidate who represented the men we had been fighting, and I could not bring myself to continue in my position.

Later I had a talk with our attorney, who was a friend of both Crothers and myself, and he persuaded me to talk again with Crothers. This time Crothers spoke in a very mollifying way, urging that we ought not to quarrel over such a small matter. We were both very nervous. What he said at the time gave me the impression that he had abandoned Crocker, but a day or two afterward he brought Crocker up to my office and introduced him to me.

I asked Crocker whether or not he would support the graft prosecution if he were elected. He evaded the subject, quibbled and dodged, while I became more insistent upon a direct answer. He would not give it, and at last I lost my temper and dismissed him very curtly.

The interview was so stormy and I was so determined not to stay with the paper if I were to be forced to change my attitude, that Crothers finally yielded and I had my way. The *Bulletin* supported Heney and Leland, the opponents of Fickert and Crocker.

So we went into the final battle of the graft prosecution. It was fought bitterly.

Labor, because their mayor, Schmitz, had been exposed by our investigation was, I think, largely on the side of Fickert. The bribery and graft and rotten city conditions that we had revealed did not greatly concern them. All this was too far removed from their own personal, immediate interests for them to become partisans in the struggle. And the clear issues had been very skillfully clouded by Calhoun's efforts. All through the campaign our meetings were largely attended. Heney spoke to packed audiences in every district in the city. Of course, we believed that two-thirds of San Francisco would be in our favor. We did not dream until the day of the election how greatly mistaken we were.

The United Railroads made a wonderful campaign. Money was poured out with no thought of cost. The *Post* and the Oakland *Tribune* issued big editions which were left at every doorstep in San Francisco. Women's clubs were organized and women went about among the people whispering the vilest scandal about Heney.

The United Railroads had a complete card index of every voter in the city, and toward the close of the campaign the betting at the poolrooms should have shown us that Fickert would win. But we could not believe it; I refused to believe it. I still had too much faith in the people to believe that such a calamity could possibly happen, that any city would actually vote for men who had been proven to be exploiting it.

Up to the day of election I was certain that Heney would win. Late in the afternoon, however, Burns and Spreckels came into my office, both of them white. They had been out in one of the Mission districts where only laboring people lived, and they had been jeered from the sidewalks as they drove along in an automobile. That convinced them that we had lost.

It was a terrible blow, but we bore it as best we could. The returns came in that evening, showing Fickert far in the lead. Heney, I think, polled only 26,000 votes; Fickert beat him by 10,000 or 12,000.

That was really the end of our hopes of convicting the men who had debauched San Francisco.

Hardly had the election results been announced when Gallagher's brother came to me and demanded the $4,500 I had promised to pay Gallagher for the flats that Calhoun's men had dynamited. I told him that we were not through with Calhoun yet. The jury had disagreed at the one trial, but there were still other indictments and other trials.

"The bargain was that your brother was to stay with us till the case was definitely ended. It has not ended yet. When it does, I'll pay him the money."

Gallagher's brother left, dissatisfied. It was too well understood that Fickert was to take program from the Calhoun crowd for him to have any faith in our ability to try Calhoun again. I was still doggedly hanging on, hoping in spite of hopelessness, but he may have believed that I was about to break my promise. I do not know.

I only know that a very short time after this interview Gallagher disappeared. None of us knew where he was, nor could we locate him. No doubt he received help from some one and went away—not to return until Fickert had carried the Calhoun program through.

Fickert went into court with a written document, obviously prepared for him by the attorneys for the United Railroads, asking the dismissal of the Calhoun cases, and they were dismissed. All the other big defendants were also dismissed. The graft prosecution was over.

It had been a hard three years' struggle, three years of incessant effort, battling against every kind of opposition. It was over, and we had just one thing to show for it—Ruef in jail. Of all the men who had bought and sold San Francisco and the people of San Francisco, we had put just one behind bars, in stripes.

To this end Heney had given three years of his life, of hardest possible work, without receiving one penny for it, paying his own living expenses from money he had saved. He had been shot through the head and made deaf in one ear. He finished the fight almost without funds, with his practice gone, and with nothing but defeat at the hands of the people of San Francisco to repay him for it all.

He stood stripped, but still full of fight and fire, with a determination to succeed in life. The contest, of course, had increased the national reputation he had begun to earn in the Oregon land fraud cases. Though rejected by San Francisco, he had become a national character, which he still is, with a large following all over the United States.

Roy was ruined by the powerful people behind Fickert —people who were interested in clearing Calhoun. His restaurant failed, his skating rink failed, he lost all his money. He had a large family, to which he was deeply devoted, dependent upon him; and, without money, ostracized by the business men who might have helped him, he became so desperate that he disappeared from San Francisco. He went without a word, and not even his family knew where he was.

But Roy had not lost heart. He found employment in the East, and when he was established there he communicated with his family. In time he made a moderate success, and later returned to California and became a prosperous business man in San Jose.

Burns, who received all the credit for obtaining the confessions of the eighteen supervisors—the feat that made the graft prosecution possible—became the nationally known figure that he is to-day, and accumulated a large fortune. So far as I know Roy has never received the smallest credit for his work, although—as I have already shown—he not only formed the plan which trapped the supervisors, but carried it out himself in every detail.

The failure of the graft prosecution was a bitter disappointment to me. I had hoped that we would be able to reach the big men, the men at the top of the whole pyramid of civic corruption. I felt that they were the men responsible for the shameful conditions in the city, and I was not satisfied that we had been able to get only Ruef, one of the less important men.

Still, I was glad that we had got him. That was a small triumph. I felt that our efforts had not been without some result, though we had failed in our real endeavor. This feeling, hardly formulated, lasted in my mind for some time after the end of the graft prosecution. Then one day in New York I learned something that had upon me the effect of an earthquake.

I was standing in the lobby of the Waldorf-Astoria, idly talking with Burns and S. S. McClure, the publisher, when McClure happened to inquire:

"Why did you fellows break the immunity contracts with Ruef?"

"Because he refused to play fair with us," I said. And I told about the letter that Gallagher had carried from Ford to Ruef, to which Ruef had first testified, and then refused to remember when it was needed in the Ford trial.

"Hell, no!" said Burns. "That wasn't the reason at all. Where did you get that story?"

"You told it to me," I said.

"Oh, I never told you a story like that! That didn't have anything to do with our breaking the immunity contracts."

"You did tell it to me," I insisted. "And I've told it to a hundred others. What was the reason, then?"

"Ruef wouldn't testify that the money was paid him to use in bribing the supervisors. He wouldn't testify that Ford had ever said anything to him about bribing. He insisted on going on the stand and saying that the money was paid him as an attorney's fee."

A light burst upon me. I remembered the message Louis Byington had brought me from Ford.

"Maybe it was paid as a fee," I said.

Burns would not listen to it a minute. He insisted that there must have been some verbal understanding that the money was to be paid as bribes to the supervisors. Anyway, he said, such testimony from Ruef would have been ridiculous. Of course, the money was not paid to him as an attorney's fee. Of course it was bribe money, even though they had called it an attorney's fee. But Ruef had been stiff-necked, and had refused to swear that Ford had said a word to him about bribery. For that reason the immunity contract had been broken, and Ruef had been sent to San Quentin for fourteen years.

I returned to San Francisco with a great deal to think about.

CHAPTER XIX

My Attitude Toward Ruef Undergoes A Startling Change. I See Our Reform Activities In A New Light. Ruef A Victim Of Social Conditions; His Crime That Of Being Found Out. I Am Humbled In My Own Sight. I Go To San Quentin To Visit Ruef. He Tells His Story. Asking Mercy For Ruef, I Bring Myself Into Disfavor. After A Long Fight, He Is Eventually Paroled.

The longer I considered the story Burns had told me, coupling with it Byington's statement and with other small incidents that now occurred to me, the more convinced I became that Ruef had not broken faith with us but that we had broken it with him.

It became apparent to me that Ruef had promised to tell the truth in return for the promise of immunity, and that later, when he refused to tell more than the truth, the immunity contract with him was broken and he was sent to the penitentiary.

This seemed to me a terrible thing. Yet I could not escape the conclusion that we, who had been working to purify the city, had done this terrible thing. And as I thought more about it, other things that we had done came into my mind. I realized that many aspects of them were neither virtuous nor praiseworthy.

I reasoned that our goal, reach it as we might, was praiseworthy. It was our intention to rid the city of men who were corrupting every nook and corner of it, who were linking up the lowest dives with the highest places in the community, who were selling the rights of our children and the morals of our young men and women. If, in the heat of our enthusiasm, we had done questionable things, at least we had done them for a good cause, and with a good end in view.

It came to me then that doubtless other men justified themselves in the same way. I thought of Ruef in a new light. I recalled him as a young man, just out of college, ambitious, clever, energetic, desiring to make a place and an honorable name for himself in the world's affairs. I realized the conditions he had found around him; the price he had seen other men paying for success; the temptations pressing upon him to win popularity, honor and acclaim by the only methods open to him, methods boldly used by other men who were successful and admired.

Ruef did not make those conditions. It was we, the people, who had made them. We had made money our measure of success, regardless of how the money was acquired; we had been bad citizens, careless who controlled our city or how they controlled it, if only each of us was left alone to bend all his own energies toward getting wealth and the honor that inevitably follows. We were responsible for the environment in which Ruef found himself; we had set up the standard of success that he tried to reach.

We did not question the methods by which a man got money; we only demanded that he get it. Even now, we were not punishing Ruef so much for what he had done as for being found out. Other men, equally guilty, were walking abroad in the light of day, enjoying friends, success, popularity. We had not altered the conditions in the least; we had not changed our standards of value;

we had not ceased to flatter and fawn upon the man who had money, no matter how he got it.

It came to me that Ruef, seeing these things, justified to himself the things he had done, just as I justified to myself the things I had done. I had been fighting for a clean city, but my motives had not been all pure, civic devotion. I had not been unaware that I was making a great, conspicuous fight, that it was making me a big figure in men's eyes, and that if I won I would be something of a popular hero.

All these motives had mingled to give me one strong, burning desire—to win the fight. It had seemed to me that many questionable acts were justified if they would contribute toward that end. I knew Ruef and Ford and Calhoun and Schmitz were guilty; I wanted them convicted, and I had not greatly cared how it was done. If I had cared I should have failed.

Doubtless Ruef, with his keen insight into human nature, also knew these characteristics, and therefore had no difficulty in justifying to himself his various actions. No doubt many motives had entered into his desire for success. He wanted to stand well in men's eyes, he had wanted to repay the affection of his parents by making them proud of his achievements. He had come from college, a young man, to find San Francisco what it was, and he had made his place in it, doubtless justifying himself at every step.

When I thought of Ruef in this way, a change came in my attitude toward him. I thought of the years I had spent in doggedly pursuing him, with the one idea of putting him behind bars. It seemed to me that I had been foolish and wrong. It came to me that I should your mother and to your gray-haired father. It is because of what you have done that your mother lies here, as you see her now. Will you not try to spare them further shame and disgrace?'

"My mother said, 'Listen to our friend, my son. Do as he tells you, for my sake.'

"Then for the first time I broke down. I wept, and I said that I would do anything they wanted me to do.

"After that Rabbi Nieto and Rabbi Kaplan saw Burns and Heney and Spreckels and made the arrangements. I was to be given immunity if I would tell the truth. So I told them everything. I felt bitter humiliation as I did it. I knew that I was betraying my old associates. I was torn between loyalty to them and my love for my family. I felt that in confessing I was doing a worse thing than I had ever done before, but I did it.

"Then, before the Ford trial, when the evidence was being arranged, I was told that I must testify that Ford had given me the money for the purpose of bribing the supervisors, that something had been said between us to that effect.

"This was not true. Nothing was ever said as to the way the money was to be used. We spoke of it always as an attorney's fee. The understanding between us was never put into words. I assumed that Ford supposed I was to use the money as bribes wherever it was needed to get the overhead trolley franchise; I knew he didn't pay me $200,000 in the belief that I would keep it all, myself, as my fee. But nothing was ever said that indicated this understanding.

"I was willing to go on the stand and tell the whole

truth; but I would not go beyond the truth. I felt bitterly ashamed that I had gone so far as I had, and nothing would persuade me to go further. I had betrayed my old associates badly enough, without swearing to falsehoods against them.

"I refused to testify that Ford had ever said anything in regard to bribing the supervisors, and for this reason the immunity agreement with me was broken, and I was sentenced to San Quentin for fourteen years."

This was Ruef's story, and I believed it absolutely. I began at once, through the *Bulletin,* to plead for mercy for Ruef. I wanted to tell this story fully and publicly, and base my demand for Ruef's parole on the ground of simple justice; but I was unable to do so.

Crothers was unwilling that the halo resting on us for our share in the graft prosecution should be disturbed. We had won considerable credit in the fight, we were looked upon as disinterested, ardent crusaders, incapable of wrongdoing. With all his power as owner of the paper, Crothers refused to allow this impression to be disturbed. So I was obliged to make my appeal for Ruef on purely sentimental grounds.

My changed attitude toward Ruef displeased all of my former associates in the graft prosecution. For me suddenly to ask for mercy for Ruef caused them to say, and perhaps to believe, that I had in a measure renounced the fight that was so dear to them all.

This was Judge William P. Lawlor's attitude. Shortly after his last election to the Superior Bench he called to thank me for the help the *Bulletin* had given him in his campaign, and to say good-by. He was about to go East than a life sentence at the end of one year. The Board had made this law inoperative by passing a rule that each prisoner must serve half of his net sentence before his petition for parole would be given a hearing. Prior to my efforts in Ruef's behalf, this rule had been broken frequently, but as soon as I tried to make it apply to Ruef the Board endeavored to live up to the letter of their rule, and only in rare instances violated it. The power against me was too great to overcome. The Governor insisted that Ruef should serve half of his "net" sentence, four years and five months. Not a day was subtracted. The fight to free him was long and bitter.

Ruef was finally paroled, but not until he had served every hour of half of his net sentence. Even then he was not allowed to return to San Francisco, but was instructed by the Board to spend a month at Vichy Springs, near Ukiah. Evidently they still feared him, and were reluctant to allow him to return to San Francisco. At the end of the thirty days, however, he came back to his home in San Francisco and went into the real estate business, in which he has continued ever since, accumulating, I understand, a good-sized fortune.

CHAPTER XX

My Address To The Council Of Jewish Women. I Review My Activities In The Graft Prosecution. Lessons Of The Ruef Case. A Confession Of Misdirected Ambition, With An Outline Of My Philosophy Of Tolerance.

In the midst of my fight to secure Ruef's parole, I was invited to address the Council of Jewish Women. Having nothing in my mind but the Ruef case, I chose that as my subject, hoping against hope that I could yet accomplish Ruef's release. My talk before the Jewish women was rather in the nature of a confession. It was as follows:

"I feel out of place in facing you in the rôle of a public speaker. I am not an orator. I don't know the tricks of oratory, and if I did I would feel none the less queer, because I am not sure that I know anything important that you don't know, or that I have any message that is worth your time. I have an idea, however, that I have learned something about myself, but nothing that I can be sure of about others, or the motives that prompt the actions of others. I feel reasonably certain that outside of being kind, and tolerant, and merciful, and forgiving, there isn't much that can be done in this muddled, baffling world of ours. So I am appearing here to-day to confess, rather than to teach or preach. What I have learned about myself has come from a long struggle and a hard fight, and what I have learned is that I am just an average human being, no better, no worse, and no wiser than others.

"All of you are familiar with the struggle that I refer to—the fight against municipal corruption in San Francisco, which was begun some ten years ago. Perhaps the *Bulletin* started it. At any rate, it was in that contest that I learned my lesson. In those days the city was governed by what the world called a corrupt Mayor and a corrupt boss. I was the managing editor of the *Bulletin* at that time, as I now am, and I raised a great hue and cry over the acts of the administration.

"As I think back to those days I can see now that there was no altruism in the motives I had when I began the fight. It was temperamental of me to become indignant against the men, or the cause, I was opposing. Before a fight was well under way I became an intense partisan and could see nothing but good on my side and nothing but evil in my opponents. I am trying to analyze truthfully the motives I then had. I have frequently said to my old fighting friends that I was prompted by no high motives. But they have protested against such frankness, and endeavored to convince me that I made the fight because, as a good citizen, I was indignant at civic corruption.

"Indignation no doubt formed some part of the motive. I think all motives are mixed. But looking back, I must confess that the compelling force in my activities was the success of the newspaper that employed me. I think I was just striving for material gain and the prestige that inevitably goes with that kind of success, and so I pointed out the sins of others, unconscious of my own, and in vivid stories tried to inflame the public imagination against what the conventionally minded believed to be wicked.

"Of course, nothing was happening then that had not happened before, and is still happening in all city governments. The administration was responding to privilege. That is, the powerful corporations and the powerful property owners were asking and demanding an advantage over the mass of the community.

"There was nothing new about it, but Schmitz and Ruef went a little further, perhaps, and were a little more picturesque and more open in bestowing privileges than the community had been accustomed to. You all know what finally happened. Heney came here, and Burns, and the exposures followed. Some of the city's most prominent and influential men were caught, among them the Mayor and Abraham Ruef.

"You know the bitterness of that fight, the persistence with which we pursued them. We felt that failure to encompass their complete ruin and conviction and imprisonment would have been regarded as a defeat. I was perhaps the most zealous of the group. Filled with bitterness and hate, I went on writing articles, or inspiring them, filled with much that was true and much that was assumed to be true, and at all times justifying myself, if I stopped to think at all, on the theory that these men that I was fighting were wholly bad, and that all of the men in pursuit, including myself, were wholly good. It never occurred to me in those days that these men were very much like all other men in our civilization. They were not especially evil men. They were just doing evil things. We made the great mistake then in assuming that it was a moral question. It was not. It was economic pressure—a desire for money to meet the one standard by which society measures success—which is possession and the private ownership of the valuable things of the earth.

"And so the battle went on, as you know, and out of it all came the conviction and imprisonment of just one man, Abraham Ruef. He was sent to the penitentiary for fourteen years. That was what we all wanted. That was what we had all been hoping for, striving for, and fighting for. Of course, we should like to have sent others there, too, but failing in that we centered on this one man, and we triumphed.

"I shall never forget the morning that Ruef started for the penitentiary. All the bitterness and hatred of all the years of pursuit came into my mind to reproach me. I thought, 'Is this success, or is it utter failure? Is this a real victory or an appalling defeat? After all the years of mad pursuit, is this the harvest?—the imprisonment and branding of one poor, miserable, helpless human being?'

"In imagination I followed Ruef on his journey to the prison. I saw him being taken inside the walls. I saw him being shaved, and photographed and striped and numbered, and degraded and humiliated. I thought of his tears, and his suffering, and of those who were near and dear to him. And then it dawned upon me for the first time that my life, too, had been filled with evil; that I had done many cruel things; that I had at no time been fully fair to him, or to the others who were caught with him; that I had been striving, as he had, for success; that I had been hurting others in order to make money out of a successful newspaper; that I had been printing stories that made others suffer that I might profit; pandering to many low instincts in man in order to sell newspapers;

that I had told many half truths, and let many lies go undenied.

"And when I thought of all that Ruef had done and of all that I had done, I could not see that I was any better than Ruef, and so I asked for and pleaded for mercy for him with the best arguments that I could command. I asked for his parole at the end of one year. I urged it on the ground that it was a legal thing to do, that the State's statute provided for parole at the end of one year.

"In making the plea I encountered a rule of the Prison Board which forbade any prisoner applying for parole until he had served half of his net sentence. That, according to my view, nullified the spirit of the law, and was, therefore, illegal and wrong. The campaign went on for his parole. I was met on every hand with protests and objections, expressions of hatred, and at best this, 'He is not repentant. Why doesn't he repent?'

"I wonder if any of us has repented. What is repentance? Certainly no man can fully repent in prison. Repentance must be free and voluntary. The state cannot force it by locking a man up in a cell for a term of years. It can make him suffer; it can make him weep; it can make him a craven; or it can make him bitter and resentful and vicious; desirous of wreaking vengeance upon society that is wreaking vengeance upon him. But it cannot give him humility, which is the essence of true repentance.

"I wonder how many of those who are hating Ruef and who are opposing his parole have repented. How many have that rare quality, humility? And how many are there who know that mercy is beautiful and precious, and even practical? We, who consider that we are good, can, of course, easily forgive the little evil we see in ourselves. And if we can do this much in our own case, why can we not extend this forgiveness to the greater evil we think we see in Ruef? I have tried to repent for the bitterness of spirit, the ignorance I displayed in pursuing the man Ruef, instead of attacking the wrong standard of society and a system which makes Ruefs inevitable. I may not have entirely succeeded, but at least I have reached the point where I can see the good in the so-called bad people, and can forgive and plead that mercy be shown to Abraham Ruef.

"And so I made up my mind that day that it was my duty to go to the prison and see him and ask him to forgive me. We had been enemies for many years, and it took all of the philosophy that I could summon to buoy me up for that trip. But I made it, and took him by the hand, and told him that I was sorry for all I had done, and I asked him for his friendship.

"Three years have passed since that day and that meeting, and during those years I have thought much of Ruef's career, and what happened to him, and why it happened. Ruef was a graduate of the University of California. He came from there with high honors, younger than most men are when they graduate. He looked about him for a career. He wanted to be successful, as we all do. And having a liking for politics, he chose that field for his activities.

"In those days there was only one kind of politics, and that was corrupt politics. It didn't matter whether a man was a Republican or a Democrat. The Southern Pacific Railroad controlled both parties, and he either had to stay out of the game altogether or play it with the railroad. He didn't create this situation. We created it.

"He didn't create the standard of success, which is possession. We created it. He came out of college and found these things that we had fixed through all the years. He entered our life, our civilization, and went ahead. There was no other way then to gain society's laurel wreath, except by acquiring money and power. There isn't now. There may be some day. So he went on with the game—OUR GAME. He had talent, brilliancy of mind, force and persistence. So he grew in power and prominence until he found himself in a position to grant favors to the favored. He sold them, as all men in his position had done before, and as they are still doing to-day in many of our cities.

"I think if we should all be perfectly frank we would admit that we wanted these big corporations, these moneyed interests, to have these things that they bought of Ruef. We thought they were entitled to more and more. We were awed by the power they had. Whether that is true or not we certainly were responsible for the municipal slum in which Ruef found himself. He had taken no part in its creation. He found it, ready made, entered it, and became inoculated. He was ultimately diseased, and then we took this poor, miserable victim of ours, this man who had played the game that WE had made and sent him to the penitentiary as an example to others.

"That is our explanation of it. That is the way we justify his imprisonment. I don't think it was right to send him or any other man to prison for being caught in our system. I think that what these men did in those days should have been exposed and explained, and then we should have all gone to work to rid the city of the slum and make of it a healthful place in which to live. But it still exists, and will for a long time to come, no matter how many Ruefs we catch and imprison.

"What happened to Ruef would not seem to me so cruel if the community had profited by his misery. If his degradation had awakened the people to the true conditions here it might have been worth a human life. But it did no such thing. We are still going on in the old way, believing that jails will cure our civic diseases, for which we are all equally responsible.

"But, at least, it has been a valuable experience to me, and has done me a great deal of good, because it has enabled me to discover myself, and to learn that we are all of us guilty, and that we can no longer absolve ourselves by putting men in prison. That falsehood can never fool me again. It will be a long time, I fear, before this view takes possession of the minds of men; but perhaps gradually we will begin to study ourselves more and learn of the evil that is in us and the necessity for curing ourselves before we set out after the other fellow. That is a big job in itself. It can hardly be done in a lifetime—even a long lifetime. There would still be much left that is wrong in all of us, no matter how hard we strive to rid ourselves of it. And if we work diligently at it we will have no time to devote to the purifying of others.

"That is the way I feel, and hereafter I am going to let the other fellow severely alone, and permit him, if he chooses, to work out his salvation in his own way.

I feel sure I am not fit to judge him, nor to hunt him, nor to criticize him, nor to put him in jail. We cannot make people good by law, by mere legislative enactment. Men and women must *want* to be good. The feeling must come from within. The Legislature can never do it. We must not want to do things that are harmful to others. We must not want to say cruel and unkind things of others. We must not want to gossip about our neighbors, and scorn those who have been caught doing things we ourselves might have done, or perhaps have done and have been successful in preventing the truth from being known.

"You can imagine how Ruef and the other men who were indicted with him viewed us, who were in hot pursuit of them. You can imagine that they knew enough of us to know that we were not what we pretended to be, that we were not fit to preach to them from a pedestal. They knew that we were full of evil, too. They knew that our lives had not been perfect, and you can well understand how deeply they resented our self-righteous attitude toward them, and our abuse of them, and our hatred of them, and our intemperate invective and relentless warfare upon them.

"They knew us, because they knew that we were human, and that it is human to err. They knew that we were no better and no worse than the average human being, and while they perhaps were conscious that they had done wrong they knew we were bad, too, but we had not been found out. Perhaps our misdeeds may not have involved the breaking of the Penal Code. But perhaps they had, and we had escaped detection.

"Ruef and the others had merely been found out and

caught. Being found out was Ruef's chief crime. I feel sure that if he had escaped detection, even though we were possessed of a general knowledge of all that he had done, he would still be honored and respected in this community. So Ruef, after all, was punished for his failure, and not for what he did.

"Ruef suffering in prison caused me to pay him many visits. It was while waiting to see him on one of those visits that I first met Donald Lowrie. The warden showed me an article Lowrie had written for a magazine. I detected in him real ability as a writer, and I made his acquaintance and secured his parole, and suggested to him that he write his 'Life in Prison.' That was the beginning of a change in our prison system in California.

"Lowrie's revelations awakened the people to a realization of what they were doing to men convicted of crime. They brought me into touch with hundreds of so-called criminals, and taught me that they are very much like all the rest of us. Some of them, of course, are hopelessly anti-social, but I think they have been made so by the way in which we have treated them. I have gone on trying to intercept them when they come out of prison, show them some consideration, give them some help; and I have been able to change many so-called criminals into useful members of society.

"This has been called—mistakenly, of course—maudlin sentimentality. I am quite willing it should be called that. But it has been a practical work. Changing men from highwaymen into farmers and orchardists is practical. Every time a desperate man is halted in his career and given a new point of view there is one less criminal in the land, and the security of the commonwealth is increased just that much. This has been an interesting work, and has been filled with wonderful experiences. Most of the so-called criminals that I have met and associated with, and helped, have responded to kindness and fair treatment. And the fact that they have has convinced me that kindness and tolerance will do more for the uplifting of humanity than legislatures and jails and dungeons and straitjackets and the gallows.

"I am trying to change the attitude of mind that exists toward our so-called bad people, our criminals, and the scarlet women. I am sure there is good in all of them if we could only find it, and help it along. I don't see how we can ever make much progress in this direction until we change our belief—a belief that has come down to us through the centuries, that the outcasts are wholly bad. We must also change our attitude toward them. We must not feel superior to them. We must meet them on common ground, and in a spirit of true humility.

"To change this point of view, even if it were only in a small degree, was uppermost in my mind when I planned to publish the life story of Alice Smith. I believed that even women of the underworld were not beyond being helped. They are not abandoned, except in so far as we have abandoned them. With this thought in mind I chose a typical case of a girl who had gone wrong. I decided to portray her young life, her childhood, her early hopes and desires, and to show that she was like all other girls until something happened which she was unable to control, something which changed her and caused her to leave the better life and join the army of the forlorn. This, I thought, would convince some people at least that she and her kind had been misjudged.

"To some extent I was successful. But, of course, not wholly so, because of the inherent prejudice that so many have against turning on the light in the dark places in our social life. I realize that I have gone rather far in touching upon this forbidden subject, but I thought that it ought to be done, and I have done it at some cost. There has been much misunderstanding of my motive in giving publicity in a newspaper to the life of the underworld. I am glad it has been done, however, because I think it brings us a little nearer to the truth. And the truth is what we are searching for.

"As I have said before, there isn't much that we can do beyond being kind, merciful, forgiving and tolerant. And I don't think it would be necessary for much more to be done. After all, we are just poor, helpless creatures, all of us, on a vessel adrift on an uncharted sea. We don't know where we came from, or why, or where we are going, or why.

"Instead of mingling together with a tender, sympathetic realization of our common lot, and being kind and helpful to one another, we are broken up into scornful 'sets' and 'cliques' and 'classes.' Thus divided we snarl and sneer, we judge and revile and condemn. Let us hope that some day we will adjust ourselves to one another, and even though the purpose of life remains veiled and the great mystery unexplained, the voyage may yet be a happy one."

CHAPTER XXI

The Story Of Sam Leake. A Picturesque Personality Drowned In Alcohol. A Modern Miracle. Sam Relates His Amazing Experience To Me. His Useful Work For "Down-And-Outs." An Inside Story Of His Earlier Political Days.

Perhaps the most sensational single revelation that burst upon the community during the period covered by these chapters was the unearthing of convincing evidence that Fred W. Henshaw, Justice of the Supreme Court, had received a bribe to influence his decision in the Fair Will case in 1901.

While the trolley briberies and the other public utility graft that came to the surface through the confessions of the supervisors were startling, and to thoughtful people disturbing enough, yet when it was found that the Supreme Court had been reached with money and influenced in its decision, people were genuinely terrified. The Supreme Court was their "Sacred Cow," the bulwark of all their institutions. Now there was a widespread feeling that no form of government was safe from being undermined by greed and passion for power.

Oddly enough, the Henshaw exposure was indirectly the result of the healing of Sam Leake by Christian Science.

Leake was a picturesque figure in the political life of California for a great many years. In politics he was a Democrat, but in those corrupt days, when the Southern Pacific Railroad controlled both parties, it did not make much difference which party you belonged to. You were ruled by the same power. The Southern Pacific dominated the conventions of both parties, dictated their nominees and secured the election of the officials believed by them to be most subservient to their interests.

Sam Leake was powerful through the late eighties and nineties, and on into the early part of this century, not only in the legislatures as a lobbyist, but in all the various official activities of the state. For many years he was assistant to the State Librarian in Sacramento, but later he came to San Francisco and became the managing editor of the *Morning Call* when it was owned by John D. Spreckels. During the years that he held this position the liquor habit gradually grew upon him until it finally mastered him completely.

When he gave up his position on the *Call,* he continued his connection with politics, and his power remained undiminished. But King Alcohol finally gained complete control of him. For several years he was intoxicated most of the time, and utterly incapacitated so far as keeping up his old connections was concerned. He drank to such excess that his friends began to avoid him, and I was accustomed to see him staggering about the Palace Hotel barroom, a lonely and deserted figure.

In the earlier days, when he was in the State Library at Sacramento and I was the correspondent for one of the San Francisco papers, we became good friends. He had a charming personality, was intelligent, interesting and magnetic; wiser about politics, perhaps, than any other man in California. Whenever the newspaper men wanted the "low down" on any political situation, Sam Leake was the one they sought for information. Later, when I joined forces with the graft prosecution, our ways parted and I became antagonistic to all the interests that he was friendly with. My attacks in the *Bulletin* against corrupt government frequently led to violent excoriations of Sam Leake.

Thus we became enemies; at least we stopped speaking when we met. The old relations were at an end. As I continued to see him drinking at the Palace bar when I passed in to lunch at the men's grill, I wondered how long he could keep up such a pace and live.

Suddenly he disappeared. The fact that I no longer saw him around the bar made no particular impression on my mind at the time. I was busy with my own fights and made no inquiries about his disappearance.

One day in my office James H. Wilkins, a well-known writer, who at that time was working for me, said something which reminded me of Sam Leake.

"Jim," I said, "I haven't seen Leake around the Palace bar for several months. What has become of him? He isn't dead, is he?"

"I should say not," Wilkins replied. "At this moment he is probably at the Mechanics' Library, reading. He is clear-eyed, rosy-cheeked and in perfect health. He is completely cured of the drink habit."

Of course I was amazed.

"How did that happen?" I asked.

"Christian Science," said Jim.

"That," I said, "would make the greatest serial ever written. Can't you bring him up here?"

The next morning Jim Wilkins and Sam Leake appeared at my office. Sam and I hadn't spoken to each other in many years. I had attacked him bitterly all through this period of our enmity. We shook hands as if nothing had ever happened. I said:

"Sam, you have a great story and you ought to write it. It will encourage others—give them hope."

Sam said: "Fremont, I think I have had quite enough notoriety."

"Yes, I know what you mean. But this will be a different kind of publicity, Sam. I feel sure if you will write a frank story of your redemption you will do a great service to your fellow men."

"If you feel that way about it I am ready to start. I'll bare the whole story of my degradation, and tell of the influences that reclaimed me."

Within a week I published the first chapter of "The Healing of Sam Leake." Nothing I had hitherto published made quite the same appeal. The entire town was stirred. Each morning when I came to the office the *Bulletin* building was swarming with mothers of drunkards, sisters of drunkards, fathers of drunkards, wives of drunkards—all waiting to see Sam Leake, to plead with him to help save those they loved. Sam responded in every instance, and spent the greater part of each day at the *Bulletin* office talking with callers and meeting those who needed treatment privately and helping them in every way he could. In addition to this unexpected task, he had a chapter a day to write on the serial. He was the busiest man in the city. This crowd of people seeking help increased as the serial went on, and before it ended he had opened an office in a downtown building and was there receiving and treating alcoholic patients.

In his story he did not spare himself. He gave all the shocking details of his life as a drunkard. He told how he went to his home in San Anselmo (a suburb of San Francisco) drunk every night, taking with him two quart bottles of whisky. One of them he usually hid among the rosebushes in the garden, as his wife would not permit more than one bottle to be brought into the house. He soon finished the first quart, then in the early morning hours he staggered out into the garden, tumbling around among the rosebushes, searching for the hidden bottle, frequently not being able to find it on account of his dazed condition.

In the morning he was so nervous that he was unable to dress himself. He had to be helped out of bed and dressed. But he continued drinking, gradually growing weaker and weaker. It was when he was at his worst that a woman friend looked him up and asked him if he would go with her to a Christian Science practitioner, a Mrs. Lomax.

"Out of friendship for you," Sam said, "I'll go if you will promise me she won't ask me to stop drinking, because if I stop drinking it will kill me."

His friend assured him she would not ask him to make any such promise.

With his friend he called on Mrs. Lomax. She did not ask him to stop drinking. Instead, she said:

"When you leave here, if you feel like drinking, drink; but I don't think you will have the desire much longer."

Sam said in his story that he drank, when he left her, as usual, but kept returning to her office to talk with her. He was usually drunk when he called. He continued these visits for some time, gradually becoming interested. Occasionally he went to the church and listened to the testimony that people gave who had been cured of various diseases, saying to himself: "Well, I haven't heard any one yet tell about being cured of anything so horrible as the thing I am afflicted with." He thought he was beyond all help.

In his story he said the talks Mrs. Lomax gave him began to affect him. "One morning I woke up, feeling as well as I had ever felt in my life. I wasn't nervous, and my mind was clear for the first time in years. I was strong and able to get up and dress myself. Wild with joy I cried out to Mrs. Leake: 'Come in here. I am healed! I am healed!' And I was."

He has never taken a drink since, and to-day sits in his office in the Sharon Building in perfect health, physically, mentally and spiritually.

Leake's story, when it was finished, went all over the world, into many languages—I think even into Chinese. Hundreds of thousands of copies of the pamphlet containing the serial have been sought from different parts of Europe, Australia and other far-away parts of the world; and Leake has had letters—thousands of them—from mothers and sisters and wives whose dear ones have been helped through his story, and from drunkards who have been restored by his influence and example.

There is a typical and colorful story of the old political days in California in which Sam Leake was a conspicuous figure. I shall tell it so that those who have become interested in his regeneration may get a glimpse of the man when he was at his keenest as a power in the secluded byways of politics.

The story happened at the session of the legislature that opened in Sacramento in January, 1891. Up to that time, and through all the preceding years of the railroad's control of the politics of the state, no man had appeared brave enough to dispute with the railroad its right to name the United States Senators, who were to be sent to Washington to represent California.

At this session Colonel Dan Burns came to Sacramento and opened headquarters in the Capitol Hotel and announced he was going to elect Morris M. Estee, a prominent San Francisco attorney, to the United States Senate. Colonel Burns was fresh from Mexico, where he had made a fortune in a silver mine. Having all his life been deeply interested in politics, he decided to try his skill against the big powerful railroad machine.

He picked Estee for two reasons. First, he had a personal liking for him and a belief in his ability and integrity. Second, because Estee was exceedingly popular with the Republicans of California, having a few years previously secured the Republican nomination for Governor against all efforts of the Southern Pacific to stop him. The managers of the railroad machine, however, were able to prevent his election by stepping over into the Democratic party, which they controlled as completely as they did the Republican party. Thereby they secured the nomination of George Stoneman for Governor. With the full power of the railroad behind him, Stoneman was elected.

In a short time after Burns' arrival, he organized the Estee fight so well that the railroad became slightly alarmed, and cast about for some man who could defeat him, who would be agreeable to them.

M. H. DeYoung, owner of the San Francisco *Chronicle,* entered the fight, with Judge Dibble as his manager. Dibble, a San Francisco Assemblyman, was a powerful leader in the Assembly. DeYoung shrewdly secured Dibble's service as manager of his fight. Of course, the railroad did not want DeYoung.

Charles N. Felton, who had served one term in Congress, was the other candidate. The railroad would have been satisfied with Felton's election.

At the start Estee showed the greatest strength. I attended this session of the legislature as the correspondent of the San Francisco *Evening Post,* sent there by George Heazelton, the supposed owner of the *Post.* As a matter of fact, Lieutenant-Governor Leland Stanford had furnished the money and financially backed Heazelton in the purchase of the *Post.*

For some time I received no instructions from Heazelton about coloring my articles in favor of any one of the three candidates, and this gave me the impression that the railroad was not interested in who succeeded. Personally, I wanted Estee to win. I knew his character and his public activities, and had a very high opinion of his integrity and independence of spirit. This bias was reflected in my letters to my paper. That lasted only a few days. Before the fight became very warm, I received a letter from my boss telling me to be outright for Charles N. Felton. It was then that I learned the railroad's choice. I felt very badly at being compelled to desert the Burns-Estee fight but frankly explained to them that while I was personally with them I could no longer help them with my articles—that I had been ordered to support Felton.

At this time the voting strength of the three men was as follows: Estee, 47; DeYoung, 20; Felton, 13. It required 61 votes, a majority of both houses, to elect.

Several ballots were taken and the votes did not change.

Early in the session the usual number of "cinch" bills were introduced into both houses, and among them was the time-worn bill making a common carrier of the Western Union Telegraph Company. I was told at the time that this bill had been regularly introduced for many sessions, and had always proved profitable to the boodlers who introduced it. But the patience of the Western Union people was exhausted at last. Word was received at the legislature that they were through with paying money to kill that bill, and they were going to try to defeat it without money.

The bill first came up in the senate, and passed to second reading by a vote of 21 to 20. Instantly after the vote was taken, John Hamill, a senator from San Francisco, moved for reconsideration. When the vote was taken he voted against the bill, thus hanging it up for another twenty-four hours, to give Jaynes, the manager of the Western Union Telegraph Company, time to come through with the coin. But Jaynes remained obdurate and allowed the bill finally to pass. Jaynes, knowing the bill would be highly damaging to the finances of the Western Union, did not feel justified in allowing it to become a law. He started an active fight in the Assembly, declaring to his friends that at least he would punish the crooked Senators who tried to hold him up.

He explained that while there were twice as many Assemblymen to win over as there were Senators, they could be got for less money.

Judge Dibble and Assemblyman Marrion were the chosen leaders of the movement to defeat the bill in the house. One day, while the senatorial situation was at a deadlock, Sam Leake, who was at that time Assistant State Librarian, saw Dibble and Marrion pass through the library into a private room adjoining the room occupied by Leake. They closed the door and remained in the room for some time. Leake shrewdly guessed that this meeting was in some way related to the senatorial fight. When they went out, Leake entered the room to see if they had left any evidences of their conference.

His quick eye detected some scraps of paper in the wastebasket, which stood alongside the desk where Marrion and Dibble had sat in conference. Leake emptied the wastebasket on the desk and put the torn pieces of paper together. He was rewarded by finding before him a complete printed roll call of the Assembly. After several names of members he discovered crosses and amounts of money, some $250 and some $300. He then put the other pieces of paper together and they turned out to be several wrappers that had been around packages of greenbacks. On each wrapper was the amount of money in that particular bundle. He figured up the amounts, and they totaled $7,500.

It did not take Leake long to determine that this money had been sent up from San Francisco to defeat the Western Union "cinch" bill. He knew that Dibble was holding twenty votes for DeYoung in the senatorial fight, he saw how Burns could win Estee's fight by sending for Dibble, showing him what had been discovered, and demanding that he withdraw DeYoung from the fight that day when the two houses met in joint session to vote. That would elect Estee. Leake sent for Dan Burns, showed him this precious evidence and pointed out how he could win his fight. Burns, of course, saw the point at once, and was wildly enthusiastic over the victory that he saw would come to him within the next day or two.

Estee was sent for. When he came into the room the Colonel said:

"Estee, you are the next United States Senator. I congratulate you."

"Great," replied Estee. "But how is it going to be accomplished?"

Then Burns explained to him that all that was necessary at the present time was to send for Dibble, show him what they had, tell him to withdraw DeYoung's name and instantly swing his votes to Estee or there would be an exposure of the entire story—which would, of course, have finished Dibble politically, even in those wicked days.

Estee said: "Colonel, it has always been my ambition to represent California in the United States Senate. It would be a fine finish to my career. But I don't want it that way. It has got to come clean or not at all."

Burns made a strong plea to Estee to change his decision or at least think it over for a while before deciding definitely, urging that this was nothing more than a political move and all political moves had some such background; as they did in those days, and still have. But Estee refused to yield and flatly declined to go on with it. So the two houses met in joint session that day at twelve o'clock, and the vote was the same as it had been on the previous day.

That evening about eight o'clock, while I was sitting in the corridor of the Capitol smoking an after-dinner cigar, I saw Chauncey Clark, a well-known lobbyist, approaching me. He was smoking a big fine Havana cigar, his eyes were bright, his cheeks were flushed, he was smiling happily, and I thought I detected the smell of champagne on him before he got within ten feet of me. I knew something had happened.

"What's the news, Chauncey?" I asked.

"Felton," he cried, flourishing the Havana cigar above his head. "It's all over, Fremont. Felton to-morrow at twelve o'clock."

"Has the sack been opened?" I asked.

"Never mind. Don't ask me any embarrassing questions. I tell you, 'Felton to-morrow at twelve o'clock.' That's enough for you to know."

Chauncey was right. Charles N. Felton was elected at the joint session on the following day

All kinds of rumors flew about that afternoon as to who had put up the money. Felton indignantly denied that he had spent any of his money, and I feel certain it was an honest statement. Some time afterward I learned from an absolutely reliable source that a well-known California millionaire paid the money—a man in no way connected, directly or indirectly, with the Southern Pacific Railroad. He was merely a friend of Felton's and wanted him to go to the Senate; and as Felton was not in any way hostile to the railroad's interests no opposition was made by the railroad people.

But, by way of returning to Sam Leake's indirect connection with the Henshaw affair—to which I referred at the beginning of this chapter—it becomes necessary to speak of Sam's reclamation of William J. Dingee.

CHAPTER XXII

What Leake Did For Dingee. He Urges Him To "Come Clean." Dingee's Devastating Confession. Echoes Of The Fair Case. Henshaw's Plea For Mercy. I Learn Later That He Is Not Keeping Faith. Happiness Found In A Clear Conscience.

William J. Dingee was another picturesque and colorful figure in the political life of California. Many years ago he quickly acquired a large fortune through a cement plant that he owned near Santa Cruz. With this fortune he spread his activities into other fields. He became interested in the Oakland Water Company and in real estate down the peninsula, and in many other enterprises. He built a very showy and expensive residence in San Francisco, and another one on Fifth avenue, New York. His connection with the water company in Oakland brought him directly into contact with the politicians of Alameda county. He had to keep in close touch with them in order to safeguard his water interests from being hurt by the raising of rates.

When Dingee was at the high peak of success, he was perhaps the most outstanding figure in California. Suddenly he began to go down. His fall was rapid. His fortune of many millions seemed to vanish overnight. He lost the San Francisco mansion, as well as the one on Fifth avenue in New York. About eight or nine years ago he came from New York to San Francisco, shattered in health and ruined financially. He was flat broke. He blamed a group of powerful financiers and public men for the disaster. He believed they had conspired to take his wealth from him. He was very bitter. At this particular point in his life, when he had become utterly desperate, he thought of his old friend, Sam Leake.

He crossed New Montgomery street from the Palace, and called on Leake in the Sharon Building.

"I am sick in soul and body, Sam. You have done so much for yourself. Can't you help me?"

Sam replied: "Dingee, I can't do a thing for you until you clean yourself up inside as I did. When I was cured I became introspective, and after making an honest diagnosis I discovered that I wasn't fully cured. I realized that I, in my political life in California, had committed about every crime except murder, and I knew that people were not going to accept my reclamation unless I 'came clean.' They were going to whisper me to death: 'Oh, this fellow Leake hasn't reformed. This attitude of his is all pretense. He is the same old Sam Leake.' So I wrote my confession and gave it to Older to publish, and in that way got all that old stuff out of my system. I felt clean. That's what you must do, Dingee. Go over to your room at the Palace Hotel and write your confession and put into it every wrong act you have committed during your career here in San Francisco, and let me give it to Older to publish."

Dingee agreed, returned to his room at the Palace, and began writing the story of his public life. He was not accustomed to writing, but he kept at it faithfully and at the close of each day he took the finished pages over to Sam Leake who kept me in touch with the story as it progressed. We met every morning at six o'clock breakfast at the Fairmont Hotel. One morning Sam came in very much excited.

"Dingee's confession tells of the bribery of Judge Henshaw of the Supreme Court in the Fair case," he said.

James G. Fair was one of the group of four men who in the sixties and early seventies were known as the "Bonanza Kings," Mackay, Fair, Flood and O'Brien. These men got control of the big silver mine in Virginia City, Nevada, and by manipulating the stock market became multimillionaires.

Fair, fearing that when he died his children would dissipate his fortune, tied it up in a trust allowing his heirs only the interest. There were four children,—two sons and two daughters: James G., Junior, Charles, Theresa and Virginia. James G., Junior, died before his father. Charles was killed in an automobile accident in France, shortly after his father's death. Theresa married Herman Oelrichs, of New York, and Virginia married William K. Vanderbilt, Junior.

Not long after Fair's death the daughters brought an action to set the trust aside. The trust was upheld in the lower court. The case was then appealed to the Supreme Court. The first decision of the higher court was in favor of the trust, four to three, Henshaw voting with the four. A rehearing was asked.

It was then that negotiations were opened with Henshaw, and the contract was made and signed, Henshaw agreeing for $10,000 to change his vote. In the rehearing, Henshaw reversed himself. The vote then stood four to three in favor of the heirs. In the final decision the vote was the same, Henshaw voting against the trust.

For this vote he received $400,000. The trust was broken and the money distributed.

The bribe was paid to Dingee in checks by S. G. Murphy, the president of the First National Bank of San Francisco. Some of the checks were for $50,000 and I think one was for $100,000. These checks were turned over to Dingee's bookeeper, Mr. Losch, who, under instructions from Dingee, entered them up in the ledger under the name, "J. Brown." But this blind was not fully carried out because Henshaw's name appeared in the account as having drawn portions of the money. Thus the evidence of the bribery became a matter of record.

After Dingee finished the confession and signed it, he gave it to Sam Leake. One night about eleven o'clock, after I had gone to sleep in my room at the Fairmont, there was a rap at the door. I opened it, and in came Sam Leake with the confession, signed. He handed it to me, and said, "Fremont, it's yours to publish." I took it with me to the office the next day, with many misgivings.

Knowing R. A. Crothers, the owner of the *Bulletin,* so well, I could not believe that he would allow me to publish a story that would involve a Justice of the Supreme Court. Being a lawyer, he had the old-fashioned notions about courts, especially the Supreme Court. But I told him about it and urged its publication, saying that it would be very timely, as I was then finishing Martin Kelly's confessions. Kelly was an old-time sub-boss, long since dethroned, and now dead.

Kelly's story, which had been running for some time as a serial, told many interesting things about the Fair case; but it touched only upon one phase of it, which was Mrs. Craven's claim to having a later will written by Fair in which he left his property to her. As I feared, Crothers refused to allow me to publish the Dingee confession, saying that the paper could not afford to make such a revelation against a distinguished member of the Supreme Court of California. I sorrowfully put the confession away in a drawer of my desk.

Shortly afterward, I met ex-Mayor Eugene E. Schmitz on the street, and he said:

"Fremont, I understand you have in your office Dingee's confession. Go ahead and publish it, so far as I am concerned. I haven't any interest in it any longer since my friend George Knight died."

He seemed to know what the confession contained. A few days later he called at my office and told me that Judge Henshaw had heard I had Dingee's confession in my possession and had said to friends of his that if I published it he would kill me. I think it was later that same afternoon when Judge Henshaw rang me on the telephone and asked if I would not come down to his chambers. He wanted to have a talk with me.

"No, I will not go to your chambers," I said, "but you live at the Fairmont and I am stopping there to-night. I will meet you in the lobby of the hotel at six o'clock." The meeting was arranged for that hour.

I was there a little ahead of time, but I was not there before Henshaw. He was nervously pacing up and down the lobby of the hotel in evening dress. He took me up to his rooms and into his library. He said we could talk there undisturbed.

He opened up the subject by saying:

"You know how these things are done, Older. Men in public positions are sold out as legislators are, without their knowledge. You must be aware of that. You have had a lot of experience in legislatures. You know that frequently men find out how legislators are going to vote and then sell this knowledge for money. The same thing happened in the Fair case. Some one learned that I had changed my opinion of the legal aspects of the case and sold the knowledge to the Fair heirs."

"That isn't true in this case," I replied. "I happen to know from Dingee's ledger that you received the money for your decision."

Up to this time Henshaw had believed all of Dingee's books had been destroyed in the fire. He had his office in the Crocker Building and the Crocker Building was gutted. This made him feel secure. But I had learned from Losch, Dingee's bookkeeper, that he had taken two books over to his home in Mill Valley the day before the fire, and one of them was the ledger that contained the accusing evidence of the bribery.

I related these facts to Henshaw. At this point his wife entered the room and our conversation ceased. He asked me to meet him at the same place the next morning at eight o'clock.

At that meeting his entire tone changed.

"I'm getting on in years, Older," he said. "I haven't much longer to live. The publication of this story would ruin me. If you will promise not to publish it, I will resign my position on the Supreme Bench. I can give a reason that will be accepted by my friends and the public. I can say that I am interested in war work, as I have been and shall continue to be, and that I want to give all my time to it. I will resign at once. I know you are very much interested in the Mooney case. I will help you in that. The Supreme Court cannot give any relief because the law forbids it, but I will willingly go to the Governor and use such influence as I may personally have and ask him to grant Mooney a new trial. I will urge it because I really believe he is entitled to one. Further, I will sever all my connections with Fickert, the District Attorney. Of course, you know we have been very friendly. I will have nothing more to do with him."

"I'm getting on in years, too," I replied, "and I've got to a point where I do not desire wantonly to hurt any one. There was a time in my younger life when I might have acted otherwise—when I should probably have refused to agree not to use such an important story. But if you will do as you have promised, I will not publish it. I want you to know, however, that I am not the sole custodian of this Dingee information. Matt Sullivan is Dingee's attorney, and I understand that Dingee told it to him, and Sullivan had it taken down in shorthand. I have also heard that he gave a transcript of it to Hiram Johnson. I can't promise you that he will not make some use of it."

"I'll see Matt myself," said Henshaw.

"No," I said, "I'll speak to him about it. I think he will be satisfied not to give it publicity if you will resign from the Supreme Court."

With that we parted.

I related to Matt Sullivan what had transpired between Henshaw and myself, and he agreed with me that if Henshaw would resign from the Supreme Court it would be sufficient and the story ought not to be published.

Not long after the interview, Henshaw carried out the first part of his agreement and resigned from the Supreme Court, giving the reasons he had indicated to me he would give, and the public saw no significance in the resignation.

A year or so afterward, I left the *Bulletin* and became editor of the *Call.* My reason for resigning was that Mr. Crothers had grown more and more impatient with my radical activities, especially with what I had done in the Mooney case, and I realized if I remained much longer on that paper I would be entirely shorn of power and the paper would gradually sink under the heavy competition that it then had in the evening field. I did not want to be identified with its failure, which I felt sure would occur within a few years. Among the letters and papers which I took with me was the Dingee confession, which I put in a drawer of my desk in the *Call* office. There it lay for several months. About the first of November, 1918, Police Captain Goff, then Lieutenant Goff, brought a man into my office and introduced him to me as George Parson. After the introduction Goff left the room. Parson had a package under his arm which he opened and laid on my desk. It was a box containing a stack of typewritten manuscript about two inches thick.

I said, "What's this?"

Parson replied, "Secretary of Labor Wilson employed Densmore to come to San Francisco to establish a dictaphone secretly in District Attorney Fickert's office. The Secretary believed that by that method the truth about the conspiracy to convict Mooney and Billings of the bomb outrage which occurred on Preparedness Day will be disclosed."

This manuscript that Parson laid on my desk was the unfinished report Densmore was preparing for Secretary

Wilson. Parson turned to a portion of the dictaphone conversations and showed me talks over the telephone between Henshaw and Fickert which revealed very clearly that Henshaw not only had not detached himself from Fickert as he said he would, but was conspiring with him at that particular moment to introduce a new witness—a "framed" one—into the Mooney case to help establish the guilt of Mrs. Mooney.

"Now," said Parson, "here's the point. I understand you have Dingee's confession in which he gives the details of the bribery of Judge Henshaw in the Fair case. I also understand that you did not publish it because of his promise not only to have nothing more to do with Fickert, but to use his influence in the interests of Mooney. Does this authentic record here prove to you that Henshaw has broken his word?"

"Yes," I said, "it does."

"Well, then," said Parson, "I am here to ask you to let me have that confession so that I may incorporate it in this report that I am writing for Densmore, to be submitted to Secretary Wilson."

I gave him the confession and it was incorporated in the report. The report was finished, signed by Densmore, and given to me—that is, a copy of it was given to me, the original being forwarded to Washington. When it was delivered I asked Parson why he had given me this report.

"Because," he replied, "I think you have the courage to print it."

The Densmore report was published a few days later in the *Call,* including the story of the Henshaw bribery.

Many efforts were subsequently made by very powerful

people in California to get possession of the incriminating ledger. Dingee was offered a large sum of money if he would turn it over to certain people to be destroyed. Dingee was in close touch with Sam Leake, and together they managed to hold on to the book, both resisting all importunities and all temptations to allow the evidence to be destroyed.

It was later used in two suits brought to recover money by some of the heirs of the Fair estate who had been injured by the breaking of the deed of trust. Both suits were settled out of court, a considerable sum of money being paid in each case.

Dingee has re-established himself in business and is doing well. After his confession was published, efforts were made to get him to relinquish documentary evidence that he held establishing Henshaw's guilt. In fact, large sums of money were offered him. But he declined these offers and remained true to his confession and to those who had been responsible for its publication. He made his confession solely to clear his own conscience, and in the interests of his physical and spiritual health.

Sam Leake goes serenely on with his work, meeting his patients daily, talking them out of their fears, restoring them to health and doing, in his quiet way, perhaps as much good as it is possible for any one to do in this world of ours. All of the fine qualities that have been developed in Sam Leake's nature since he broke away from drink were no doubt always a part of him, but they were not given a chance in the wild days of his political career. He is the happiest man I know.

CHAPTER XXIII

While Visiting Ruef At San Quentin, I Meet Donald Lowrie. A Convicted Burglar Who Is Also An Excellent Writer Excites My Interest. I Secure A Parole For Lowrie, And Run His Story In The *Bulletin*. My Reawakened Interest In The Welfare Of Prisoners Recalls An Earlier Experience. Pat Sullivan's Tragic Story.

After Ruef and I became friends, I frequently visited him at the prison. Upon one occasion, while waiting in the warden's office for Ruef to be brought from the main prison, Warden Hoyle handed me a typewritten article to read. The subject of it was the indeterminate sentence. It was an exceedingly good piece of writing, the arguments in favor of the indeterminate sentence being the best I had ever read. Assuming that it must have been written by a prisoner, I became keenly interested in the author of it, and asked if I might meet him.

"It was written," said the Warden, "by a man named Donald Lowrie, who is doing fifteen years for burglary. He is a bookkeeper in the next room. I'll call him in."

Lowrie was brought in and introduced.* He was in a complete suit of stripes. He seemed shy and very much embarrassed. It was the first time I had ever heard of him. I said:

"I've just been reading an article that the warden tells me you wrote. It is very well done, indeed. If you could get out, I believe I could make use of you on the *Bulletin*."

* An earlier reference to my first meeting with Donald Lowrie will be found in Chapter XX.

Lowrie's face brightened at once. He suggested that perhaps I could secure a parole for him. I told him I should be glad to try and would ask the Board of Prison Directors immediately. I did so, and encountered no difficulty in securing a unanimous consent for his release at the next meeting of the Board. When I learned this I called at the prison, saw Lowrie, and suggested to him that I should like him to write, under his own name, a straightforward, truthful story of his life in prison. I had already decided that if I could get him to write this story I would publish it as a serial in the *Bulletin*. Perhaps it would give the people of the state a better idea of prison conditions than they had ever had before.

A short time after this visit Lowrie was released and came direct from the prison to my office, with the first two chapters of his book, "My Life in Prison," already written. I started its publication at once, and it took both the city and state by storm.

Two weeks after his release he was invited to address the Commonwealth Club at the Palace Hotel. He hesitated when I told him that he was to be the speaker, fearing that he would be too nervous and too embarrassed. I told him I would sit next to him and buoy him up as much as I could. I was sure he would succeed.

Lowrie wrote the speech in full and began reading it to one of the largest audiences the Club had ever had. After reading two or three pages, he dropped the manuscript and made an informal talk which fascinated the crowd. When he finished, a hundred people, men and women, swarmed around him and congratulated him on his very interesting and enlightening talk. Subsequently he spoke before the Federation of Women's Clubs. From that time on he made speeches before high schools and in halls throughout northern California. Lowrie's name will appear frequently in these pages; his after-history I shall recount fully in a later chapter.

My interest in Lowrie and his story reawakened an old interest I had in prisoners in my early days as a reporter. It recalled my meeting with Pat Sullivan many years before, while I was doing police reporting for one of the city newspapers. I found Sullivan convalescing in the Emergency Hospital from a severe case of delirium tremens. As usual, I was searching for interesting stories. When I saw Sullivan in the hospital I asked him something about himself, and how he came to be there.

He told me he had been on a big spree, was gathered in by the police, and wound up with a severe attack of delirium tremens.

"This has just about finished me, and I am desperate. I have lost my job and also my wife."

At the thought of his wife, he broke down and wept for several minutes. When he had regained his composure, he said he wanted to write to her, but did not know how to write—had never learned. He asked me if I would write the letter for him. I sat down, and wrote—on a piece of copy paper that I had in my pocket—as appealing a letter to her as I could, telling her that he was sorry for what happened and would try to get another job and go on as before. The letter pleased him very much. He then gave me the story of his early life.

"I was born in Ireland, but came to America when I was a small boy. As soon as I was old enough I enlisted in the American Navy and was put to work as a stoker. I remained one for twenty years. In that time I had saved $7,000, and with that I left the Navy and came ashore in San Francisco."

Evidently he knew nothing of the world, having spent so many years in the dark stoking hole of a man-of-war; and, as sailors often do, he drifted immediately to the Barbary Coast and became fascinated by the life he found there. He had discovered a world that suited him, and he invested part of his money in a saloon. The place he bought was a dive, where women of the underworld congregated. Shortly after he took possession he met a young woman who had been divorced and was then living a fast life. She had run away from her husband and her little boy, and at this time was hanging around the dives of the Coast.

To Sullivan she was the loveliest creature he had ever seen. Shortly after he met her they were married. He first took her to a dry-goods store and fitted her out with a complete wardrobe. He rented a flat and established a home, the first he had known since childhood. But he soon got to drinking heavily, and it was not long before he become enslaved by the habit. This shortly resulted in his losing the saloon and his means of livelihood. The woman left him and returned to her old habits. He pulled himself together, however, got another job, hunted up his wife, and started housekeeping again. This occurred many times. It was after one of these disasters that I met him at the city prison.

He pleaded with me to try to find him something to do, so that he could be in a position to start life again with this woman he had learned to love very deeply. As I had a little influence at that time with the Republican boss, I secured him a position as coal heaver on a state tug. He soon found his wife, rented another flat, and again resumed the old life.

Within a few weeks the woman was back "cruising" on the Barbary Coast. Sullivan came home and, finding her gone, broke out in one of his sprees and was soon in the gutter once more. A few months afterward, while I was riding on the dummy of a California street car, the gripman said cheerily, "Good morning, Mr. Older." I looked up. It was my old friend Sullivan, in a new uniform, looking prosperous and happy. He answered my inquiring look with, "Well, we are all right again, Mr. Older. I've got another little flat and some furniture. This time we are going to make it. She has promised never to leave me again." He was full of confidence.

I lost track of him for a year or more. Meanwhile, [illegible]d become city editor of the *Evening Post*. One day [illegible]d in the morning paper the story of a ghastly mur-[illegible] A man lurked in a dark doorway at midnight. When [illegible]oman came out of a Pacific street underground dive [illegible]passed him, the man sprang upon her with a knife and [illegible]er to pieces. The assassin was described as a hard-[illegible] and degenerate brute. The three morning papers [illegible]te of it as the most cruel, brutal murder that had [illegible]rred in San Francisco for many years. Arrested, [illegible] murderer shouted blasphemies, declaring that he was [illegible]ad he had killed her, that he would do it again if he [illegible]ad the chance. This man was Pat Sullivan.

I called at the city prison to see him. Before I reached his cell I could hear him yelling, raving, shouting oaths. When I saw him he was pacing up and down his cell like a madman. He was hideous to look at; unshaven, eyes bloodshot, hair matted—he certainly was all that the papers had described him to be. As soon as he saw me he became quite calm. An officer allowed him to pass out into the corridor, where we sat on a bench together.

"She drove me mad," he said. "You know how I kept on forgiving her time after time. It was no use. She grew worse. Finally I decided to try it with her in the country. Perhaps it was the city, the love of the red lights, that caused her to fall down. I would rent a piece of land far away. Maybe we could still be happy together.

"I rented a small farm near Fresno and went into the business of truck gardening. Before we left the city she refused to go unless I could get her boy. So I went over to Oakland, kidnaped her child from the father. Together we went to the farm.

"It was all right for some time, but one evening [illegible] I came home from town I saw a man leaving the c[illegible] I suspected the worst. I went in and found her lyi[illegible] the bed dead drunk.

"In the morning, when she was sober, I told he[illegible] couldn't stay there any longer. Country people wo[illegible] put up with that sort of thing. I gave her some m[illegible] and sent her back to the city, promising to follow he[illegible] a few days after I had settled up my affairs. Wh[illegible] came to the city I had a few dollars, enough to s[illegible] again. But I had great difficulty in finding her. I search[illegible] through every dive on the Barbary Coast and in othe[illegible] parts of town. I kept this up for weeks. Meanwhile, my money was nearly gone. I took to drink in my desperation. At last I found her in an underground saloon on Pacific street. She was chatting with some men, drinking.

"I walked up to her and asked her to come home with me. She laughed at me and went on drinking and talking with the men. I urged her again, and she cried out angrily: 'Go on, you drunken bum!' and went on with her laughter and conversation with her men friends.

"So I went up the stairs and into the nearest doorway. I waited until she came along. Then I jumped out and killed her."

We were sitting together on a bench outside in the corridor while he told me his story. He had got this far when two or three nicely dressed women came along with some religious tracts they were distributing to prisoners.

When they saw Sullivan they recognized him from the pictures in the papers. One of the women held out a tract to him and said: "Poor man, aren't you sorry f the dreadful thing you have done?"

Sullivan sprang from the bench like a wild beast and yelled:

"Sorry! No, I'm not sorry. I'm glad, I'm glad, I'm glad! If she came back to earth I'd kill her again. God damn her soul! It's all over now but hanging, and I want it done quick."

His voice must have carried out on to Merchant street. The woman rushed away frightened. It took two or three men to drag him back to his cell.

I returned to my office and wrote the story of Sullivan's life as he had told it to me; the many times he had forgiven this woman and tried again to live a decent life with her, his many failures, and his great patience through it all. It was a sympathetic story. At that time, more than thirty years ago, a sympathetic story about a murder of this kind was practically unknown.

Sullivan did not engage an attorney. He made no effort to escape the rope, pleaded guilty in court and urged the judge not to delay his execution. He was the first prisoner hanged at San Quentin.

So when I joined Lowrie in an effort to help ex-prisoners, it was not entirely a new thing to me. Rather it was a return of a train of thought never wholly forgotten, now brought strongly to the surface of my mind by a new interest in Ruef and Lowrie. I was convinced that much could be done for ex-prisoners, believing that they were only men like other men, who by some accident of fate had fallen upon harder lives than others. The next few years were to alter considerably that point of view.

CHAPTER XXIV

Lowrie and I Organize A Prisoners' Relief Bureau In The *Bulletin* Office. My First Reaction To The Criminal Mind. More Intimate Knowledge Alters My Early Beliefs. The History Of Charley, A "Lifer" For Stage Robbery. I Succeed In Obtaining His Parole. Charley, At Seventy-One, Becomes Foreman Of My Ranch.

Lowrie and I organized a little relief bureau in the *Bulletin* office. We aimed to help men who came out of prison. We did help many. We got positions for paroled men and for men who had done their time. In that way I became acquainted with many of the desperate characters of California.

In the beginning, before I understood as much as I do now, I believed that men in prison were just like men out of prison, except that at some period of their lives something had gone wrong in their affairs. Some accident had overtaken them, and they had been caught. I still believe there are very few men out of prison that have escaped doing something, at some time, that broke one of our many laws.

With many convicts, I felt that environment, drunken parents or poverty had caused them to drop out of line with the rest of us. I felt that they had had no opportunity to develop into what we call normal human beings.

It took a long time for me to learn differently, and I still am undecided as to just what it is that causes men to become professional criminals. I am convinced that they are in some way different from the rest of us. They see life from a different angle. There is something peculiar about them—some twist in their brains.

We cannot see what it is, because men's brains are hidden by a cap of bone. We cannot look into a man's mind, and see what is happening there. We can see a club foot, for instance. We can see that a club-footed man is not normal; we do not expect him to walk like other men. But when a man has some abnormality in his brain we cannot see that. We expect him to act like the rest of us, and when he does not, we punish him. That is because we do not understand. We do not punish a club-footed man because he does not walk normally.

For many years I have known criminals intimately, have watched and studied them. Many of my first beliefs have been altered or destroyed in those years. Now I can only say that I do not understand their motives, I do not know what makes them what they are. Until we do understand, I believe we should withhold judgment, we should be patient and try to understand.

The story of Charley comes to my mind. He was a man of unusual force and character. I used to visit the prisons often and talk to the men. On one occasion I was shown into the execution room of San Quentin by Warden Hoyle. A prisoner made a little talk to me, explaining the various trappings of death. He talked in a mechanical, singsong way, as if he had made the speech many and many a time.

He started with the rope, which was tied to a heavy weight. He said this was kept at the end of the rope for a certain length of time to take all the elasticity out of it, so that when the man dropped through the trap the rope would not stretch. It would hold firm and crack his neck quickly.

He went from this rope to other features of the death process, explained the trap and how it was sprung by three men cutting three different cords, so that no man knew that he had been the one to cause death. The prisoner's matter-of-fact manner made the death scene very vivid and terrible.

I was interested in him. He was an old man, very fine looking, erect, strong, notwithstanding his age—he was nearly seventy. I asked the warden who he was. He said:

"That's Charley. He's in for life for murder. He was a stage robber, one of the most desperate men among the criminals of California. He's been here twenty-nine years."

I said: "My God, why isn't he paroled?"

Warden Hoyle replied: "I wish you could get him paroled. He's a fine character. I would trust him with a million dollars to go around the world with. I know he would keep his word and return when he said he would, with every dollar intact."

I talked with Lowrie about him. It turned out that Lowrie and he were great friends. Lowrie was very eager to have him paroled. I found this was difficult to accomplish.

Charley and his partner had robbed a Nevada county stage in the late seventies. They took $15,000 from the strongbox. The money was owned by a banker who was a passenger on the stage. When he saw the money in Charley's hand he could not control himself. He leaped from the stage and tried to grab the money. He threw his arms around Charley.

Charley's partner told him to stand back. The banker

making his escape when it rained. Charley did not know the man who drove the cart, but he found in the prison a man who wanted to escape and was willing to take a chance.

Charley unfolded his plan to this man, and said:

"If you could get the job of driving the cart when the winter season begins, we could make it."

His friend said: "That's easy." Immediately he began work on a beautiful inlaid cribbage board. When it was finished he presented it to Director Filcher. Filcher was delighted and said:

"I'll make my wife a Christmas present of this. Is there anything I can do for you?"

"Well, yes."

"What is it?"

"I'd like to have the job of driving the cart."

"Sure!" said Filcher. "I'll get it for you in fifteen minutes."

It was done. Then Charley got an extra pair of striped trousers, took them to the tanner, and had them dyed. He put them on under his striped trousers and wore them constantly. His partner had only striped trousers, but he wore high boots and had a raincoat that came to the top of his boots. Charley said:

"Now all we have to do is to wait for a rainy day."

The rainy day came. It rained nearly all winter. California was flooded. The first day it rained heavily. Charley told his partner they would make their attempt that day. At the proper moment he crawled under the tarpaulin, and they started. On the way the driver said:

"I have to stop at the commissary office. They may have something to take down to the Point."

"My God!" said Charley from under the tarpaulin. "Why didn't you tell me that? We're caught."

"Well, maybe they won't have anything."

Charley lay hidden in the cart while the driver went into the office. The commissary did not have anything to send to the Point. The driver went on toward the Point. As they approached, he saw a guard, and reported this to Charley. Charley, directing the escape from under the tarpaulin, said:

"Make a detour. Drive over to Mrs. Mahoney's and ask her if she doesn't want some coal."

Mrs. Mahoney did not want any coal. Her suspicions were aroused immediately. She said:

"No, I don't want any coal, and you know very well I don't want any coal."

By this time the guard had disappeared and Charley whispered:

"Drive on to the Point."

When they reached it, they both jumped out and disappeared around the Point and along the bay shore, toward San Rafael. They broke quickly into a barley field, wandered into some deep ditches, and covered themselves with barley and straw. Within an hour they heard the guards on the hills.

The guards were out with guns, combing the country. Charley and his partner heard them coming and going all day, while they lay hidden. When night came they slipped out, and made their way along the coast line of the bay in the darkness. It was raining hard. They walked several miles until dawn, when they hid again and remained hidden all day.

They continued this for several days and nights, in

the rain, without food. They became desperately hungry, and one evening about six o'clock Charley made an attempt to get some food. He walked toward a little cottage. A woman was standing in the door, calling her husband to supper. Charley could smell the hot food, and through the window he saw the table spread. It drove him frantic, but he did not dare go nearer, for he knew that by this time the whole state was placarded with notices of a reward. The desperate Charley was at large, one of the most dangerous men ever known in California.

He lay hidden until the husband went in to supper. Then he crept to the chicken house, grabbed two chickens by the neck without letting them make a sound, wrung their necks and carried them off. His partner had found a few potatoes in a garden, and together they went away with the chickens and potatoes. In the brush they found an old tin can, built a fire and boiled the food.

Charley was so hungry that he drank from the can. There was a scum on it, and he became deathly sick, with terrible pains. He probably had ptomaine poisoning. His partner, seeing his agony, said:

"Well, Charley, I guess we better go into San Rafael and give ourselves up."

Charley was able to say, "Give ourselves up, Hell!"

"What can we do?" said the partner.

"Die in the brush, of course."

All night and all the next day he was desperately ill. The next night he was able to go on. He had now eaten nothing for almost a week. They made their way to Benicia, stole a boat and crossed the Sacramento River to Port Costa. Here they hid in the railroad yard among the freight cars. In their wanderings, his partner had lost one of his boots in the mud, and the stripes on one trouser leg showed beneath his coat. About nine o'clock Charley walked up into the town of Porta Costa and went into a little shop, run by a woman.

There were several men standing around the store, discussing the escape of Charley. He walked bravely up to the counter and said:

"I want a pair of 28 overalls and a pair of number 8 shoes."

The woman eyed him suspiciously.

"You don't wear 28 overalls," she said.

The men in the store stopped talking and looked at Charley. For a moment he thought everything was ended for him. However, he carelessly flipped a $20 gold piece on the counter and said coolly:

"*I* don't, no; but my sheep herder does."

Charley's manner and the show of gold quieted the woman's suspicions. She sold him the shoes and the overalls. He also bought some cigars and lighted one before he left the shop. In another place he bought a flask of brandy and some food and then went back to his partner in the freight car. Charley took one swallow of the brandy. His stomach settled at once, the last of the ptomaine symptoms disappeared, and he was able to eat heartily.

They took the midnight train to Sacramento, one getting on at one end of the smoker and the other at the other end. Charley sat with a passenger. They began to talk, and before they got to Sacramento became good friends. The passenger invited Charley to his house in Sacramento to spend the night. Charley said:

"No, my wife will be at the station to meet me."

Arriving at Sacramento, he rejoined his partner and went to a saloon, bought a couple of drinks, and looked at all the papers of the last few days to see whether or not the detectives were on their trail. They found they were not. Then Charley bought a pistol—a .44—and some cartridges. The partner said, "Let's go out and get a decent meal, Charley, for once."

In telling the tale, Charley said:

"In a weak moment I consented. We went into a restaurant on K street. No sooner were we seated than two policemen walked in, stepped up to the counter and lighted their cigars, and stood there talking.

"I got out my .44 and laid it on my knee under the edge of the table and kept it there. The policemen walked out. When we finished our meal we went out and walked toward the railroad yard. On the way I saw a policeman following us. I drew my gun, hid it under my coat and turned and said to him, 'Are you following us?' The officer said, 'Where are you going?'

"I said, 'We are going home.' The officer walked away.

"That man never knew how close he came to Kingdom Come."

The two went on to the American river and took possession of an old hut in a deserted vineyard. They lived there all winter, going over to a little town occasionally, pretending to be woodchoppers, and buying such food as they needed. In the spring they boarded a freight car, made their way to New Mexico and from there to Chicago, where they separated.

Charley went to work, saved his money, and finally

went into business. He accumulated $800 in money, and bought a gold watch and chain. He was doing well.

In the family where he boarded there were two sisters. Charley fell in love with one of them, and she with him. She was a good girl, and pretty. They became engaged to be married. Charley was prospering. He was going to build a little home and settle down. They picked out a lot, and Charley bought it.

Then his partner was caught in a robbery, and in order to save his credits in San Quentin he confessed where Charley was. Wells Fargo detectives found Charley and arrested him.

Up to this time Charley's girl did not know that he was a fugitive, but as soon as he was arrested he sent for her. She came to the city prison, and there Charley gave her the lot, the $800 in money and the watch and chain. He told her what he was, that he had to spend the rest of his days in San Quentin.

The officers brought him back to the prison, and when I saw him he had been there twenty-nine years.

When I undertook to get him paroled, I found it necessary to get some signatures in Nevada City—those of the District Attorney and others. There was still a great deal of feeling there against him. It was most difficult to get the signatures, but finally I prevailed upon them to sign, and Governor Johnson, as a Christmas present to me, paroled Charley.

The day he came out of prison he dined with Mrs. Older and me at the Fairmont. In our rooms, after dinner, he told us the story of his escape. I asked him about the girl in Chicago, what had become of her.

He said that she had corresponded with him for eleven

years, but that finally he had written her and told her that some day she might want to marry some good man, and that if he learned of this correspondence it might cause trouble. So he had advised her to stop writing.

"That," said Charley, "was eighteen years ago, and since that time, until you came into my life, I have never heard from a living, human being."

I said: "Were you very much interested in the girl?"

"Yes; we intended to marry. I think I've got her picture here with me now." He put his hand down in his inside pocket and drew out a photograph.

He thought he had it! He knew he had it. It was the only thing he did have, the only thing he had brought with him out of prison. It was the picture of a gentle, sweet-looking girl.

He looked at it for some time, and mused, more to himself than to us:

"Of course, she doesn't look like that now. She's probably an old woman now. That was thirty years ago. I wish I knew what has become of her."

Mrs. Older and I had taken up our residence on a ranch in Santa Clara county, in the foothills, near Saratoga. It comprised two hundred acres. It was a fruit ranch, and there was a great deal of work to be done upon it. It served a good purpose, because I took men from prison down there and helped them regain their foothold. I made Charley foreman of this ranch.

He was seventy-one, but one of the strongest men I ever saw. He plowed from daylight to dark, never seeming to tire. He ran everything connected with the ranch, made all the purchases, paid all the bills. He was perhaps one of the most exacting men in the way of honesty that I ever encountered.

There was a young man working on the ranch—not a prisoner, just an ordinary citizen—whom Charley soon discovered was what he called a petty pilferer. He had no use for that young man.

"That kind of a fellow," he said, "would get a whole neighborhood in trouble. He'd steal a whip, or a buggy robe, or some little thing." His contempt was indescribable. "If he'd go out and get some big money, I wouldn't mind it so much; but he's just a petty thief," he declared, with scorn. "They're the curse of the earth."

Charley and I were living in a tent at this time, and I had a community box of cigars there; that is, I told Charley they were as much his as mine, and to smoke them whenever he wanted to. He was working up on the hill one day, and he saw this young man smoking a cigar down in front of the tent. He knew it had come from this box.

He said that he thought of a necklace that Mrs. Older had left on the table Sunday evening before she went to San Francisco. He had put it in a bureau drawer under some clothing. When he saw the young man smoking that cigar he thought of the necklace. He rushed down to the tent, went in and opened the bureau drawer and the necklace was there.

"It was a good thing it was," said Charley, "because if it hadn't been, I would have taken an iron bar and got it."

CHAPTER XXV

"Buck" English Tells Of Charley's "Going-Out Dinner." One Reclaimed Prisoner Who "Went Straight" To The End. Charley's Strict Social Code. Fritz Bauer First Shakes My Belief In The Normality Of Criminals; But Even He Shows Himself Capable Of Gratitude.

There was another stage robber, of a similar type to Charley, serving a life sentence in San Quentin. This was "Buck" English, a great friend of both Charley and Lowrie. Through them I became interested in him, and finally succeeded in getting him paroled. He, too, went straight as long as he lived.

After "Buck" came out, he told me much about Charley; for one thing, the story of the "going-out dinner" that the prisoners gave when Charley was paroled.

"Buck" English and Lowrie were room mates in prison. They had a room with a bathroom, had accumulated a good library, and were very comfortable together. The reason why "Buck" was allowed to occupy this room was that he was not locked up at night. He was in charge of the electric lights. As they might go out at any time, it was necessary that he be able to attend to them.

When "Buck" heard that Charley was leaving prison, he was in a position to celebrate the great occasion. He got together his friends among the prisoners. It was decided to give Charley a farewell dinner. Each prisoner was detailed to get some portion of the feast by stealth from the prison kitchen; one man the roast beef, another the potatoes, another the soup meat, another vegetables, another the pies, another the cigars. "Buck" said, "I'll provide the drinks."

Having access to the kitchen at night, he took several pounds of dried apricots to his room, boiled them, squeezed them and bottled the juice. He got hold of some hops and put them in, with other things that I have forgotten. After the job was done he corked the bottles, tied strings around the corks to hold them in, as is done with champagne, and put them away for the great event.

The night before Charley was to go out the guests assembled quietly in "Buck's" room. At midnight, when all the prison was asleep, the feast began.

"It was some dinner!" said "Buck," in relating the story. "We opened up with soup, and wound up with dessert, black coffee and cigars. Then I stepped into the closet and brought in the bottles and cut the cord. The corks hit the ceiling. Then I poured our glasses full and served the drink."

Standing, they gave Charley a toast, and the more eloquent among them made suitable speeches. It was a great occasion, still remembered in the prison.

"Charley sat back then, lighted his cigar, and with the influence of the apricot wine or brandy, or whatever it was, he glowed and talked," said "Buck," "more interestingly and fluently than he had talked in the twenty-nine years. He told the story of his life, and of his different escapades. It was a great evening.

"The old man had never talked much in all the years, but now he opened up. He told one story that might interest you.

"He had held up a stage in the Sierra Nevada mountains and was in hiding until the trouble blew over. Making his way through the mountains, he came across a cabin where the man was sick in bed. There was a wife and several children, without money and without food.

"So Charley went down in the night to a near-by town, stole a team, broke into a warehouse and loaded the wagon up with all kinds of food, bacon, ham, flour, sugar, coffee, and such other things as he thought they would need. He took some calico for dresses, and some ribbons for the children. He drove up with these things to the famishing family.

"In telling the story, he said that he felt they now had everything but money. He was thinking this when a Chinese vegetable wagon came along, and the peddler displayed \$40 or \$50 in gold. When he had gone on, Charley went down a short cut through a gulch, intercepted the Chinaman, held him up, took the money and carried it back to the family. He now felt that they were well provided for, and he could leave, so he went on his way through the mountains."

I tried frequently to find what started Charley off wrong. He may have given a clue to it one evening at our ranch. He had come in from a hard day's work at the plow. It was a cool evening, and we had a hot fire going in the stove. When Charley had lighted his pipe I asked him to tell me something about his boyhood.

"I was raised on a farm in one of the Southern states," he began. "When I was ten years old I was accused of stealing a swarm of bees. I didn't do it, but the story spread around the neighborhood that I was a thief. I was disgraced. I knew the boy who did steal the bees. I lay in wait for him and threw rocks at him with a slung shot. One of the rocks hit him and hurt him badly. This disgraced me more than ever, and I got the reputation of being a bad boy."

Charley then bent his head and wiped his eyes on his shirt sleeve. The strong emphasis he put upon "bad boy" convinced me that in his own mind he believed that this accusation which had so embittered him was the important turning point in his life. But for that incident, he thought, he might never have committed a crime and might have lived a relatively happy life like other men; might have married, prospered and had children to comfort him in his old age. He may be right, but somehow I can't quite believe it. He had character and great ability, qualities that might have made him a very successful man, but they were offset by a violent temper and an independent and rebellious spirit.

I doubt if he would have been able to live a life without violence.

At twenty years of age Charley enlisted in the Confederate army and fought in the Civil War. He was chosen by Quantrell for one of his wild band; picked, no doubt, for his courage and daring. Quantrell headed a large body of carefully selected men, good shots, good horsemen, quick and ready for any raid. They were marauders, robbing farmhouses, stealing cattle and carrying off whatever was needed. They robbed and killed as a band of guerillas under the sanction of war.

When peace came, Charley, accustomed to this kind of life, came West and continued it single-handed as a stage robber. This was in 1865. He passed at least two-thirds of his life in prison, or as a fugitive from justice. He spent nearly forty years in the penientiary at San Quentin.

"Buck" English joined Charley at our ranch. Their friendship was very deep, but "Buck" was taken ill, and I had him sent to the relief home, where he could have the care he needed. He was there for a year before he died. Charley visited him regularly every Sunday and carried him something nice to eat, whatever delicacy he thought "Buck" would like.

A short time before "Buck's" death, when Charley was with him, he said:

"Charley, I am going over the hill."

"Well, what of it, 'Buck'? That's nothing. Death is only a leap in the dark. Why regret it?"

"I don't," said "Buck." "I don't care anything about that, Charley. But I owe you $80, and I would like to get well and work long enough to get the money and pay you back. I don't like to go out without doing that."

Charley took "Buck's" hand and said:

" 'Buck,' you know damn well you don't owe me a cent. Forget it."

"Buck" smiled and seemed happy. A day or two later he died. On the day of the funeral Charley appeared in my office with his best suit on and a rose in his buttonhole.

"Everything is arranged, Mr. Older," he said. " 'Buck' will have as good a funeral as any man ever had. I've taken care of that. The services are up at the undertaker's at ten o'clock."

"It's ten now," I said.

"I know," he said. "I know. I want to be a little late. Some of 'Buck's' friends have stuck a preacher in, and I can't stand preachers, so I'm going to hang around outside till he's through."

Charley saved his money and prospered. He grew too old for farm work, but I got him some work in San Francisco that he could do, and he continued to save money, to live frugally and do well. After he left the ranch he still had a very kindly interest in our affairs, and was very strict as to what kind of prisoners we allowed to come there. He had a stern social code.

While he was still at the ranch I brought down a Mexican who had just come out of the penitentiary. He was what Charley regarded as a petty larceny thief. Mrs. Older and I had moved up the hill into the new house, and Charley had refused to take his meals with us there. He said the new house was too stylish for him. He preferred to cook for himself in his own cabin. After the Mexican came, however, he appeared at our house for dinner.

We were surprised, and asked him why he had changed his mind. He said:

"Well, you know I can't eat with that Mexican. He's a low-down thief; he's not in my class. You know, over in San Quentin there are just as many classes as there are outside, and more, too. I can't associate with a fellow like that."

So after Charley moved to the city he still maintained his interest in the social standing of our guests, and in this connection some interesting incidents occurred.

Upon one occasion, a paroled burglar who was living at the ranch visited the city one Sunday for a little recreation.

During the day he got to drinking, and that evening he went to Charley's room to call on him. Because he was drinking he probably was more talkative than other-

"Oh, yes, there is. Has any one hurt your feelings or wounded you in any way?"

"No."

"Well, why don't you go up to breakfast and go on with your work as usual?" Silence.

"Of course, if you want to leave the ranch you are free to go. Your remaining is no advantage to me. I am only urging you in your own interest. Why not work another month and add that money to what you already have? That would put you just that much farther away from starvation."

He did not answer. He hung his head and looked sullen.

"Tell me, Fritz, just what is the matter. Has any one been unkind to you, or said anything to hurt your feelings?"

"No," he answered. "I boiled up."

I didn't understand what he meant, and he would make no further explanation. However, he remained at the ranch and the next day behaved normally. The following Sunday, Jack Black came to visit us. Jack was a wise ex-prisoner who had lived at the ranch with us, and whose story I shall give later on. When Fritz saw Jack his face lighted up.

"Say, Jack, you know why I 'boiled up,' don't you? You understand."

"Yes," said Jack. "I understand."

Later, Jack explained to me that men in prison frequently get into a state of mind where they will not talk to any one for a week or more, and sometimes will not eat. Jack did not know what happened to them, but he knew that it was a common occurrence.

Fritz stuck it out for twenty days and then quit. I brought him to the city with me and paid him. A few days later, a policeman rang me up and asked me if Fritz had ever worked at my ranch. I said: "Yes; why?"

"Well, we think he stole a suit of clothes from a ship."

Fritz was a sailor and had been down on the water front. Being an ex-convict, of course, he had been suspected when the theft was discovered. He may have been guilty. I don't know. At any rate, I got him out of the scrape. Later he was arrested and I got him out again.

He met Jack Black one day and said: "The big fellow may have to get me out again," and Jack replied: "You keep this up, Fritz, and the first thing you know the 'big fellow' will stop getting you out. Then you know what will happen. You'll get twenty years when he gives you up."

Later I got Fritz a job as a sailor on a sailing vessel, and he was greatly pleased. This seemed to be the thing he needed. Months afterward, he came up from Central America and brought us a parrot, which showed that in his muddled head and through all his boilings up, he remembered the kindness we had shown him.

I don't know what became of him. I am still puzzled as to why he acted as he did. He had a comfortable place on the ranch. He had as good a chance as Charley to save money and to make his way in the world. He certainly hated prison, and had no desire to be hungry and cold and friendless. Nor was there anything vicious about him.

CHAPTER XXVI

George Fisher, "100% Right When In Jail, 90% Wrong When Out." A Lover Of Nature, Animals And Children, But With A Strange Perversity That Refuses To Be Mended. Tim O'Grady, Incorrigible Thief, Comes Our Way With His Pet Linnet.

Among the numerous ex-prisoners who found their way to the ranch, George Fisher was one who deepened my doubt of ever getting very far in determining why some men break the penal code and seem unable to keep pace with the rest of us. George was an especial friend of Jack Black, who urged me to get him out of Folsom prison, where he had been many years.

"Here is one man," said Jack, "that I know is all right. I lived with him in a cell at the county jail for three years, and we never had a word. That is the severest test there is. A loving husband and wife could hardly pass that test, locked up for three years in an 8 x 10 space. They would probably quarrel some. George and I never did. Get him out if you can. He is 100 per cent."

Shortly afterward I secured a parole for George, and he came to the ranch to work.

"Here is one of your prisoners I can't make out," said Mrs. Older, after he had been with us two or three days. "I can't understand how a man who looks as George does, with his kind disposition and wonderfully honest eyes, could ever get into prison."

Every one on the ranch grew fond of George. He loved little children and his sympathies for suffering people were keen. He had never drunk liquor or used tobacco. Yet he was a burglar and had served four terms in the penitentiary.

He was an especial favorite with the children at the ranch. They did not know he had been in prison. We thought it best for them not to know. It might prejudice them, and they might thoughtlessly tell the neighbors. This would hurt George, because he was very sensitive about his past life and never referred to it.

One evening Mrs. Older and I returned from the city. We asked the children how they had amused themselves while we were away.

"Oh, we had such a good time!" they said. "George showed us such wonderful secrets!"

"What secrets?" we asked, full of curiosity.

"He took us up into the forest and showed us a beautiful little waterfall he has built. He called it his 'Little Yosemite.' Then he showed us where he had planted a peach tree and an almond tree in the woods, and he told us lovely names he has for the trees and the little hollows. He asked us not tell any one, because those are his secrets. He goes there all by himself to look at them, and nobody knows. We promised him we wouldn't tell, but we know you won't tell if we tell you."

The wild animals on the ranch all seemed to love George, and had no fear of him. The beautiful bush-tailed squirrels came to him when he gave a certain rap on the base of their favorite trees. He always carried nuts in his pockets for them. Nothing wild was afraid of him, and all the domestic animals loved him. The cows and pigs came to him whenever they could, and he petted them and stroked their backs.

One evening, as I was returning from the city, Mrs. Older met me on the road. She was very much excited. Her hands were trembling.

"George has turned queer," she said. "You know you told me to tell him to turn the calf into the pasture; you said I had kept it in the pen too long and it was time for it to learn to eat grass. I told George what you said, and he refused to do it. I urged that you wanted it done.

"George said, 'I know he wants it done, but I won't do it for him or for any one else. The calf might eat too much grass, take sick and die.' He absolutely refused to obey me."

I asked Mrs. Older not to be disturbed, to let George have his way.

Jack Black, who had said that George was 100 per cent right, came to visit us, and one evening after dinner, as he was going down to the farmhouse to see George, I decided to let him discover for himself George's queerness. I did not want his mind to be influenced by any prejudiced word from me.

The pump was run by electricity. It forced the water up to the top of the hill above our house. It furnished our house supply. We used a great deal of it for irrigating the flowers. Starting the pump involved no work, just pushing in the switch.

Next morning Jack came to me and said, "Mr. Older, George is 90 per cent wrong. I asked him to start the pump. He said he wouldn't do it.

" 'Mr. Older wants you to start it.'

" 'I don't care if he does. I won't.'

" 'Why not?'

" 'Because they're using too much water on the hill. They use too much on the flowers. Besides, they will wear out the pump.'

" 'That's none of your business,' I said. 'They wouldn't live here without flowers, and if the pump wears out they will buy another.'

"George said, 'I won't do what's wrong for Mr. Older or any one else. Supposing he were to order me to kill Frank, the horse. Do you suppose I would do it? Of course not.'

" 'I would,' I said. 'I wouldn't care what his reason was. He might want to stuff the hide and put it in a museum. I'd burn his house if he asked me to. There isn't anything I wouldn't do for him.'

"George said, 'I won't start the pump.' That was his final answer.

"I tell you," said Jack, "George is off his head."

George stayed on until he expressed a desire to leave. When he left I got him a job in the city. Finally, he decided to go East. He came down to the ranch to say good-by to us and his wild animal friends and to leave with us Bessie, his beloved dog.

He was very sad. He rapped on the tree and no squirrels came. They had all been shot by thoughtless boys. His chipmunks, grown older, did not come at his call. He visited his "Little Yosemite" and his secret places in the forest. As we drove away from the ranch, his dog sobbed on the hilltop and looked lovingly after him.

He is in the East now. For several Christmases he sent us a box. Every one was remembered, every one he ever met at the ranch, and Bessie, his dog. Her present was usually a box of chocolate, of which she is very fond. Bessie never seems to be her old self since George left.

I am sure the penitentiary never reached George's trouble. It is beyond us all. Until we know why he is so different from the rest of us, the best we can do is to be kind to him.

There were other characters as baffling as George. Tim O'Grady was one of them.

Tim walked into my room in the *Bulletin* office one morning early. A linnet was perched on his shoulder.

"I'm just from Quentin, Mr. Older, and I brought my little friend with me. Of course, I know I can't keep the bird now that I am out. I didn't like to leave him in the prison, and so I said to myself, I'll give him to Mr. Older. Perhaps his wife will like him. So here he is."

The bird hopped from Tim's shoulder to my desk and chirped gaily.

"He's been a great comfort to me," said Tim. "The only friend I had in the world. I raised him from the nest, and trained him. When I left the cell in the morning, the bird flew away over the wall and played all day with other birds, but as soon as the bell rang for the lockup he'd fly in and light on my shoulder and go to the cell with me.

"Take him to your home, Mr. Older. I'm sure Mrs. Older will take good care of him."

Tim was a thief and had been in San Quentin twice. Not at all a bad fellow. Kindly, full of fun and mischievous. For his pranks in prison he had spent a lot of time in the dungeon and in the "sash and blind," the old house of torture that Governor Johnson abolished.

"What are you going to do, Tim? Have you a trade?" I asked.

"Yes," he replied. "I am a good waiter, and I guess I can get a job all right. I'll go out now and hunt one and leave the bird with you."

I sent out and bought a cage and put the bird in it with water and food, and left it on my desk. It remained there overnight. That evening I told the story to Mrs. Older and she urged me to bring it home. When I entered my office in the morning I was startled to find the cage empty. I thought some one in the office had stolen it. But in a few minutes Tim entered, smiling, with the bird on his shoulder.

"I was lonesome last night, Mr. Older, and hated to go to bed alone, and so I came into your room after you had gone and took him with me to my room. But I won't do it again. You take him home with you and then I can't."

"How about the job, Tim?" I asked. "You must get work, you know. If you don't you'll be tempted, and the first thing you know you'll be back in jail."

Tim assured me that nothing of that kind would ever happen again. He was through with stealing forever.

Mrs. Older was delighted with the bird. "Little Tim," she called him. We soon grew very fond of him. He sang two or three beautiful little songs and flew from her shoulder to mine in the happiest way. At night he made his bed in a geranium pot.

Meanwhile Tim disappeared. One morning I saw in one of the papers that he had been arrested for attempted theft. I told Mrs. Older that evening that Tim was in jail. While she had never seen him, her sympathy went out to him because of his bird. She looked at Little Tim through her tears, and said: "Poor Little Tim, your father is in jail." Then she turned to me and said: "You must get him out."

The following day I called on Chief White and told him Tim's story and the story of the bird. He sent an officer for Tim. He was brought into the chief's room in handcuffs.

"Take off those handcuffs," said the chief to the officer. "Now, Tim, sit down. You are with friends who want to help you. I'll get you a good job in a work camp in the mountains and will pay your way up there. You may go to-night. Try to make good, Tim," said the kindly chief, "and I'll do everything I can for you."

Tim was strong with promises, and no doubt he meant them at the time.

"Chief," he said with tears streaming down his cheeks, "I'll never steal again, so help me God."

There were tears in the chief's eyes, too, as he sent for an officer to take Tim back to the city prison.

"Let me go back to the jail alone, Chief. Please do. Let me go on my honor. I want to show you I can be square."

The chief dismissed the officer who had come to take him, and Tim started down the corridor alone, with his head high and his chest out. He went up in the elevator and gave himself up at the prison.

That afternoon he was free and on his way to his new job in the mountains.

I took the good news home to Mrs. Older. My first words were, when I entered her room, "Tim is out."

"So is Little Tim," she said. "He flew out the window

an hour ago. I am sorry to lose him, but I am glad he is free. He'll join the other linnets and make his way."

Tim held his job for a few weeks, but finally quarreled with the Chinese cook and had to quit. He returned to the city. I saw him a few times, and then he disappeared.

A few weeks later I received a postal card from him, sent from a little town in Iowa: "Kind regards to you, Mr. Older, and thanks for your help. Love to Donald Lowrie. I shall be here for about four weeks. Yours, Tim."

I showed the card to Lowrie. He smiled and said: "He'll be there four weeks. To me that sounds like 'thirty days.' "

Lowrie was right. Tim had taken to stealing again. Later we heard from him from other jails, and if he is alive is probably in one now. He just can't keep step with the rest of us.

CHAPTER XXVII

The Peculiarities Of Pedro. A Vivid Imagination, A "Grand Seigneur" Appearance And An Ingratiating Manner Make Havoc With My Pocketbook. I Undergo A Sad Awakening. We Entertain Charles Augustus Boggs, Real-Life Version Of "The Crew Of The Nancy Brig." Hopeless Mental Twists That Prison Discipline Is Powerless To Straighten Out.

Pedro had the soul of a poet and the habits of a sybarite. His eyes were large, dark and languorous. His skin was olive, his features regular, his figure perfect. He dressed in excellent taste and simulated the air and manners of a young man of wealth and leisure. He was twenty-six years of age when I met him in my office eight years ago.

"I live in Los Angeles, Mr. Older," Pedro began. "On the train coming north, I met a young man who is a very dear friend of mine. He was in great trouble, and, wholly trusting me, he told me his story. Two years ago he forged a check for a small sum, was caught, tried, convicted and sentenced to five years in the Colorado penitentiary. His conduct in prison was excellent. His youth and good behavior appealed to the kindly warden, who paroled him after he had served one year of his sentence. He was allowed to return to Los Angeles, where his father and mother lived.

"They did not know he had been in prison, and he determined they never should know. He got a job in a laundry and was earning $75 a month. In a short time, a deputy sheriff in Los Angeles who knew he had been in prison and was out on parole called on him and threatened him with exposure if he didn't give him $60. My friend paid the money. A month later the deputy sheriff made another demand for money. This he also met, although he had to borrow a part of the sum.

"The deputy sheriff waited a month or two and made another demand for money. This time he wanted $90. My friend did not have it and could not borrow it. He was desperate, and, fearing immediate exposure, he passed a forged check and paid the man what he asked. Feeling this new crime would soon be discovered, my friend bought a bottle of poison, removed all identification marks from his clothing and took the train for San Francisco.

"Arriving here he intended to commit suicide. His body would not be recognized. It would be buried in an unknown grave, and his parents would never know what had become of him. On the train he read a chapter of Donald Lowrie's story, 'My Life in Prison.' Believing that the editor who was publishing Lowrie's story might be sympathetic with him, he decided to call on him and tell him his story."

"I am sympathetic," I said, "and will help him. Where is your friend?"

"It is my story," said Pedro.

I called in Lowrie. I wanted him to hear the tale and give his expert opinion on it.

Pedro told his story over again to Lowrie. Lowrie believed it and confirmed me in my judgment that I should go at once to Los Angeles with Pedro, expose the deputy sheriff, pay the man who had cashed the forged check, reinstate Pedro in his job, and give him a chance to make good.

Pedro agreed to go with me on the train that evening. He had only $8 in money. I told him he could pay for his berth with $5 and I would provide the railroad tickets. We were to meet at the station in time for the eight o'clock train. Meanwhile, Lowrie took Pedro over to the Argonaut Hotel and got him a room so that he could change his clothes. He had a long talk with Pedro and was further convinced that he was telling the truth. He took the bottle of poison from Pedro and brought it to my office.

The train for Los Angeles left at eight o'clock. I arrived there at a little before eight. I saw Pedro walking up and down the waiting room, immaculately dressed, his hands gloved. He was carrying a very large and very beautiful bouquet of roses.

I was staggered, but I had said good-by to Mrs. Older, and had also confided my errand to my friends, and I still hoped, in spite of the bouquet of roses and the gloved hands, that his story might stand up.

"I have your ticket, Pedro. Come with me and buy your berth."

"I am sorry," he said, "but I spent the $8 that I had this afternoon. I needed a new pair of gloves, and I am very fond of roses. I couldn't resist this bouquet."

Still I didn't weaken. I bought his Pullman ticket and we went to Los Angeles together. Arriving there in the morning, I sent Pedro to the law office of a friend of mine and instructed him to remain there until he heard from me. I would go first and settle with the manager of the taxicab stand at the Alexandria Hotel, who had cashed the bogus check.

I called at the hotel and introduced myself to the taxicab man. I told him I had come from San Francisco to straighten out the Pedro transaction. He stared at me as if he thought I were mildly insane.

"What do you mean by straightening it out?" he asked.

"I mean," I replied, "I am ready to pay the $90 Pedro owes you. You probably know the boy was hard pressed for money."

"Hard pressed, hell," he said. "He's a crazy fool. He hired an automobile from me, with a driver, at $30 a day. He drove around in it for two days."

"Where did he go?" I asked.

"Oh, nowhere in particular. Down to Santa Monica and back and then around town, showing off. He owed me $60 for the machine for two days. He gave me a check for $90 and I, thinking he was the son of a rich man, out for a time, accepted the check and gave him $30 change."

"Did he seem to have been drinking?" I asked.

"No; he showed no signs of liquor. He is just a damned fool."

So the taxicab man was the cruel deputy sheriff who was threatening with exposure a poor, hard-working boy if he didn't pay him hush money!

I was pretty weak by this time, but I took a taxicab from the hotel and drove out to the suburbs and found Pedro's brother. I asked him if he knew what his brother had done.

"Yes," he said, "the poor boy flooded the town with bogus checks and skipped out."

Pedro had bought the poison to be used as an effective part of the story he planned to tell me.

I rang him up at the attorney's office and told him what I had learned and added that I could do nothing for him.

I took the train home that evening feeling rather cheap. A day or two later I received a bill for $90 from the Alexandria taxicab man. He had evidently become convinced that I was insane.

I never heard from Pedro again. I suppose some prison warden has him and is solemnly at work trying to make him walk straight by a form of punishment which would make a strong man stagger.

One evening, about dinner time, Charles Augustus Boggs suddenly stepped out of the darkness into our kitchen at the ranch. Mrs. Older and I were away, and Lowrie and George were in charge. The boys recognized Boggs at once as an ex-prisoner. They knew him by the cut of his suit of prison-made clothes and the squeak of his prison brogans.

"I have walked over from San Jose," said Boggs. "I haven't had anything to eat in three days. I know Older will give me a meal and put me up for the night."

"Sure he will," said Lowrie. "He isn't here, but George and I will cook a dinner for you."

The boys started a fire in the cookstove and began preparing the potatoes.

"By trade I am a cook," said Boggs. "Let me get the dinner."

Lowrie and George stepped aside, and Boggs soon had a fine dinner under way. He ate ravenously, proving at least that he was very hungry.

When the dishes were washed and the kitchen swept

Mrs. Older arrived from the city. Lowrie presented Boggs to her as a starving man they had just fed.

Mrs. Older asked them to give him a room at the farmhouse, and they went away together.

In the morning, after breakfast, Boggs insisted to Mrs. Older that he wanted to do some work to pay for the two meals.

"What can you do?" Mrs. Older asked.

"By trade," said Boggs, "I am a locomotive engineer."

There were no locomotives on the ranch and Mrs. Older was puzzled. "I have only gardening work here," she said.

"I am a professional gardener," said Boggs.

Doubting, but curiously interested in this new type of "nut," she said, "Very well, I want some flower beds made." She pointed to the spot.

Boggs seized a spade and Mrs. Older left him at work and went about her own affairs. Later he asked her if she wanted the flower beds in the form of stars or heart-shaped. She looked down at the garden and saw that he was making both designs, and executing them beautifully. For the first time, she realized that he had done landscape gardening in prisons.

She told him she wanted just the ordinary flower beds, and he quickly transformed them to suit her taste. He was wonderfully skillful, and when I returned from the city that evening Mrs. Older excitedly related to me the story of Boggs and admiringly pointed out the work he had done. He was undoubtedly a genius gone wrong. She was glad to employ him permanently at good wages.

A few days later, as I was motoring home, George, excited, stopped me at the barn.

"The yearling steer has broken his leg. What are we to do?" said George.

Knowing no answer, I made none, but drove on up the hill to the house. I met Boggs coming down the hill. I told him my trouble. He was smilingly calm. "Don't worry, Mr. Older. By trade I am a butcher. I'll take care of the steer."

An hour or two later he showed me the carcass, hung on a tree, dressed as might be for a Christmas stall in a city market.

"If we leave it here overnight, Boggs," I said, "the coyotes will get it. We would better hitch up the team and haul it to the farmhouse." The farmhouse was two hundred yards distant.

"It will not be necessary," said Boggs buoyantly. "I am a trained athlete; been in the professional game for years."

The steer weighed two hundred and forty pounds. Boggs, five feet six inches in height, swung it lightly on his back and trotted away with it.

The plumbing in the house went wrong. The nearest plumber was four miles away. We consulted Boggs.

"Don't distress yourself," he said cheerily, "by trade I am a plumber."

He did the work easily, skillfully and quickly.

When the first rain came, water in torrents poured down the hill, threatening the very foundations of the house. Frightened, we summoned Boggs.

"I have specialized in cement work," he observed reassuringly. In a day he had made a long cement drain at the back of the house, which carried away the water. It is still in operation and in perfect condition.

The paint in the dining room needed retouching. It was a delicate shade of gray. Mrs. Older approached Boggs. There was genuine doubt in the tone of her voice.

"Mr. Boggs, you don't happen to know anything about painting, do you?"

"Four years' experience as an interior house painter and decorator," he replied.

Boggs mixed the paint, caught the shade exactly and painted the dining room.

One of the cows was taken ill. Boggs was called in. "Yes, I am a veterinary," he said. "I'll treat the cow." He did. She was well in three days. He built culverts for the road, criticized the plowman's work, and gave valuable hints to the men who were pruning the orchards.

Late Christmas Eve we heard Friend, the dog, barking violently on the porch. He barked so earnestly that we thought there must be some one in front of the house. There was. When we went out in the morning we saw stretched across the front of the house the words, "Merry Christmas." They were lettered in red toyon berries, surrounded by garlands of fir gathered from the hillsides. Boggs had done it.

We were delighted, thanked him for the surprise and complimented him on his skill in lettering.

"It comes easy to me," he said. "I am a woodcarver by trade."

Of course we wanted Boggs to stay with us forever and ever, but we were sure he wouldn't. He had been with us nearly two months, when he suddenly told Mrs.

Older that he never stayed anywhere more than two months.

"Why not remain with us?" she urged. "We like you and will pay you well. You could save some money."

"No," he said. "I feel I must go. I came up here to get away from pursuing women. I thought if I grew a full beard, perhaps I wouldn't be so attractive and they would leave me alone. My beard is grown now, so I'll leave when my month is up."

We paid him, and parted with him sorrowfully.

Two weeks later little Mary, a member of our household, was reading a San Jose paper. She suddenly looked up, startled.

"Mrs. Older, was Mr. Boggs' first name Charles Augustus?"

"Yes; why?"

"He's in jail," said Mary.

Boggs had attached himself to a matrimonial bureau in San Jose in the rôle of a professional husband. He had married a young Swedish woman with intent to swindle her out of a sum of money. He got out of the scrape, but did not return to the ranch. He was evidently ashamed of what he had done. A few weeks later he called on me at the *Bulletin* office and wanted to come back. In fact, he agreed to go down with me that afternoon; but he did not appear. There were two ex-burglars with us at that time, and Boggs, I reasoned, feared to face them, knowing that his was a kind of crime that even burglars would not forgive.

Some time later he wrote me from Lodi. He was in jail on a serious charge. He asked me to help him. But this time his was a case in which no one could help him.

I wrote him and told him so. I have not heard from him since. No doubt he is now doing time in some prison.

Boggs was one of the most useful men I have ever known. He could do so many necessary things, and could do them well. He said he had been a woman's dressmaker and had taken prizes for his skill. He had given us such proof of his ability in so many ways that we were inclined to believe he could even make women's dresses.

Boggs has the misfortune to have some twist in his mental processes that he is no way responsible for. Whatever the twist is, it is as yet far out of the reach of and beyond science. Being abnormal, he does abnormal things, is judged by the standards of normal men, is condemned and sent to prison to be corrected and made better by a stupid form of punishment. In fact, a sick man is subjected to a treatment that would make a sound man ill.

Thus, in this cruel way, the human race slowly gropes toward the light.

CHAPTER XXVIII

How The Innocent Suffer For The Guilty. John Ward, Sentenced To Thirty Years In San Quentin For An Eight-Dollar Robbery He Did Not Commit. No Parole For The Man Without A Suit Of Clothes And A Hat. The Case Of Fate Against John Byrne. Innocent, But Condemned For Murder. The Death Sentence Commuted To Life Imprisonment. Paroled After Fifteen Years, He Comes To My Ranch To Die. My Idea Of A Christian Burial.

Soon after I started publishing Lowrie's "My Life in Prison" some one told me there was an innocent man in San Quentin who had served eleven years. His name was John Ward. He had been arrested in Watsonville for robbing a man of $8, was convicted and sentenced to serve thirty years in San Quentin.

I had heard and investigated many stories of innocent men being in prison, and as a rule they had turned out to be untrue. I hadn't much faith in the Ward story. But I sent a man over to see him and get his version of the affair.

He said the reason he was selected by the police for the crime was because he was the only ex-convict in the town and they naturally suspected him. "But," he said, "I wasn't within two miles of the scene of the crime and knew nothing about it. The man who was robbed was very drunk and after he left the saloon he fell in a near-by alley and some one picked his pockets. The police took me to him the next morning, when he was sober, and he identified me. I have no way of proving my alibi because the woman I was with has disappeared and I cannot find her."

I did not go any further with the investigation at that time. Some months afterward, a young man called on me at the *Bulletin* office, and after getting me to promise that I would not publish what he intended telling me, said:

"John Ward is innocent."

"How do you know?" I asked.

"Because I am the one who robbed the drunken man in Watsonville. I was only a boy at the time. Since then I have grown up, married, and got a good job here in town and I can't afford to have it generally known that I committed this crime. I'd lose my job. But I'll give you an affidavit with all the facts. That ought to get him out. Gee, but I've suffered a lot over Ward being in prison eleven years. He sure got a dirty deal."

I secured his affidavit, and through other information he gave me I succeeded in establishing a perfect alibi for Ward. I mailed all of this evidence to the prison directors, expecting, of course, that Ward would be released at the next meeting. I waited three months, and nothing was done.

Some time afterward I was dining with Governor Johnson at his residence in Sacramento. When we had finished a very fine dinner and the Governor had lighted his pipe and had comfortably settled back in his chair he looked over at me and said: "Older, this is a bully world."

"Yes," I replied. "It is, for you and me and some few others, but it is not a bully world for a fellow named

Ward. He has done eleven years in San Quentin, and he's innocent."

He asked me for the facts as I knew them, and I told him the Ward story. He did not say anything, but I felt it made an impression.

Shortly afterward I visited San Quentin, and while Warden Hoyle was showing me through the prison I turned on him abruptly and said: "You have an innocent man in here, haven't you?"

"Oh, you mean that fellow Ward."

"Yes," I replied, "I mean Ward."

"Well," he said, "he's no good, you know."

"What's that got to do with it? None of us is much good either," I said. "What could you expect of a man after having been locked up for eleven years, innocent?"

"Why don't you get him out on parole? We'll stand for that."

"Isn't that rather odd," I said, "paroling an innocent man?"

"That's the best we can do. That's more than he deserves. He's a bad egg."

"Parole is better than nothing," I said. "Let me have a talk with him."

The warden took me to his office, sent for Ward, and had him brought into the room.

"The warden tells me, Ward, you're no good. What about that?"

"I know they say that. But let me tell you my story and you'll know.

"I was first arrested at Watsonville, for fighting on the street while I was drunk. I got thirty days in the county jail. I was to go out on a Monday morning, and the Saturday afternoon before that it was very hot. The gardener brought a pint of whisky into the jail and passed it through the bars to me and said, 'Here's a drink for you boys. It's a hot day. Maybe it will cheer you up.' I took the bottle and passed it to the other fellows. I didn't care to drink myself because I wanted to go out Monday morning perfectly straight. For that bottle I got a year in Folsom.

"I served the year, came back to Watsonville, and one afternoon while I was driving a spring wagon from Salinas over the San Juan grade to San Juan, with a couple of fellows, we stopped to get a drink of water at a farmhouse. My companions went in for the water and came out with a piece of harness and an old raincoat, and threw this junk into the wagon. I said: 'Don't take that stuff. It will get us into trouble.'

"They replied: 'Oh, it will be all right. There's nobody in the house. It doesn't amount to much, anyway.'

"Foolishly I drove on into San Juan. The next day we were all three arrested and charged with burglary. The District Attorney sent word to me that if I would plead guilty I would get off with ninety days. I followed his advice and got three years in Folsom.

"That's my record. That's how bad I am."

I got a parole blank from the warden, filled it out and gave it to the warden to file with the Board. Before leaving, the warden said I would have to send the prisoner a suit of clothes, otherwise he could not come out.

I said: "I thought the state furnished clothes."

"No," he replied, "we only furnish a suit of clothes to men who have finished their terms. All the clothes of men who are brought here are taken from them and not returned, and there is no provision for a paroled man getting a state suit, so we have to rely upon the friends of the paroled man furnishing the clothes for him."

"Very well," I said. "I'll send him one of my old suits."

The next day I sent by express an old suit of clothes to the prison; and assuming, of course, that Ward would be out, his story faded from my mind. Two months afterward, I happened to be over at the prison to see some one else, and the captain of the guard said: "Your friend Ward is still here."

I was amazed. "Why, I thought he had been paroled."

"No, he is still here. I don't know what the matter is. Perhaps you had better see him."

Ward was sent for and came into the captain's office.

"I thought you were paroled, Ward."

"No," he said. "They wouldn't let me go. You sent me the suit of clothes, but you didn't send me a hat." He had been kept in prison two months because he had no hat.

When I returned to the city that evening I expressed one of my old hats. He was paroled—not pardoned—to work in a stone quarry at Watsonville for $15 a month. I never heard from him afterward.

Theodore Roche, the well-known San Francisco attorney, now a Police Commissioner, first called my attention to the case of John Byrne. Roche had been his attorney and was convinced of his innocence. Byrne was a Reno printer and had come to San Francisco directly after the fire of 1906 to find the body of his father, believed by him to be hidden under the ruins of a rooming house where he lived.

In those days, while the city lay in ruins, it was difficult to find lodgings, and John Byrne, knowing Patrick Sullivan, who had a saloon on the corner of Sixth and Brannan streets, was offered a bed in a rear room back of the bar. In his younger days Byrne had known the Sullivan crowd quite intimately, having been reared in the neighborhood. Byrne accepted Sullivan's kind invitation and was asleep in this back room when two masked bandits held up a saloon on the opposite corner.

One of the bandits, Burke, was shot and killed by George O'Donnell, an ex-policeman, who happened to be in the saloon at the time. The bandits shot and killed the barkeeper. Another man was shot and he nearly died. The other bandit escaped, ran across the street, and entered the back door of Sullivan's saloon. His name was Hogan, and he belonged to the Sullivan gang. Evidently, in planning the holdup, he had this Sullivan retreat in mind as a get-away. He hurried through the rear door on into the front of the saloon. Byrne saw him pass and noticed that he was wounded in the chin.

A short time after the thing happened, a squad of police appeared on the scene, headed by Captain Duke. They made hurried inquiries of eye-witnesses and were told that the living man crossed the street and went into Sullivan's saloon. They immediately made an investigation of the saloon and in the back room found John Byrne. His height and general appearance corresponded to the description given by some of the eye-witnesses. Captain Duke searched him and found in his pocket a bandanna handkerchief similar to the one worn over the face of the bleeding bandit. That was enough. Byrne was arrested and taken to the police station.

Evidently Hogan had gone on into the saloon and had been carefully hidden by his friends who congregated there. Byrne remained reticent, merely claiming that he was innocent. He was raised with this gang and did not want to be regarded by them as a "snitcher." Some time passed and he said nothing. Meanwhile, he discovered that the Hogan crowd was going to allow him to hang for the murder. He sent for Theodore Roche, who had acted as his attorney in settling the estate of his father, whose body had been found in the ruins of the rooming house. He told the entire story to Roche and convinced him that he was innocent. Roche defended him at the trial, but the gang had spirited away all witnesses that would have been helpful to Byrne, and he was convicted of murder in the first degree and sentenced to be hanged. His execution was delayed while his attorney appealed to a higher court.

After the conviction Roche had told me in detail this story. He was very much disturbed by his failure to save Byrne's life. I had heard so many stories of this kind that I gave little credence to it. I believed, of course, that Roche believed Byrne was innocent.

Years passed before I thought of the case again. In 1913, shortly after Jack Black came to live with us at the ranch he told us Byrne was innocent. "I know," he said, "because when the crime was committed I was occupying the same cell with Hogan's brother. The day after the holdup a sister of Hogan's called on her brother at the jail and told him that the older brother committed the crime that Byrne was charged with."

Jack's first thought was that he should not interfere. He argued that Byrne would alibi himself out of his trouble, and he did not want to inform on any of his own crowd. Shortly afterward, however, Willie Hogan, his cellmate, revealed a plot that he and his brother had hatched up for poisoning Byrne's food. When Jack heard this he became very angry and his sympathies turned entirely to Byrne. He warned Byrne against eating any food brought him or any of the jail food.

"I went to Byrne's cell," said Jack, "and told him of the plot. I urged him not to eat anything that was brought him; I told him if he didn't have any money I would provide him with enough to buy his food from the outside. This 'horning in' of mine saved his life, for I learned afterward that they had tried to get him to accept food that undoubtedly contained poison.

"I was so indignant," said Jack, "at the heartlessness of the Hogan crowd in their attitude toward Byrne that when I made my escape from the county jail I had a wild idea in my head, as I approached Sacramento, of leaving the train and rushing into the Governor's office, and saying quickly: 'I have escaped from the county jail in San Francisco. John Byrne is innocent and I know it,' and then rushing out and getting away if I could. But, of course, I abandoned that thought as too dangerous, and went on my way to British Columbia."

Jack made the innocence of Byrne so clear to me that I again sought out Roche. Together we prepared a serial story of the Byrne case for the *Bulletin*. It was written by James H. Wilkins. In this serial we named Hogan as the murderer. No word of protest ever came from the Hogan family, which was further corroborative evidence that Black's story was true.

With all this evidence we were unable to convince

the Board of Pardons that Byrne should be released. The admission that the state had railroaded an innocent man to the gallows involved too many powerful people. There was the judge who tried the case; the police department who furnished the evidence; the warden at San Quentin who was more or less tainted because he was an innocent man's keeper.

These influences prevented the Board of Parole from believing Roche's story and the story of Jack Black. Nothing was done. Meanwhile, Byrne's sentence to be hanged was commuted to life imprisonment by Governor Johnson—not because Governor Johnson believed Byrne was innocent, but because of his strong friendship for Theodore Roche. Roche had made a very earnest appeal to the Governor, and Johnson decided to save the feelings of his friend Roche, even though he did not have complete faith in his story.

Byrne served five years in the county jail before he was taken to San Quentin. This was followed by ten years at San Quentin. His health broke under the strain. At the end of his fifteen years of confinement, the Board of Prison Directors paroled him to work in a road camp in the northern part of the state. He was not strong enough for that heavy work and was allowed to take a position in a printing office in Eureka.

His health grew steadily worse. He realized that he had only a short time to live and took the train for San Francisco, wiring me that he was coming to my ranch. He wanted to die with his friends around him, meaning Jack Black and myself. When he arrived in San Francisco I had him examined by a good physician, who held out no hopes for his recovery. I telephoned the parole office and asked permission to take him to my ranch. It was at first denied by the parole officer on the ground that my ranch was in Santa Clara county and bordered the bay.

"This," said the parole officer, "would be a technical violation of the parole. It was understood that he must not return to any of the towns or cities bordering the bay. We are afraid he will again connect up with the old gang."

"But there isn't any old gang," I replied. "That story is a myth and you people know it."

After some argument it was agreed that he might go to the ranch. I took him on the train with me that afternoon. He was hardly able to walk, but I got him into the machine at the station and motored him up to our home in the hills.

Jack Black was there to receive him. We placed him in a room at the farmhouse and made him comfortable. He died five days afterward, Jack sitting by his bedside night and day, tenderly caring for him.

During the days he liked sitting out in a deep cushioned chair on the farmhouse porch, looking out on the hill line. His patience was remarkable. Injustice had not made him bitter. He died without a word of complaint against the cruel fate that had murdered him slowly through fifteen years.

Mrs. Older, Jack Black and Charlie, our houseman, took the body over to San Jose and arranged for its burial. Aside from Byrne's two brothers they were the only mourners. There was no clergyman to officiate. As we were laying him away, a clergyman came over from a near-by grave where he had been officiating, and asked us if we would like him to say a prayer. This was the Reverend Frank Linder of the First Methodist Church of San Jose. He had read the story of Byrne's death and was sympathetic. He stepped to the edge of the grave, and said:

"We pause at reverent attention when a brother man has passed into the great silence. We give hearty thanks for every kindness shown to and for every service done to this man, and for all who have hurt and harmed him we pray that in the divine economy it may be forgiven them. We give special thanks for those who wait here this afternoon because they care. We rejoice to believe that there are so many in this world of men who do care. May their tribe increase until we shall become really a society of folk who care. We remember the One who said: 'Into Thy hands I commit my spirit.' We would scarcely care to trust the final destiny of human life with any human person. We see not at all. We know only in part. We rejoice in the belief that at the center of life there is a Divine Spirit, which sees all, and knows, and understands. Into that Divine Intelligence we would commit this life, and may the peace which passeth all understanding abide with him and with all."

This is my idea of a Christian burial.

CHAPTER XXIX

I Find A Poet In Prison—Douglass, Driven To Forgery By The Drink Habit. His Sentence Expired, Mrs. Older And I Take Him In Hand. He Falls Again. I Send Him To The Alcoholic Ward At Stockton. Recovery, Followed By Further Relapses. Douglass Publishes His Book. The Woman Who Never Lost Faith. An Amazing Marriage. Love The Greatest Force In The World.

While visiting Donald Lowrie at San Quentin, a short time before his release, Warden Hoyle showed me some excellent verse published in one of the magazines and written by a prisoner. Douglass was the name signed to the poems. It was not the author's right name, but it is the name I shall use in this story.

There was a rare poetic quality to the lines. Douglass interpreted the sufferings of the men in prison in a very dramatic way. He caught the prison atmosphere as no other writer to my knowledge had ever done. This perhaps was more clearly shown in a poem of his the warden showed me, "The Garden of Death." It was a passionate protest against capital punishment.

I give it here:

Safe bound by locking waters,
  Within the Golden Gate,
A fortress stands, remote and gray,
  A prison of the state.
The flanking walls that round it sweep,
  A massive portal scars
Where warders grim their vigils keep,
  With locks and bolts and bars.

In old San Quentin's garden
  The morn is sweet with blooms;
A little square in God's pure air,
  Amid a thousand tombs;

And in a fountain's mirrored depths,
As you are passing by,
Bare, mocking walls on either hand
Seem reaching to the sky;
And through that glimpse of Paradise
A youth was led—to die.

Above San Quentin's garden
The loophole grates look down,
Beyond the walls and castled keep
Where shotted cannon frown;
And just within a little gate
Along a steel-bound tier,
In cells of death men hold their breath
When unseen steps draw near.
For death is in the air they breathe
And in each sound they hear.

Through old San Quentin's garden
They led him to his doom,
While rose and lily sighed for him
An exquisite perfume;
And in the prison yard beyond,
Men spoke with bated breath,
Of laws that mock the law of God
And strangle men to death,
Of men who send God-given life
To godless, brutal death.

O'er old San Quentin's garden
A stately pine tree sighs;
A lonely captive from the wild
Where Tamalpais lies;
And seated by its rugged trunk,
A convict, old and wan,
Was reading from a little book
He held in palsied hand—
And on the title page I read:
"The Brotherhood of Man."

At once I became deeply interested in Douglass and asked the warden about him.

"Drink brought him here," said the warden. "Running out of money while under its influence, he would forge a check for a small sum, pass it on a barkeeper and continue his spree. When sober, he is a fine, honorable man, highly cultivated, a gentleman. His family is prominent in Southern California. When quite young he formed the drink habit, got into trouble and was cast off by his people. That was more than twenty years ago. Since then he has been in prison several times, always under the same conditions and for the same offense. He always gets a light sentence, because he pleads guilty, and the courts have had pity for him."

Douglass was brought into the warden's office at my request. He was very nervous and embarrassed, and not inclined to talk. He told me his time would be up in another month, and he intended to make a supreme effort to conquer the habit that had so wrecked his life. I asked him to call on me when he was released and I would help him to make a new start.

He came directly to my office from the prison. He was still very nervous. His lips twitched, and his voice was broken. But there was a resolute look in his eyes which reassured me.

"Are you quite sure you can hold out this time, Douglass?" I asked.

"I am positive," he said; "I shall never drink again."

"It will be a hard fight," I said. "You have fallen so many times, you know, and each fall makes your will weaker."

"That is true, but this time I have the sustaining influence of a woman's love. This woman has stood by me through two prison sentences, and now I am going to make the battle for her sake."

Somehow his words convinced me and gave me perfect

confidence in him. Ordinarily I should not have been so easily convinced, because I personally knew how insidious the habit is and what tricks the mind would play in its behalf.

Douglass had no money. He needed $50 to tide him over until he could get a position. A portion of the money he wanted to use to pay the expenses of a visit to the woman he loved. I gave him the money and asked him to dine with Mrs. Older and me at the Fairmont that evening at six o'clock.

He did not appear at the hour appointed. We both became nervous with fear that he had fallen. I reproached myself for having given him such a large sum of money. We waited hopelessly until six-thirty. He came at that hour, but was quite drunk. We made the best of it.

He could eat nothing. When we had finished we took him to our rooms and kept him in conversation for several hours until the effect of the liquor had partly passed away. He promised me faithfully that he would go to his room in a downtown hotel and see me at my office at eight in the morning. He did not come, and I felt that he was beyond help.

Early on the following morning, however, he called me up on the telephone.

"I am drunk in a Barbary Coast dive, Mr. Older," he said. "I am right on the verge of sliding back into hell again. Will you hold out your hand and help me?"

He gave me the location of the saloon. I sent a reporter for him with instructions to rent a room, put him to bed and keep him there until he heard from me. This was done.

That evening I had him removed to the Emergency

Hospital. He passed the night there. Early the following morning I called on him.

"Douglass," I said, "you are again heading straight for the penitentiary. I know of only one way to save you. That is to have you committed to the alcoholic ward of the Stockton Asylum for six months. I'll see that you have good treatment."

He was glad to go. He left that evening. Each Sunday Mrs. Older and I motored to Stockton to see him. Meanwhile, Donald Lowrie had been paroled and was writing his story for the *Bulletin*. Having similar literary tastes, Lowrie and Douglass had become fast friends in prison; therefore, on one of our visits to the asylum, we took Lowrie with us. Douglass was overjoyed to see Lowrie. He was getting strong again. In fact, he was quite himself, and, being normal, the queer people he was compelled to associate with in the asylum began to affect his nerves. He longed to get out and go to work.

In a short time after this visit I secured a suitable position for him in a near-by dry town. I had him discharged from the asylum as cured and took him to his new job.

"Now, Douglass," I said, "this is your last hope. You can't get a drink in this town and I want your word of honor that you won't leave it."

Of course, he solemnly promised, and meant to keep his word. He was sober for several weeks. He made some kind friends in the town, and they helped him to make the fight.

Finally the evil day came. He found a bottle of wood alcohol in the office where he worked and drank it. The effect of it on him was dreadful. For days it was thought he would become totally blind. Fortunately, he recovered, resumed his work and kept straight for a short time. He fell again, this time in a near-by city which he visited. He spent all of his money, borrowed all that he could, sold his clothes and went down into the gutter. But the battle was to go on.

Again we put Douglass on his feet—only to find that his employer, disgusted, had discharged him. Douglass' friends paid all his bills; and this making his employer feel that he, too, should do his part, he took him back. Nor was this all; for, in order to strengthen Douglass in his fight, his employer arranged for the publication, in book form, of Douglass' prison poems.

Our Prison Reform group—and especially Lowrie—became very much interested in preparing the book for the press. It finally made its appearance under the title of "Drops of Blood." Lowrie wrote for it the following foreword:

"A strain of music, the scent of a flower, the ripple of running water—how often they sweep a chord, mute but yet attuned, awakening the pent floods of memory. It is thus with this little book of verse, wrung from the silent gloom of unending prison nights—nights we spent together in the semi-darkness of a forgotten world.

"Behind the graven figures '19173,' I see you to-night as I saw you then, seated at the tiny deal table in our little eight by four cell, the dim light from the smoky oil lamp falling fitfully upon your face as you wrote in silence line after line, page after page—and I, lying on the narrow bunk against the wall, wondering what you were wresting from the universal source and setting into words amid such somber surroundings.

"To the art of 'setting words prettily together,' as Ruskin puts it, you have added the color which can be drawn only from the fountain of hard experience. May the message you are sending out find its way to the heart of the world, and there plant the seed of a deeper, larger and kindlier understanding.

"In those years of the past, we studied the theme of life together. To-day we labor apart, and yet together as before—you in your way and I in mine—to turn the thoughts of men and women toward the needs of the 'proscribed,' seeking to redeem ourselves, and in so doing to encourage others."

It is rare, indeed, for a book of verse, even though of fine quality, to have a large sale. Only a few hundred copies of "Drops of Blood" were sold. Perhaps this fact discouraged Douglass. He fell again. It was then that the woman who loved him, and who had never lost hope, decided to marry him, relying upon the strength of her love to sustain him. Then began our preparations for the wedding.

It was decided that Douglass' wedding should be held at Medora's home in the mountains, in the open air and under the trees that she loved. At last Douglass was to be reclaimed. This was to be our triumph. We all motored over for the great event—Donald Lowrie, "Buck" English, old Charley, Clarence Darrow, John D. Barry, and Mrs. Older and I. The aged father and the other members of the Douglass family that had been estranged from him for nearly a quarter of a century were there.

CHAPTER XXX

The First Act In Ruth's Sordid Tragedy. The Recital Of Babe's Vivid Life-Story Makes Her Pause. I Help Her To Open A New Door. Back To The Old Life. At Twenty-Three Ruth Takes The Suicide Way Out.

When Hugo came to me on his release from prison, his wife—Ruth—came with him. She was young—not more than twenty—and rather pretty. Hugo had the weakest face of any of the men who came to me from prison; he had a receding chin and forehead, and a pug nose.

His wife did most of the talking. Hugo, she said, was a fairly good musician, and if he could get a trombone and join the Musicians' Union he would be able to make a living for her and himself.

Lowrie had collected a small fund to be used for similar requests. Together we started Hugo on the way to making his own living. His weak face, however, prevented my having much faith in his making good.

I never saw Hugo again, but I learned, through Lowrie, that he was not doing well.

More than a year afterward a young, over-dressed woman called on me. Her face was painted and diamonds worth several thousand dollars glittered on her fingers. The brand of the underworld was on her.

"You don't remember me," she said.

"No," I replied.

"My husband and I called on you more than a year

ago. He was the one you bought the musical instrument for."

With difficulty I recalled her. She had completely altered.

"I have gone into a sporting house," she said. "My husband left me to starve. I stood by him all the time he was in prison. I worked in Oakland as a waitress, earning very little. I went over to the prison every visitors' day all the time he was there. I was as faithful to him as a wife could be. When he came out, I brought him to you, but even with the help you gave him, he could not make a go of it. He took to drink, left me at home frequently without food. Finally he disappeared altogether. I was so disheartened that I didn't much care what became of me. I am now in an uptown house and doing very well. I have $1,300 in the bank and $3,000 worth of diamonds. I'm all right now, I guess."

Ruth mentioned the name of the house she was living in. I had just been reading a wonderful life story written by a young woman of the underworld. She was known in the world in which she lived as "Babe." While the story of Alice Smith was running in the *Bulletin,* I had received a most remarkable letter from a woman who had signed herself: "From A to Z." While the writer was evidently illiterate, there was a Zolaesque realism in her description of the horrors of the life she was living. Later I learned that Babe had written the letter.

Babe became so much interested in the subject that she wrote her entire life story, beginning with her early childhood. She was one of several children. Her father died when she was four years old. Her mother was poor, and when Babe was twelve she went out to work. It was the old struggle. Scant wages, no pretty clothes, no schooling; only long hours of hard, grinding work.

At seventeen, Babe chose the course that forever shut her out of the respectable world. Once under way she went down rapidly. In her story she did not spare herself. She told the truth; all of it. In the course of her narrative, she gave a vivid picture of the horrors of her life in the very house in which Ruth was living.

"Let me read you a chapter out of a story I have here," I said to Ruth. I took the manuscript from a drawer and began reading aloud.

Before I had finished, Ruth leaped to her feet and shrieked: "Stop! Stop! I can't hear any more. It's all so horrible. I never dreamed it was as bad as that." Sobbing and almost hysterical, she left the room.

A few days later, Ruth called me on the telephone and asked for an appointment. Her voice betrayed excitement. I told her I would see her at once. She came rushing into my office, out of breath.

"The story you read me the other day has haunted me," she began. "I have made up my mind to quit the life forever. I think I have some dramatic talent. I have gone to a dramatic school and I am studying for the stage. The manager tells me I have real ability and is very much interested in me. He is going to cast me for a leading rôle in a comedy. He wants to know my address. Of course, I can't tell him. I am still in that house. I told him I lived in Oakland. He asked me who I knew in San Francisco and I gave him your name. He says he is going to ring you up. I gave him my name as Ruth Maynard. I was afraid he would call you before I could see you, and you would say you didn't know me."

Ruth made rapid progress, and in two weeks the play in which she was cast for the leading part was put on at the naval station in a big hall with fifteen hundred young men as an audience.

Our little group accompanied Ruth to the island. Donald Lowrie, Bessie Beatty, Sophie Treadwell, John D. Barry and myself made up the party. The audience liked the performance. Ruth was crude and amateurish, but she did well enough to warrant our giving her a favorable notice in the *Bulletin.*

That night Ruth left the house and took an apartment by herself. We all hoped she would succeed.

At about this time, Pantages was planning to put on a new one-act play. I succeeded in having Ruth employed in it to play a minor part. She did well in rehearsal, the manager was satisfied, and her new career began. The play ran two weeks at Pantages, and then went on the circuit for several months.

I heard nothing from Ruth in the meantime. When the play was dropped, she returned to the city and called on me.

I noticed her lips were scarred. I asked her the cause.

"I took carbolic acid several weeks ago," she said. "They thought I would die. I was saved by a young physician who attended me. He said my recovery was a miracle."

I couldn't believe her. She told the story lightly and laughingly. She seemed happy enough.

"Why did you do it, Ruth?"

"Oh, I slipped once. I became intoxicated. It discouraged me, and I wanted to die. But I am all right now. I have a little play of my own. There are three of us in it, and Pantages is going to put it on. I am to be the star. You'll see Ruth Maynard up in the electric lights, Sunday night."

I couldn't reconcile her manner as she sat talking to me of her future with the attempt she had made on her life only a short time before. I doubted the suicide story.

After Ruth's engagement at Pantages ended, she took the play and the little company to New York. It was an ambitious venture and ended in failure. The money she had saved melted and the diamonds went to the pawn shop.

She had been educating her twelve-year-old brother and caring for a younger married sister whose husband was unable to support her. She wrote me from New York that her play was a failure and that she was leaving for New Orleans to be with her sister, who had typhoid fever. When the sister recovered, she brought her and her little girl to California with her. She left them in Pasadena and came alone to San Francisco.

She called on me to tell me that she had gone back into the old life, and into the same house which she had left in such horror only a year before.

"Why did you do it, Ruth?" I asked her. "You have talent enough to make a living on the stage. You could have got a position. Why didn't you ask me to help you? I am sure I could have found a place for you."

"I was out of money. I had to have $50 a month

for my brother, and my sister is on my hands. I was desperate for money. I won't stay there long. As soon as I get a little money ahead, I'll go back to the stage."

I did not hear from her again for three months. Then I came into my office one day to find a memorandum on my desk, saying:

"Ruth Maynard called up. She is dangerously ill. She wants to see you."

I went at once to the address Ruth had given in her telephone message. It was a large apartment house in an uptown street. I assumed that it was the sporting house to which she returned after her failure in New York. I took the elevator and asked for apartment 64. I pressed the button at the door. A pretty little four-year-old girl opened it. I was shocked to find a child in such a place. A woman appeared. I asked for Ruth. "She is very ill in bed," she said. The woman took me to Ruth's room. She was propped up on pillows. Her face was thin and pale and her eyes seemed large and unnatural.

"This is a strange place for a little child," I said.

Ruth laughingly asked me if I thought I was in a sporting house.

"Yes, I had thought so," I said.

"Well, you are not. You are in a perfectly respectable apartment house. This is my sister's apartment; the little girl you met is her child. You saw my sister when you came in."

Ruth said she was better. In fact, she was getting well. She had been ill, dangerously so, for a month.

"I had a breakdown," she said. "To deaden the remorse I felt for having returned to the life, I commenced taking morphine and cocaine. I had always felt that I had too much sense to fall for the habit. But I saw other girls around me taking it. It did not show in their manner, or, so far as I could see, in their health. I decided to try it. It braced me up for a time. I daily increased the doses, until I completely collapsed. The doctor thought I would die, but I am too wicked to die, I guess."

I tried to cheer her up by urging her to keep away from the drug. I told her that when she was well enough I would try to get her a place in a theatrical company that was then playing at one of the local theaters. She agreed to make another effort, and before I left she had become quite interested in life. She expressed a hope that she might yet succeed as an actress, and so break away from the life that had brought her so near to death.

In a day or two I telephoned her that if she were well enough she could commence rehearsing for a small part on the following Monday. She was delighted, and spoke most cheerfully of her future. This was Wednesday.

Coming up from the ranch on Friday morning I read in one of the papers that Ruth had killed herself the night before. She had made sure work of it this time. In the midst of her dinner with her sister, Ruth suddenly left the table and ran into the bathroom. A few minutes later her sister found her there, dead. She left a note saying it would be useless to try to save her. This time, she said, she had taken a poison that no physician could overcome. She was twenty-three years of age.

CHAPTER XXXI

Babe, Truly A Brand Snatched From The Burning. Mrs. O'Connor, Big-Hearted Policewoman, An Angel Of Mercy. An Unknown Friend From The East Provides For Babe, Dying Of Tuberculosis. A Pathetic Letter From The Good Samaritan Who Cared For Babe During Her Last Days On Earth.

Babe, whose pitiful history had driven Ruth out of the life a year before, was also dead. When I learned that she was writing her story, I wanted her to come to the *Bulletin* office. I knew that Bessie Beatty, a writer on the *Bulletin,* could help her, not only with the writing of the story, but with her wonderful sympathy. I knew neither Babe's true name nor her address; but I wrote her a letter, and Mrs. O'Connor, the policewoman, delivered it to her. This was the answer I received:

My dear Mr. Older:

I received your kind note through Mrs. O'Connor, and I want to thank you for your kind thought of me. I have every confidence in you, but I can't possibly trust any living being further. I can tell my story better and honester when I think I don't have any person who knows me. Just put yourself in my place and honestly ask yourself if I am to blame.

If my story comes out people are bound to suspect, and what protection would I have if I went to your office and was seen? You know we are a novelty even if we are shunned. But, Mr. Older, if ever the time occurs when I can leave this life I will come to your office and see you if possible under some guise or another. I never want to discuss it with any person or want to go where any person will know my history. I have perfect confidence in Mrs. O'Connor, and if she fails me I don't think I would want to live. If the time ever comes that I can see my way out it will be under her direction. Miss —— has offered me a home with her, but I have had to refuse, as I once lived on charity and it is one reason why I am what I am to-day.

I am continuing my writing as you told me, and have let no person influence me. No person except Mrs. O'Connor and Miss —— knows I am writing. So I am perfectly safe.

If you print my story you will be doing something for every young girl in San Francisco that even thinks of entering this life, and as I write my story something seems to be at my back urging me on. I can't sleep nights thinking about it.

Mr. Older, urge the people to leave us unfortunates alone. We can't leave the life. If they didn't have the traps could we poor rats crawl in? And now we are in why make us squeal? Mr. Older, we are done for. But try to keep others out of the life. Let the people who have the bringing up of children tell them the truth. Tell the boy. Preach to him as you would tell him not to kill. Tell him not to go near a girl only as he would his sister. Tell the girl what the life means. Don't be afraid to preach it from the house tops. We are the most miserable creatures on God's earth. Talk about the black slaves!—free the white slaves. If we are a necessity, then give us a crown of roses, for we are certainly martyrs—martyrs to men.

I have every faith in your loyalty. Believe me when I say I thank you from the bottom of my poor heart.

Sincerely,

BABE.

Shortly after Babe had completed her story, the life she was living began to undermine her health, although at the time she was only twenty-two. Mrs. O'Connor, the policewoman, was Babe's only woman friend. She dearly loved Mrs. O'Connor and fully trusted her. Mrs. O'Connor had the girl examined by a physician, who reported that she was far gone with tuberculosis. Her life might be prolonged, the doctor said, if she was sent to the country, and lived in the open air. Mrs. O'Connor interested an Eastern woman in the case. This woman had some money and she was glad to provide the means for Babe's care.

Together, the two women looked for a suitable place, and finally decided upon a farm near Napa. The woman who owned it agreed to take her. There was a tent on the place that she could occupy. Mrs. O'Connor did not dare tell the country woman all of the truth about Babe's life, for fear she would not receive her. She was merely told the girl had made one false step, and that the man who was responsible for the wrong had deserted her.

We learned afterward that the woman who received Babe could have been trusted to be kind to her even if she had been told everything.

Babe was very weak when she arrived and rarely left her bed. The kind woman from the East provided her with everything she needed and wrote her almost daily.

Suddenly we learned that Babe was dead. The news came to Mrs. O'Connor in a letter written to her by the woman in whose care Babe had been. The letter is here given:

Dear Mrs. O'Connor:

It is with a sad and a very lonesome heart that I write to you and try and tell you about our dear child that has passed to a higher and better life. No more old cough (as she would call it), no more pains and aches, though she suffered very little; in fact, she had no pain to speak of, only getting weaker and the loss of sleep. It is so pitiful to think of the way she clung to life; such a thing as not getting well never entering her mind. It was always "When I am well, I will do this or that."

The way she looked forward to the time that she would study and go to school, never a word about death. It seems that God must know best when he takes a child like her, for I never met a dearer or sweeter disposition in my life. The way she endeared herself to us all; there was not one here who did not love her; even the cook, a Chinaman, has hardly talked since. She was such a loving, lonesome little thing, never having any advantages that she should have had, being left without a mother's care so young. I little wonder that she never went further, poor darling.

I am so thankful for having had the chance of knowing and loving her, and to have been in the position to be able to return to God one of his little children, for she was well prepared to meet Him. She would lie for hours and never a word. I always said she was praying. I will try and tell you all that will interest you, for she loved you and the young lady who was so kind and good to her. She never discussed her friends to me, only an occasional word; she was so quiet and close about everything connected with her.

You understand that she had been moved from the tent to the house ten days before she passed away, and was to go back to her tent the next day, before the fatal illness that has taken her from us. We had moved her much against her wishes. She did not want to come into the house, she so loved her tent—they are taking it down as I am writing. We felt after the last hemorrhage that at any time she was liable to have another, so we were afraid to leave her alone; it was well we had insisted, as it all happened for the best. The last I saw of the child was last Sunday, as I was ill on Monday and unable to leave my room.

When I saw her on Sunday she was very cheerful—all that worried her was to get back to the tent, and I had promised to ask the doctor on Monday—he being satisfied, she was going back the next day. My nurse was last to talk to her on Monday evening about 9 o'clock, when she was playing cards. Taking the cards from her, she fixed her for the night, leaving her door open so if she called she could answer. The last thing, in fact, all she talked of that evening, was "When I go back home." She called her tent "home." She wanted to go early in the morning, as she had a letter to write and wanted to be back in the tent before writing it. I awoke and called the nurse about 12 o'clock, thinking I heard something, I don't know what. After going out in the hall I called, "Go and see if Margaret wants you." On going to her room she found her breathing very hard, and, trying to awaken her, she found her unconscious and from that time until she died, on Thursday at 7:15 P.M., she never regained consciousness and never suffered. The life just gradually left her. The doctor called it a cerebral hemorrhage.

If she had recovered from this illness she would have been paralyzed, so God was good to take her. Think how bad she would have felt to be in that position along with her other handicap. On Friday morning I tried to get you on the wire; was unable on account of your being out of town. I talked with your husband, and on his advice I have taken on myself all the arrangements to bury her. I felt in your nervous state you were better not coming here and taxing yourself more than necessary. You did all you could for her when she needed you. We buried her on Friday afternoon. We kept her home until she went to her last resting place. I did not want to take her to an undertaker's parlor, so the early funeral, when I heard you were unable to come. I was able to place your flowers on her casket—so peaceful—just a mass of flowers. I was unable to get the violets Miss —— wanted, as the message came while we were gone with her. May the child's soul rest in peace. I will see that the violets are placed on her grave, so kindly tell Miss ——. I cannot write much more, as I am not strong and these last days are telling on me.

Now, Mrs. O'Connor, I want you, if you know of another girl like this dear child, I would like to help another just for her dear sake. Maybe take her up here or help financially. Please help me to help some girl for her sake and my own, for I feel I should try to do something for others, but my health being so poor I am not able to come in direct contact with them.

I am going to send you a few trinkets and some pictures and books that were hers. You will be better able to know what to do with them. There are some clothes and things you will be able to give some one. There were some letters she had in bed with her, and a letter which came on Monday. We burned them. Mrs. O'Connor, I would like to hear from you after you read this, as I feel I should help some other girl again. I must not learn to love them as I did this poor child, as I feel it too keenly. God bless you, and pray for me.

CHAPTER XXXII

"A Voice From The Underworld" Creates A Sensation Throughout Northern California. Men Readers Evince Disapproval Of The Story. A Crusade Against "The Line," San Francisco's Social Barricade, Is Led By A Methodist Minister. A Woman Of The Underworld "Puts It Up" To Dr. Smith. Social Outcasts Hold A Meeting In A Christian Church. One Of Them Gives A Straight Talk.

An immense amount of agitation was stirred up, not only in San Francisco but throughout Northern California, by my publication of "A Voice From the Underworld," which was the life story of a prostitute.

By having this girl, Alice Smith, tell her story from her earliest childhood recollections on through to the time when I met her, I thought perhaps it might soften the harsh attitude that most respectable people had toward women of the underworld. They would discover, I reasoned, that Alice Smith's earlier life was very much like the life of the average girl. She was fond of dolls and the same toys that other girls played with. She led the same kind of life until something happened to her that caused her to leave her home and join the ranks of the forlorn.

Of course, there was great opposition to the story. I expected it. But most of it, I think, came from men rather than women. I received, during the progress of the story, many abusive letters from men, but hundreds of sympathetic letters from women.

By focusing the mind of the people on this subject,

I think some good was accomplished, but it aroused a great deal of activity against further continuance of the restricted district for prostitutes. The agitation centered on forcing the city government to abandon what was commonly known as "The Line," insisting that there should be no further protection for them. The law against houses of ill fame, and against women carrying on their trade as prostitutes, should be enforced in the entire city.

Foremost in this crusade that eventually closed "The Line" was the Reverend Paul Smith, a young, ardent, enthusiastic, eloquent Methodist preacher, pastor at that time of the Central Methodist Church.

The evil influence of "The Line" upon the youth of the city was his topic every Sunday evening, and his eloquent sermons crowded his church to overflowing. It was a short crusade, easily won. Smith did not limit his efforts merely to a Sunday evening sermon, but put in his days and nights going about among prominent and powerful people, urging them to use their influence upon the police department and the city government to withdraw the privilege of protection from all women who made a living by prostitution.

The day after the resolution closing "The Line" was passed, Maude Spencer, who owned a fashionable sporting house on Mason street, rang me on the telephone and said she was going to visit all of the women of the underworld that afternoon and evening and urge them to assemble at Paul Smith's church the next morning at eleven o'clock. Then she would notify Paul Smith to open his church, and allow these women to enter and place their problem before him.

"I'm going to have them put it up to him straight," she told me on the telephone, "and ask him, now that he has taken their livelihood away from them, what he is going to do for these hundreds of women, many of them with children and mothers to support."

I told her I thought it was an excellent idea, and I would co-operate with her in every way possible. Maude Spencer's partner, Reggie Gamble, had been a great admirer of some of the writers on the paper, and had frequently called at the office to talk with them. She was a woman who had been highly educated in her youth, and had a very cultivated mind. She was familiar with some of the best literature, and loved to talk with us about books, music and art.

Soon after Maude Spencer and I closed our conversation on the telephone, I rang up Mrs. Gamble and told her that we were all very much excited over the idea of Maude Spencer's, and we had decided that she was the one to make the speech in the pulpit of Paul Smith's church. She replied that Maude Spencer had become so elated over my praising her idea that she proceeded at once to get drunk, and was at this time not in a condition to carry out the plan.

I told her not to worry about that—I would get word to the women myself to be at the church at eleven o'clock next day. I asked her to come down to the office and prepare her speech for the following morning. She came immediately, and with the help of Bessie Beatty and Rose Wilder Lane, who was then a writer on the paper, the speech was written. I then instructed her to ring up Paul Smith the following morning at eight o'clock and notify him to open his church and be ready to receive these women at eleven o'clock. She agreed to do that.

As the women of the underworld were grateful to me for printing their letters during the running of "A Voice From the Underworld" serial, I had no difficulty in gaining their consent to meet in front of the church at the hour set. I sent a messenger to all of them during the night. In the morning at eight o'clock I rang up Mrs. Gamble, fearing she might oversleep. She said, "I'm already on the job. I'm just looking up Paul Smith's number in the telephone book."

In a few minutes she telephoned me and said that Paul Smith had heard of the intended gathering and was very angry about it, but promised he would be there. A few minutes afterward he asked me on the telephone what I had put him up against in sending all these women to him. What could he do for them?

I replied: "Where else should sinners go but to a Christian church?"

"Yes," he said, "I know, but in what way can I help them? I haven't any solution of their problem."

"They consider you are the cause of their having lost their livelihood," I replied, "and naturally they would like to discuss the subject with you."

"Very well," he said, "I'll meet them."

By a quarter to eleven there were three hundred or four hundred women standing in front of the church, and at eleven the doors were opened and the women filed in and occupied the pews. Reggie Gamble took her seat in the pulpit beside Paul Smith.

"We women find it impossible to exist on the wages of $6 or $7 a week that are paid to women in San

Francisco," Mrs. Gamble declared in her opening sentence.

There was a volley of applause from the women in the auditorium.

"Most of the girls here present came from the poor," she continued. "Your sphere is among the well-to-do. These girls are better off in houses of prostitution than they would be as individuals, because at least they get what little protection can be afforded them by the house.

"The curse of us women is disease. In my years of experience in this life, I have learned why it is that so many children are born blind and so many homes made wretched.

"Nearly every one of these women is a mother, or has some one depending on her. They are driven into this life by economic conditions. People on the outside seem oblivious to this fact. One of the girls told me that her brother, a Methodist minister, when she applied for help to him, only told her to trust in God.

"You can't trust in God when shoes are $10 a pair and wages are $6 a week.

"I have the same respect for spiritual faith that any one has. Which of the members of your congregation, Dr. Smith, will take any of these women into their homes, or pay them the proper living wages, or see that they have the care and attention that they need?

"You said that you did not want women like us to come near your church. You want this section of the city to be free from their presence. That is quite different from the attitude of the Son of Mary toward the Magdalene. Jesus did not scorn the Magdalene as you have done.

"You want the city cleaned up around your church—but where do you want the women to go? Have you made any arrangement by which they can make their living elsewhere?

"There are men in your sphere of life who say to their sons that they must have 'their fling' and 'sow their wild oats.' If people in respectable walks of life had taught their sons to respect womanhood and not be content merely to be the mothers and fathers of 'young bloods' many of these women now present would not be here.

"These women do not lead a gay or happy life. Many of them hardly ever see the sunlight. It was an unusual experience for them to step outdoors to come to this church this morning.

"There isn't one of these girls that would not quit this unhappy life of illness and pain and artificiality if the opportunity was given. But these women haven't anything. How can they do differently?

"Why don't you go to the big business houses? Why don't you go to the legislature and change the conditions? Men here in San Francisco say they want to eliminate vice. If they do, they had better give up something of their dividends and pay the girls wages so they can live.

"You won't do anything to stop vice by driving us women out of this city to some other city. Has your city and your church a different God, that you drive evil away from your city and your church to other cities and other churches?

"If you want to stop prostitution, stop the new girls

from coming in here. They are coming into it every day. They will always be coming into it as long as conditions, wages and education are as they are. You don't do any good by attacking us. Why don't you attack those conditions?"

After Mrs. Gamble finished her speech, the Reverend Paul Smith showed signs of considerable confusion. He admitted frankly that in her talk she had touched on several problems which he had overlooked entirely in considering the subject.

When he finished speaking, several women in the body of the church asked him questions similar to those already asked by Mrs. Gamble in her talk. The minister replied that he would have to give these questions consideration. Soon afterward the meeting broke up, and within a few minutes the church was deserted.

None of the women expected any solution of their problem. If Paul Smith could have placed them all in positions very few would have accepted, and even those would no doubt have failed in the work given them. But the demonstration served to illustrate in a striking way what the closing of "The Line" meant to them.

Some months afterward Paul Smith, taking advantage of this dramatic episode in his church, had a moving picture made of various groupings of sporting women, scenes in dives, Barbary Coast resorts, and cabarets throughout the city. Running through the story was a thread of the drama that had been enacted in the church. I was told he had me as a figure in the picture, although I never saw the film. He called the picture "The Finger of Justice." He took it on the road and I believe the show prospered until he reached New York City, where the police forbade its production. I have heard that Smith is still in the church, in some official capacity, but is no longer preaching.

Reggie Gamble, the heroine of the occasion, sold an apricot orchard she owned in Santa Clara county and with the money opened a drug store in Oklahoma City. She made a good living there, and I believe married a respectable citizen of the town. Shortly afterward, however, she died of influenza. Maude Spencer, whose sporting house was closed, retired to her country place in Santa Clara county and, so far as I know, has since been living a very quiet, respectable life with her adopted son and daughter, who were taken by her when they were small children and educated. Her first husband died shortly after "The Line" closed, and a year or two later she married again. I think she is now living at Burlingame.

CHAPTER XXXIII

Helen Of Bartlett Alley. The Pitiful Story Of A Fugitive From New York's Ghetto. Betrayed By An East Side Cadet, She Finds Her Way To "The Line" In San Francisco. From Bad To Worse. Cast Out By Outcasts. A Queer Conception Of Happiness.

Helen of Bartlett Alley stood in the front line of underworld women who assembled on that memorable day on the steps of the Reverend Paul Smith's church. She was not there with any hope that the preacher would be able to help her. I had asked her to go, and out of gratitude to me she went. She believed I saved her from the penitentiary.

While Helen's story may not be typical of those in her class, it is interesting and revealing, throwing some light on men's behavior to women when they drop too far below the line of respectability.

Helen is a Russian Jewess and was born on the East Side in New York. There were eight children. Helen was the youngest. Like most of the Jewish people in that part of the city they were desperately poor, and their home—three small, badly ventilated rooms—was a "sweatshop," where father, mother and children, as soon as they were old enough, worked together.

When Helen was seventeen she fell in love with a young Jew in the neighborhood. They soon became engaged to be married. Marriage was delayed, Helen says, because it was regarded by orthodox Jews as bad form for a younger sister to marry before the older ones. Helen kept company with this young man for a long time, waiting for her turn to come. The delay was disastrous. Helen, trusting in the sincerity of her lover, and believing that it was only a question of time when they would be married, allowed the thing to happen that wrecked her life. When she found she was going to have a child she was so ashamed that she left her home and went to room with a girl friend. At this point, her lover revealed himself to her. He turned out to be one of the many East Side parasites who live on the earnings of the women of the underworld, and when he discovered Helen's plight he sold her as "damaged goods" to an Italian friend of his in the same business.

When Helen learned that her lover had not only deserted her but had taken money for the sale of her body, she became desperate, realizing she could never again communicate with her family. Her old life was at an end.

"I made up my mind I would go away as far as I could get, and have my baby," she said, in relating her story to me. "Every night I rushed desperately about the streets, grabbing men until I had money enough to pay my fare to San Francisco. When I got here I went to the County Hospital and had my baby. As soon as I was well enough I found a poor family that was willing to care for the child for a small sum, payable each week. Then I went down to Bartlett Alley and began my life as a prostitute."

Bartlett Alley was the lowest and vilest section in the restricted district, made up exclusively of "crib houses." Thus isolated from her old life, in fact buried alive in this foul den, Helen began to crave companionship. In a short time she took up with another underworld parasite and soon became his slave. This man was Ben Berger, who made a business of securing as many of these women as he could in order to build up his income. Helen soon found she was far worse off than before. Berger was exacting. He demanded more and more money from her. When the daily amount fell short of his expectations, he would beat her. He was especially opposed to her wasting money on the care of her little boy.

In the midst of her troubles with Berger she met a man named Frank, another Jewish parasite, who followed a different method from Berger. He was polite. Helen noticed when she met him he lifted his hat. That greatly impressed her. He also occasionally asked after her child. He was making progress. She confided to him the longing she had to see her old mother.

"Go to New York and visit her," suggested Frank. "Buy yourself a wedding ring and tell your mother you are my wife. I'll stand for that." Thus the noble-hearted Frank.

Helen was very grateful. She felt that she had at last met a real gentleman. She made the trip to her old home and had a nice visit there, all of the family accepting her story that she was married to Frank. After her return to Bartlett Alley she dismissed Berger and took up with Frank.

These parasites that lived upon the earnings of fallen women had an organization. "The Club" it was called, and the members worked in closely with the police. The police relied upon them to see that they got their "bit"

Frank was subsequently acquitted. He returned to San Francisco and to Helen. But her troubles were not to end. Berger was more furious and vindictive than ever. So were his fellow "Clubmen." So were the police who were in a conspiracy with them. Not long after Frank's acquittal Helen called at my office. She was in tears.

"What's the matter now, Helen?" I asked.

"Mr. Older," she sobbed, "I am boycotted in Bartlett Alley. The madam has driven me out of the house I work in. I have been to see all the others. None of them will take me in, and no one will speak to me."

"Cheer up, Helen," I said. "It can't be as bad as you think. Even if it is, you are young and strong and have your life before you. Bartlett Alley isn't the entire world you know, Helen."

"It's my entire world, Mr. Older. You don't seem to understand. *I'm boycotted in Bartlett Alley.*"

I sent for the police officer who, at that time, was in charge of Bartlett Alley. He happened to be a man I knew well, and he was under obligations to me.

"Jim," I said, "I want you to lift the boycott on Helen in Bartlett Alley."

His face flushed and an ugly, sullen look came into it. For a moment I feared the obligation he was under to me would not overcome his desire to serve the "Clubmen." But he finally said, reluctantly, "Send her to No. 59. She will be taken care of."

To that extent the boycott was lifted, but it turned out that No. 59 merely tolerated her. Neither the madam nor the girls would speak to her. She had become an outcast.

She was the outcasts' outcast.

Not long after Helen's boycott Paul Smith succeeded in closing "The Line," which sent these wretched people out into the city streets, shunned and homeless. Helen's case, bad as it was before, was now worse.

A few weeks after "The Line" closed, I learned that the girl had become a street walker. She called at my office to tell me of her troubles with the police. After the restricted district was closed, there was no protection for women of Helen's class. They either had to get respectable employment or leave the city. The police had strict orders to watch them closely, and not to allow them to ply their trade. Of course this order applied only to the poor women. Some of those who had been conducting "fashionable houses" had a pull with the police, and opened protected houses in various parts of the city.

McDonough Brothers, then at the high point of their power with the police, were able to protect some of the best money-makers among the women of the streets. As long as they paid, they had immunity from arrest.

Helen was not in either of these classes. She had a hard time.

"I can't walk a block in any direction from the house where I room, without the police following me," she told me the day she called. "I don't know what I am going to do. I've got my room rent to meet, my own food to get, my little boy's board to pay, and his clothes to buy."

"There is one thing you can do, and must do, Helen. You must get rid of Frank. You don't have to support that monster. Send him away and try to get an honest job somewhere. You could wait on tables in a restaurant."

"I couldn't hold that kind of a job, Mr. Older. The police would tell on me and I would get fired."

She left me with the promise that she would send Frank away. She kept her word, but not until my urging had been reinforced by Mrs. Katherine O'Connor, who later became a member of the police force.

Some time afterward, Helen came to the office to tell me about dismissing Frank.

"I told him he must go, Mr. Older, and he went. We parted friends. I'm glad of that, because I didn't want to hurt his feelings too much. You know if he had not let me call myself his wife, I could never have gone East to see my mother. I shall never forget that kindness."

She was still furtively darting around the streets at night, dodging the police whenever possible. But they pursued her relentlessly and she was frequently arrested, and I as frequently asked the police to let her go. My argument to them in her case was that so long as they allowed the "fashionable" places that got the big money to run, they should not harass the poor and friendless.

Some months later I learned why Helen and Frank parted such good friends. In order to induce him to go, so that she could keep her promise to Mrs. O'Connor and me, she gave him $700, all the money she had saved in those dreadful years. She tried to buy him off with half the sum, urging him to be a good sport and leave her something for her boy and herself. But he was not a good sport. He demanded every dollar she had, and finally got it. He then took a trip around the country for some months, enjoying himself. At the end of this time, having spent the money she had given him, he returned to the city and to Helen.

His greeting when he entered her room was: "Well, how much money have you got?"

"I've got $100 and my jewelry, in the safe deposit box."

"That's mighty little. You're spending too much money on your clothes."

"I have only two street dresses. Now that I am on the street I have to look halfway decent, don't I?"

"Well, come along with me and let's get the money."

She went with him, unlocked the box and gave him all of her jewelry, worth about $800, and $50 of the $100. He demanded the other $50, but she begged him not to take it.

"I need it to pay my little boy's board, which is overdue," she said. "Reluctantly he allowed me to put it in my purse. That night, while he thought I was asleep, he got out of bed and I heard my purse click. He had taken my last cent."

This was evidently too much, even for Helen. On the following morning she told Mrs. O'Connor about it, and Mrs. O'Connor had Frank arrested and then rang me up on the telephone and told me the story. I sent for Helen. She evidently divined what I wanted of her. As soon as she entered the door of my office, and before I had a chance to speak, she said with all the force and dramatic power she possessed:

"Mr. Older, I won't put no man in jail."

"I haven't asked you yet to put any one in jail. But wouldn't you like to get your jewelry back? The money you could get for it would help you to educate your boy. For his sake you ought to be willing to let me try to force Frank to return it."

"You may," she said, "if you will promise me you won't send him to jail."

I promised her I would let him go if he would give back the jewelry. I sent a reporter to the jail to see Frank and we got back a portion of the jewelry. Some of it he had already given a lawyer who was to defend him. The charges against Frank were subsequently dismissed and he was released. At last, I thought, the poor girl is freed from that burden. But we were to hear of him again. Frank, burning with rage over the loss of the jewelry, in some fashion managed to raise sufficient money to pay his way to New York. He called on Helen's father and mother, informing them that their daughter had lied when she told them she was his wife.

"She is a prostitute and a street walker in San Francisco, and has been for years," he said.

The mother was prostrated when she learned the truth. The father asked Frank for Helen's address. He told him he could get it from me. Afterward I received a telegram from the father, telling me of the mother's illness and urging me to send Helen home. All would be forgiven, he said.

I sent for Helen and showed her the telegram.

"No," she said. "I can't go."

I was staggered. "Why not?" I asked.

"Because," she said, weeping, "they haven't forgiven me and never will. My mother might, but my father and brothers and sisters are different from her. If I were to go home they would make my life a hell. I couldn't endure it, and I shall never go."

After this meeting with her I did not see or hear from her for more than a year. Shortly after the war began, a letter came to me from her, from Reno, Nevada. She was in the old life there. Enclosed in the letter was a very beautifully embroidered silk flag she said she had made for me. She wanted to send me some little thing, she said, that would in a measure express her gratitude for my kindness to her. Not long afterward she returned to San Francisco and resumed her street-walking life, running the dangerous gamut of the police.

At this time I was carrying on a campaign against the corruption of the police in the tenderloin districts and was exposing some of the officials. I gave definite facts about their accepting money from prostitutes. They feared that possibly Helen was furnishing me with the information. They turned on her viciously and arrested her every time they saw her on the street. Finally they secured by crooked methods a "positive" blood test, and with this they were able to have her put away in an isolation ward in the San Francisco Hospital, where no one could see her. She was there for many months, but finally managed to send out to me an "underground" letter. After many difficulties I succeeded in getting her released. I learned definitely that she was physically well when she was sent there, and that her imprisonment was merely an effort of the police to get even with her. As a matter of fact, she never gave me any information.

Years passed before I saw her again. Only a few

weeks ago she called at my office. She was radiant, prettily dressed, smiling, apparently happy.

"Why, Helen," I said. "How well you are looking! What has happened?"

"I am not in that life any more. I have not been for two years. I am living with a man." She said it as joyfully and with as much pride as another woman would have announced that she had married the Prince of Wales.

"My man is good to me," she continued, "and likes my boy. I have my kiddie at home with us. He is fourteen now and is going to night school. During the day he has a job in a department store."

She told me she had recently received a very beautiful letter from her mother, filled with forgiveness, love and tenderness, and begging her to come home. She was very ill and could not live long. "I haven't money to go to my mother. That is my only unhappiness."

I haven't seen her since.

her son, but after I told her how much good the story had already done toward improving prison conditions in California, she withdraw all opposition and declared she was glad to know that he had at last been able to be of some use in the world. At this time Lowrie had already spoken before the Commonwealth Club at the Palace Hotel to a large and breathless audience, and had delivered a similar speech before the San Francisco Center in Scottish Rite Hall.

Nothing before published in San Francisco had aroused such widespread interest as Lowrie's story. The circulation of the *Bulletin* jumped thousands in a few weeks, and Lowrie was overwhelmed with invitations to speak, not only in the city but in interior towns and cities throughout Northern California. He was the most talked-about man in the state. We were both very happy. My dreams had come true. A brilliant career was before him.

Warnings came to me from some of the members of the police department that I was wasting my time, that Lowrie was like all the rest of the men who were sent to prison. Sooner or later he would break down and be back in the penitentiary. These prophecies were not even disquieting to me. At that time I did not know that most of the inmates of prisons were pathological cases. To my mind, Lowrie had become a burglar as a result of having developed a passion for betting on the races, and, driven wild by his losses, had plunged thoughtlessly into burglary as a short cut to getting some quick money at the track to retrieve his fortunes. If I had stopped to think about his case, I should have known that what was wrong with Lowrie lay much deeper in his nature than a passion for gambling.

Two months after the story started in the *Bulletin* I learned that Lowrie was drinking heavily. That alarmed me. Not because I feared that drink would drive him back to crime. That thought did not enter my mind. I feared only that if he were seen drunk on the streets people would lose faith in him, and also in the bureau organized by us for helping discharged prisoners. As I look back to that period, I am amazed that I should not have realized that even a stronger man than Lowrie, suddenly lifted to great popularity and fame, would have had his moral strength taxed to the utmost. I certainly had very little understanding of the frailty of human nature.

Of course, I made frantic efforts to restrain him from drinking. I protested to some of his friends against their ever asking him to drink. One of his companions whom I had rebuked told me that I was on the wrong track, that the person really responsible for his condition was a girl known as Bernice, who was living in Pearl Morton's house of prostitution. I called on Bernice and pointed out to her what Lowrie's downfall would mean to the Prison Reform movement. She admitted that she had been on several drinking parties with Lowrie, but promised never to drink with him again. Bernice turned out to be the "Ruth" who figures so prominently in Lowrie's story, "Back in Prison—Why?" From that time on, Bernice co-operated with me in trying to keep him straight; but it was useless. He went rapidly from one spree to another. The only times when he was sober were brief intervals when I was able to keep him at my ranch, vigilantly guarded by Mrs. Older and Jack Black, reformed highwayman. Jack at that time was living permanently at our home.

For more than a year I kept the knowledge from the public that Lowrie was a drunkard, but I feared every day that the exposure would come and we should lose one striking exhibit of an ex-convict who had made good.

Thomas Mott Osborne, who had been made warden of Sing Sing prison, and who had become interested in prisons after reading Lowrie's story, finally reached out here for Lowrie and urged him to come East and join him at Sing Sing as his secretary. Osborne sent a check to Lowrie, who was then at my ranch, to pay his expenses.

Lowrie did not tell me of the offer or the check because he had a spree in mind, and he knew that if he told me he was going East I would keep watch over him and try to prevent his drinking. So in the night he packed all of his clothes and effects in two trunks, in one of the guest rooms in our house; and, with the help of an ex-prisoner who was working on the ranch and who was in sympathy with him, carried the trunks stealthily out of the house and down the hill a quarter of a mile to the farmhouse. There the two hitched up the team, put the trunks on a wagon, and drove over to Cupertino, four miles away. At Cupertino Lowrie left the trunks to be sent by express, took the first train to the city and lost himself in a wild debauch.

As soon as I learned of it, I hunted him up and threatened him with a commitment to the alcoholic ward of one of our state institutions if he didn't sober up and take the train for New York that night. He had bought a railroad ticket, but had spent all the rest of his money on the spree. So I bought him a Pullman ticket, provided him with money for food, and left him in charge of a reporter, whom I instructed not to leave him until he was safely on the train. But he ran away from the reporter on the street, and continued the spree with the money I had given him. However, he did get away the next night, remained drunk on the train, and wandered off it at El Paso, still drunk; lost his Pullman ticket, and found himself stranded there. He wired me from El Paso. A woman friend of his wired him further money to continue on to Sing Sing.

At that point I lost hope of him and never regained it. He has told in his very remarkable story, "Back in Prison—Why?" all the details of his career from that time on.

My first knowledge that he was back in a penitentiary came about four years ago in a letter from him from the Western Pennsylvania Penitentiary at Pittsburgh, Pa. In this letter he confessed his downfall in Texas. He had run away, jumping his bail, left his home, wife and child, and wandered off to the East, where he played the races, lost, and finally returned to burglary. Eventually he was sent to the Pittsburgh Penitentiary. His sentence at that prison was one and a half years. He wrote me that if he could get the charges in Texas dismissed he would be released in a few months.

This was brought about and he secured his freedom, came West to Prescott, Arizona, re-established himself as a writer under the name of Arthur Jamieson, and was again making good. Shortly after his arrival there I received this very hopeful letter.

Prescott, Arizona.
Oct. 30, 1923.

My dear friend:

Thanks for your good letter. I have been here a week and have a cabin up the mountain side overlooking the town. I was in bad shape, physically—that Western Penitentiary is a man-killer, all right. The cell walls sweat moisture so that one can write one's name in it—a Turkish bath perpetual, minus the heat. It got me. It gets a good many. But aside from the physical defects, the place is not bad as such places go. I was mighty lucky to have gotten off with one year. I am now on parole, for three months.

My plan is to stay put here for a year, living in the open. I have a lot of literary material to work up and hope to connect with something local to help eke out existence. At any rate, it was my only hope. Not that I am of any particular value in the world, as the judge sagely remarked when my lawyer was pleading that further confinement would be my finish: "Of what value to society is the life of an inebriate burglar?" That sure squelched me.

But I'm no longer an "i.b." and I'm really going to try to come back better than ever and for keeps. At Cincinnati, where I remained a few days because of hemorrhages, two different strangers offered to connect me up with a booze supply, and I actually had the guts to decline. No, I'm not crowing, for I've deliberately gone looking for it in the past, when I thought I must have it. But I honestly think I'm through. This climate lessens the desire for tobacco and all stimulants, though the booze used to flow in rivers at Prescott during the frontier days.

I don't expect an answer to this. I will write from time to time, especially if I am successful.

With all good wishes to you and yours,

Sincerely,

CHARLIE.

Even this letter did not bring back my faith in him. I was not at all surprised when later I read in a Phoenix newspaper that he had been arrested on thirteen charges of burglary in Phoenix and Prescott, and was serving a long sentence in the penitentiary at Florence. A few months after I learned this, I visited him at Florence and found him a complete physical wreck. He was suffering from tuberculosis in a very advanced stage, and was hardly able to walk. But his mind was clear.

Then I asked him to finish what he had begun fifteen years before; to give to the world the full story of his failure. By frankly telling everything, withholding none of the horrible details, I was sure that a great many people would get an understanding of criminals they had never had before. They would realize that the causes of crime are in a large measure pathological, and beyond the reach of prisons to cure.

If the time ever comes when causes of crime can be studied by minds freed from hatred and the desire for revenge, something may be accomplished, but until that time comes we shall have to be content with superficial improvements in prison conditions and an occasional introduction of scientific evidence in such cases as those of the two Chicago youths, Loeb and Leopold; and of the sixteen-year-old San Francisco girl, Dorothy Ellingson, who killed her mother.

Donald Lowrie's "My Life in Prison" revolutionized the penal institutions in California and it had a softening influence upon the prisons of many other states. His latest work, "Back in Prison—Why?" will, I think, go even further than his earlier story in stimulating thought on this subject. In my judgment Lowrie, in contributing these two books, has given society far more than he ever took from it as a burglar.

He lived to write all but the last chapter of his book. He wrote me a personal letter, which came with it, in which he said: "This is the hardest job I have ever done in my life." He died a few days afterward.

CHAPTER XXXV

My Meeting With Jack Black, Convicted Of Highway Robbery And Languishing Under A Twenty-Five-Year Sentence. I Interest Myself In Obtaining His Parole. Meanwhile He Escapes, Is Caught, And Returned To Prison. Black's Speech In Court, Published In The *Bulletin,* Thrills The Community. From San Quentin To The Older Ranch. Black A Humorist As Well As A "Reconstructed Yegg."

In previous chapters I have presented the stories of Fritz, George, Tim, Boggs, Pedro and Douglass as types of ex-prisoners who would best explain how I came to realize that many prisoners are in some ways different from ourselves.

Jack Black, of whom I have made frequent mention, does not belong in that group. He is in a class by himself. That is why he is so interesting.

At the time of my first meeting with Jack, he was a prisoner in the Ingleside jail. Convicted of highway robbery before the fire, he had been sentenced to twenty-five years in the penitentiary. His case was carried to the Appellate Court. Then, in 1906, came the great fire; and all the records in Black's case were burned.

After the fire there were so many things to be done that were of more pressing importance than restoring the records of prisoners' cases then pending that Jack was neglected. As a result, he lay buried and forgotten in Ingleside jail. When I met him he had been there seven years. He had no hope. He hadn't sufficient faith in the ultimate result of his appeal to take much interest in having the record restored. He knew that if the Appellate Court denied him a new trial there was nothing left for him but the rock pile at Folsom for twenty-five years.

In my first talk with him he told me frankly that his case was hopeless, and that he did not believe it possible for me or any one else to help him. He had been sentenced by Judge Dunne. I told Black I knew Dunne very well, and that it was barely possible I might persuade him to let him go on probation. I was willing to try. Black did not discourage me, but I could see by his manner that he had no faith.

I went direct from the jail to Judge Dunne's chambers. In fact, I hadn't much more faith than Black had, but I thought I ought to try.

When I suggested to Dunne, in a tone of voice as casual as I could make it, that I thought he ought to let Black go on probation he stared at me as if he thought I had gone suddenly insane. I have forgotten the exact language used by the judge in making his reply, but I haven't forgotten that it was very forceful, emphatic, and, in spots, picturesque.

I argued the matter for an hour. I told him I was sure that Black would make good if given a chance. Mrs. Older and I would take him to the country and look after him until he regained his health and strength. Then we would get him a job and I was sure he would go straight. The judge didn't give me much encouragement. He merely said he would look into the matter, which I thought was a polite way of closing the discussion.

I telephoned the dismal news to Black at the jail, and he at once began preparations for his escape. With the

busy every minute of his time in work that he could do. After the floors had been laid, Mrs. Older said to him, laughingly:

"Mr. Black, I want you, as an expert burglar, to walk over the new floors and find the squeaks."

"In order to do that properly," Jack replied, "I'll have to walk on them at two in the morning in my stocking feet. You hear sounds at that hour that you can't hear at any other time."

After the house was finished and we had moved in, we invited two of our city women friends to visit us. The night they came a mighty storm burst over the hills from the southeast. It was the worst we had ever experienced. It was made more terrifying because the new house had not been tested by storm and wind.

Jack, who had been dining with us, was about to leave for his room in the farmhouse, when Mrs. Older, fearing that the storm might blow the roof off or pitch the house down into the gulch, asked him to sleep in one of the spare rooms.

We all went to bed filled with fear. At about eleven, just after we had fallen asleep, we heard a startling crash.

"There goes a window," I said. I rushed out into the storm. The women were shrieking for Black. Their window had blown away. Black ran from his room into theirs and leaped through the open space into the court.

"Get a hammer and nails and a ladder, Jack," I suggested, "and perhaps we can nail the window back in place."

He got the hammer and nails.

"I don't need a ladder," he said. He went up on top of a pergola, fifteen feet high, like a circus acrobat. From there he walked out on the narrow window ledge, balancing himself while I handed him the window. He nailed it on while the women looked on admiringly.

The wind was blowing seventy miles an hour. In another minute it might have torn through the open window and destroyed that portion of the house.

While Jack was putting the hammer back in its place in the basement I joined Mrs. Older in the living room. We were both laughing.

"Isn't it great to have a porch climber about at a time like this?" I exclaimed gleefully.

"I was just thinking the same thing," she replied.

The women were enthusiastic over Jack's skill, and complimented him when he came in.

"You people all go to bed," said Jack. "I'll keep watch until morning."

The next day Mrs. Older said to Jack, "You were a hero last night, Mr. Black."

"Was I?" Jack replied. "Night time is my time, you know."

On Christmas morning, Marie, a French maid, and little Mary wanted to go to Saratoga, four miles away, to Christmas mass. I said I would motor them over. They both liked Jack very much. We had not told them he had been in prison.

"You come along, too, Jack," said Marie. "You were born a Catholic."

"No," said Jack. "I won't go. A church is no place for a sinner."

"Oh, come on, Jack," the girls pleaded. "It will be a sin on your soul if you don't go."

Jack finally compromised by agreeing to go along and sit in the machine with me, outside the church, while the girls attended mass.

It was raining a little, but we put up the top of the machine, and talked and smoked comfortably.

I had been very much interested in the underworld story that had been running in the *Bulletin,* and I turned the conversation to that subject.

"I don't like women of that kind," said Jack. "None of them are any good."

"I wouldn't say that, Jack. They are a mixture of good and bad, like the rest of us, aren't they?"

"Perhaps I am prejudiced," said Jack. "Years ago I knew one quite well and liked her. I called on her one evening and found her sick in bed, without food, money or medical attention.

"I had only a couple of dollars in my pocket, but I knew where I could get more.

" 'I'll be back in an hour,' I said, and left her. I got some money in the only way I could in those days, hurried back to the girl's room, and dumped it on the table. There were $60 or $70 in the pile. She knew it was a burglary.

" 'I'll cut this even with you,' I said, 'and we'll get some food and a doctor.'

" 'I think I ought to have more than half,' she said.

"I looked at her in amazement.

" 'If you don't give it all to me,' she went on, 'I'll call the police.' "

Just at this moment, Marie and little Mary came running from the church toward the machine.

"To cut a long story short," said Jack, "I left it all."

One Sunday a prominent Superior Court judge came out to the ranch to lunch. He had been there before, knew Jack Black quite well, believed in his reformation, and was perfectly at ease in his company. After luncheon we all sat together in the living room, discussing crimes and criminals and groping about for some remedy. Jack was giving us the benefit of his wealth of experience.

Suddenly the dogs began to bark. There was an automobile coming up the hill. Jack and I stepped out on the porch to welcome the visitors. I peered closely at the driver and the occupants of the car approaching the house. I said to Jack, "They are strangers."

Jack's practiced eye made out the driver.

"Oh, it's the doctor," he said, with a glad ring in his voice.

The "doctor" stepped out of the car. "Mr. Older, this is Dr. Mack," said Jack.

I quickly recalled the doctor. I had met him before in my office. He was an old prison pal of Jack's who had made good. His wife and young children were with him. He escorted them all into the house and introduced them to Mrs. Older and the judge.

The conversation about prisons and prisoners was not resumed. The talk became general, the judge showing the deference to the doctor that his title and honored profession deserved.

Finally the judge said, "Doctor, I don't want to put Mr. Older to any unnecessary trouble. Perhaps you wouldn't mind taking me in your machine and dropping me at the station."

"I'll drive you home," said the doctor, with great cordiality. "We're only out for a pleasure spin. Where do you live, judge?"

"San Jose," said the judge.

"I'll take you there with the greatest of pleasure," was the doctor's polite answer.

Jack looked at me, his eyes dancing with the humor of the situation.

The judge took a seat next the ex-burglar, and they drove away, chatting together pleasantly.

As the car disappeared down the hill I asked Jack to tell me the story of the doctor's change in occupation.

"Justice," said Jack, "is a word that resides in the dictionary. It occasionally makes its escape, but is promptly caught and put back where it belongs. It was while it was making one of its short flights that Mack made his get-away. He was a three-time loser, and was in again for burglary. The cops had him right, with the goods on him. Apparently there was no escape. The District Attorney told Mack that he didn't have a chance to beat the case, and advised him to plead guilty. 'If you do that,' said the prosecutor, 'you may get off with five years on daylight burglary, as you were arrested about sundown. If you fight the case the judge will be angry and he will construe it as night burglary and you will get fifteen years.'

"The difference between fifteen and five years appealed to Mack, and he pleaded guilty.

"As soon as he had made his plea his lawyer hopped up and said:

" 'Your Honor, it was daylight burglary, and for that five years is the limit.' This angered the judge. He reached for an almanac, looked up the date of the crime, and announced that Mack had been arrested five minutes after the sun had set. Therefore, it was night burglary.

" 'But,' argued the attorney, 'the crime had been committed prior to that time. He had to get out of the house he had burglarized and walk several blocks to the point where he was arrested.'

"This further angered the judge. He told the lawyer to sit down, and proceeded to sentence Mack to fifteen years in the penitentiary.

"The lawyer waited until the stenographer had taken down the court's language. When he had finished the lawyer said: 'You can't alter that record now, your Honor. You forgot to arraign him. It's a felony to alter the record.'

"The judge realized he was caught.

" 'If you'll give him five years I'll let him go over, but if you insist on the fifteen I'll fight you.'

"The judge was too angry to relent, and Mack was sent back to the county jail, where he remained a year. Meanwhile the lawyer hunted up a decision which permitted the release of Mack if the judgment had not been entered at the end of one year. The lawyer swore out a writ of habeas corpus in another court and Mack walked out a free man.

" 'Jack,' said Mack to me, 'that was a close call. Lightning never strikes twice in the same place. I'm through with stealing. I'm going straight.'

"He went to work, educated himself, studied medicine and graduated. He now has a practice of $5,000 or

$6,000 a year. I don't think he would have made it except for the help of the girl he married. She stood by him, and her love and devotion held him up."

Jack finally left us to go to work in the city. He is still regarded as one of our family, and he spends many of his week-ends at our ranch. He loves the place and regards it as his home, which it is, and will be until the end.

Jack, who has been reading my story, fears my readers may get a wrong impression of ex-prisoners from the stories of Tim, Boggs, Pedro and the other weak ones. There are some really bad ones who make good, and as he regarded himself as one of the most hopeless that ever came out of prison he has written me the following letter:

Dear Friend of Mine: The last chapters of your story, portraying the "nuts" that have ripened on your ranch, have got me so wrought up that I feel I must express myself.

Your name is at the top of this letter, but I suspect I am writing to myself. You may never get it. It may prove to be one of those things we write after midnight and tear up after breakfast. Your collection of "nuts" would not be complete without me, and I want to sign up right here and now.

Your stories take me back thirteen years. Do you remember our meeting at the Ingleside jail, where you visited me at Lowrie's request? You did not ask me if I were guilty, or if I wanted to go to work, or if I thought I could make good. You said, "What can I do?"

I told you that nothing could be done; that I was convicted of highway robbery; that I had committed the still greater crime of retaining a highway lawyer to object and obstruct and delay the swift and sure processes of justice. I told you I was plastered over with prior convictions; that the police hated me, not for the things I had done, but for not pleading guilty and saving them the bother of proving them.

I told you the judge was sore, the police were sore, and the jailers were sore, and I was sore; that the whole thing was a hopeless muddle. I told you I was a complete criminal and glad of it. I told you to look on the jail register and you would find a line under my name in red ink which meant I had committed the one unforgivable crime in a jail—I had tried to escape.

You said, "It looks pretty tough, but I'll try." I've often wondered what the judge said when you approached him for me. He probably thought you were crazy. You did try, and you learned that nothing could be done and told me so.

But your trying meant as much to me as if you had succeeded. When you were unable to help me. I realized that it was tough indeed, and I said to myself, "Here's where I make them put another red line under my name," and so, with the help of friends from life's other side, I left the jail by the window—and began again where I left off.

Soon came the inevitable "pinch," and I found myself back in San Francisco. You came again, saying, "What can I do?" This time you did do something. You got my sentence changed from twenty-five years to one year.

Dear friend, that one year, the minimum, stopped me, and whatever I've done in the way of redeeming myself dates from the day I got that one year. It was the first time I ever got anything but the worst of it in a court of law. When I first met you, my mind was closed against any kindly impulse. I wanted no help except what I could take by myself. When I came back from the year in Quentin, my mind was open. I went to you, and then to your country place for six months. It is the only six months of my life I would care to live over again. Mrs. Older, little Mary, and yourself "eased" me away from the last bitter thought. And one day when you said you had a job for me in town, I was surprised to feel that I rather liked the notion of going to work. I had for twenty years been sidestepping work, not that I was lazy, but that there was "no class" there. That's twelve years ago. It did not take me long to learn working. Now I like it, and there isn't a day's work out of which I don't get a "kick."

Enough of this "I" and "me" stuff. I must get to the point. You have a big, true story. Tell your readers how to help the under dog. They are willing, but they don't know how.

Policemen, prosecutors, judges and jurors will read your story. Tell them the time to start helping the so-called criminal is when he is arrested, not when he is released.

They will never get anywhere so long as the "cop" clubs them with his nightstick and turns them in to a judge who finishes the job by giving them five, ten or twenty years in prison. They are all wrong, and are making it worse.

The "crime" thing is just a boil on the social body. I think it can be corrected, but they will never do it by opening it with a poisoned lancet.

Point out to them the value of probation, of paroles, of kindness and helpfulness to the fellow with a bow-legged mind.

These have been twelve full years for me—a wholesome home and a nice little job. It's true that I had to fight with my two fists to hold that job, but when you get one that way, you hold it.

I called on the judge some time ago, the one who sentenced me. He has traveled some himself in the last twelve years. "What can I do?" he said. I told him there was a boy in his court charged with robbery; that it was a tough case, but not so tough as mine had been. I told him if he could consider favorably a motion for probation for the boy that I would get him a job. The judge said, "I'll try to do something," and he did. The boy is working now and reporting to me.

If there is a thought in this letter that will help you in your fight for the outcast, the ex-prisoner—the prostitute—take it and use it as only you know how. They all love you and are for you, "chaps," "taps," and rawhide riata.

Sincerely,

Jack Black,
Reconstructed Yegg.

CHAPTER XXXVI

A Woman Psychologist On Criminal Abnormality. My Own Changed Point Of View. Sidelights On Modern Justice. Recalling The Mooney Affair. Mooney And Billings Both Serving Life Sentences, Yet Both Are Innocent. Clarence Darrow's Views. What The Scientists Think. My Own Ultimate Conclusions.

I was once discussing criminals with a woman who is an authority on psychology. We were sitting at a table in a restaurant at the time, eating luncheon. She said:

"The trouble is that they are not able to realize anything but the thing they see at the moment. It is a mental lack. All of us have it in some degree.

"For instance, you and I sit here enjoying our food. If there was a starving woman at the next table, a starving woman right under our eyes, we could not eat. We would have to give her our food. Now, if there were starving people at the other end of this room, out of sight, and we knew of them, we would still be unable to eat until we had fed them. Even though we did not see them, if we knew they were there we would be able to visualize them, just as though we did see them.

"But over in Poland and Russia and Palestine there are millions of starving women and children right now. We know it, but still we enjoy our food. That is because, while we know they are starving, we don't realize it. They are too far away. It's good that we can't realize all the misery in the world, for if we could, no human brain could endure it. We would go mad.

"The criminal has this same inability to realize absent objects and facts, but he has it in a greater degree. He knows when he steals that he is doing wrong, he knows that he will probably be caught and sent to prison and made to suffer. But he cannot realize it, any more than we can realize the sufferings of peoples on the other side of the world. All he can see is something he wants, and all he knows is that he wants it. He cannot realize anything else.

"That is what makes the criminal. It is a mental abnormality, just as definite as a crippled arm, only we can't see it as we can see crippled arms."

It may be that this is the explanation. I do not know. I only know that after all my experience with criminals I have come to the conclusion that their minds in some ways work differently from the minds of what we call normal men.

So, while my original opinion about them has changed, it has changed only to increase my abhorrence of our system of punishment for crime. We need the aid of science here. Punishment—revenge—is not the solution of the problem.

In the early days of the graft prosecution I must have had a blind faith that a liberal use of jails and prisons was all that was needed to rid San Francisco of corruption. Although I had lived nearly fifty years I still clung to that belief. Nor had I at that time any knowledge of the subtleties of the mind nor of the motives that govern human beings, those hidden impulses that lie so deeply buried in us all.

Here were a corrupt Mayor, a corrupt political boss, and a corrupt Board of Supervisors selling franchises and privileges to the highest bidders. The city had been betrayed. The betrayers must be brought to justice and swiftly punished. What else could be done? A long term in the penitentiary for each one of them. Then honest men of our selection would take their places. The evil ones in stripes, the good enthroned, the millennium! Some such picture as that must have formed itself in my mind. No doubt the others I worked with were seeing a similar picture. It was to be a "holy war" and a relentless one.

We had gained control of the District Attorney's office, and with two of the Superior Court judges fired with the crusading spirit, the Good, with banners flying, set out after the Wicked. My story has told you what happened. By the merest fluke we got Ruef, the corrupt boss, into the penitentiary on a fourteen-year sentence, and Peter Claudianos, a Greek boy, sentenced for life. Claudianos was employed by the wealthy defendants to dynamite the home of the chief witness.

This was the harvest gathered by us after several years of work. We made much noise, created some dramatic situations and furnished interesting "copy" for the newspapers and magazines, but we did not stop graft, nor were we crowned as the saviors of mankind by grateful, high-minded citizens. On the contrary, we were ostracized and shunned by the rich and powerful. If our intensive activities through the years accomplished any permanent good, I have not been able to discover it. Possibly they may have rendered public officials a little more cautious, but I am not sure they even accomplished that much.

After it was all over, I asked Francis J. Heney what

his conclusions were as to the effect of the prosecutions and he replied that if he had it to do over again he would not undertake to prosecute any one if he could avoid it.

"I think a better method would have been to have allowed them all to confess before the Grand Jury. In that way I could have taken their stories under oath and given them the widest publicity, so that the public would understand what was going on in their community. I believe that would have been the better way." Such was Heney's reaction at the end, after all those grilling, terrible years; deaf in one ear from a bullet fired into his head by a crazy tool of the defendants.

In the light of what seems true to me now, I find it difficult to understand how I could have been so blind in those days. The explanation may be that I stubbornly refused to analyze my own motives, fearing I should endanger my peace of mind by discovering that they were too much like those of the men I was fighting. They, too, were striving for success, as I was, and using methods not much worse than mine. But if this thought had come into my mind at that time I would not have dared express it to those who were working with me. They would not have understood, and no doubt would have attributed my attitude to cowardice or something worse.

Later, when the new point of view took possession of me, I determined to express what I believed to be true, and in a page editorial asked for mercy for Ruef. I was widely and severely criticized by those earnest followers of the graft prosecution. They were indignant. I had betrayed them in what they considered a noble cause and had fallen down in the midst of a heroic battle. To them

Ruef symbolized all that was evil in the world. There could be no good in him, and they doubtless regretted, as I did at the time, that the law limited his sentence to fourteen years. Nothing short of a life sentence would even have approximated justice to any one of us at that time.

Governor Johnson shared this feeling and was greatly incensed when I started the movement for Ruef's parole. It was not until Ruef had been sent over to the penitentiary and had been shaved, photographed, striped, numbered and thrown into a dirty cell that I fully realized what I had done. The change in my mind came suddenly, and it was only a day or two later that the big editorial, asking for Ruef's parole, appeared in the *Bulletin*.

All through the many prosecutions we inaugurated was the constant fear of the action of the upper courts. They had it in their power to undo all we had done, and in some instances they set aside our most important convictions. More than anything else that happened, the attitude of the higher courts inflamed us. We suffered days of torture and sleepless nights. It seems strange to me now that we should not have known that they would act so. But perhaps we did not fully realize that judges, after all, are only human beings, and that it was perfectly natural that they should line up, like the rest of the town, with the side that represented their class.

This truth became even more clear and painful to me in the summer of 1916, when Mooney and Billings were arrested and charged with throwing a bomb that killed and wounded a number of people, spectators at the Preparedness Day parade. The zeal earlier displayed to exonerate the big grafters was changed now to a passion to convict, class feeling still expressing itself. This crime was destined to place me in a far more unpleasant position with the articulate part of the community than I had been in when the graft fight was at its height.

The parade was on a Saturday, and on the previous Thursday evening there had been a big mass meeting at Dreamland Rink to protest against this Government entering the World War. It had been promoted under my auspices, and I had worked up the meeting through a free use of the columns of the *Bulletin*. At this meeting one of the wildest of the speakers quoted Bernard Shaw, who had said, in a published article, that the way to end the war was for the men to "shoot their officers and go home." Fortunately no special emphasis was placed on this remark in the newspapers the following day, but after the bomb explosion it was remembered by some of the newspaper men and was effectively used to make it appear that those who were responsible for the mass meeting at least had a foreknowledge of the crime that was to be perpetrated on the following Saturday. This theory, which, despite its absurdity, had grown into a belief with many people, was strengthened by an anonymous letter which was received in each newspaper office on Friday, the day before the explosion. This letter declared something would happen that would "echo around the earth."

As soon as I received my warning letter on Friday, I at once sent it to the chief of police and urged him to watch closely the I. W. W. hall on Seventeenth street. I feared something might happen. I did not have long to wait. Shortly after the parade started, in my room in the *Bulletin* office I heard the dull boom of an explosion.

A few minutes later a reporter 'phoned in the news of the bomb outrage. I told Carl Hoffman, the city editor of the *Bulletin* at that time, that I would be blamed for it.

I left the city for my home in Santa Clara county on the usual afternoon train, taking with me Hoffman and our editorial writer, Robert L. Duffus. During the discussion on the train I said I believed Tom Mooney and his crowd had thrown the bomb.

"Why do you think so?" the others asked.

"By a process of elimination," I answered. "I have a wide acquaintance with the so-called radicals in the town, and Mooney is the only one I can think of who would be rash enough to do it."

My friends agreed with me. Later, when Mooney and Billings were arrested and charged with the crime, I still held to that belief. I had no interest in their cases when they came up for hearing in the lower courts or when they later came to trial. I instructed the men who were reporting the trial to avoid writing anything that would give color to the idea of the innocence of the defendants. I was, of course, severely criticized by Mooney's friends. Worse even, I was accused of having sold them out at this critical moment, thus betraying Labor.

I even reproached Maxwell McNutt for acting as their attorney.

"I know they are innocent," was his answer.

"I don't believe a word of it," I hotly replied. Noticing that my remark disturbed him, I softened it by saying, "I do believe, however, Maxwell, that you have been convinced by them of their innocence; but I am sure you have been misled."

I did not waver in this belief until Andrew Furuseth, a Labor leader in whom I had perfect confidence, called at my office. He had just returned from an Eastern visit, and while in Chicago he said he had seen some letters which had convinced him of Mooney's innocence. From memory he told me the contents of them. They were the now famous letters that Oxman, the Oregon cattleman, whose testimony convicted Mooney, had written Rigall, an old Illinois friend of his.

In them he urged Rigall to come to San Francisco and testify in the Mooney case. Rigall came, and at his first meeting with Oxman the cattleman told him he wanted him to testify that he was in San Francisco the day of the parade and saw him, Oxman, on Market street near the scene of the bomb explosion.

"I can't do that," Rigall replied. "I wasn't there on that day. I was at Niagara Falls."

"You were here as much as I was," replied Oxman.

Shortly after Furuseth left my office, the attorneys for Mooney showed me the copies of the Oxman letters and in a day or two the original ones came. As soon as an expert had declared they were in the handwriting of Oxman, I published them in an extra edition of the *Bulletin,* with a headline reaching across the top of the page reading, "FICKERT FRAMED THE MOONEY CASE."

This publication created a sensation and intensified the feeling against me. The Law and Order Committee, consisting of the most powerful men in the city, had decided I was a disturbing influence in the community and should either be shorn of my power on the *Bulletin* or driven from the city. This was to be brought about by a concerted withdrawal of all the advertising from the columns of the *Bulletin*. This procedure was threatened, but wiser counsel finally prevailed and it was not done.

At this time my power in the *Bulletin* office was at its lowest ebb. R. A. Crothers and Loring Pickering, the two owners, turned against me and appeared before a meeting of the Law and Order Committee, apologized for me, and promised that thereafter nothing would be published about the Mooney case. But this did not stop my investigations. I continued them with even greater activity until I had established before the San Francisco Grand Jury that Oxman, who had testified he saw Mooney and the rest of the defendants drive up in an automobile near where the bomb exploded, was not in the city at all at that time. He was standing at the station in Woodland, waiting for a train to arrive to take him to San Francisco.

It was also established that John McDonald, whose direct testimony, next to Oxman's, was the most effective in the conviction of Mooney, had testified falsely. He was later brought to San Francisco, and, under oath, in the presence of the District Attorney, confessed that all of his testimony was false. The others were equally discredited.

It was ultimately revealed that the only reliable evidence given in any of the cases was the testimony of the man who made the blue-prints of Market street.

That these two men are entirely innocent of the crime is now known all over the world. No one who has heard the facts doubts it, yet Mooney and Billings are both serving life sentences, one in Folsom and the other in San Quentin, and the state seems willing that they should remain there until they die. Search criminal history back, down through the Dark Ages, and a more glaring and cruel case of injustice cannot be found. Any one who has a tendency toward pessimism, and in his gloomiest moments declares the human race incapable of any real progress, can find in the Mooney case some justification for his belief.

The little faith in human nature that I had left after the failure of the graft prosecution was considerably lessened by my experience in trying to bring about the release of these men. It was lessened still more when I discovered that ten of the twelve prominent local Labor leaders were either actively conniving at keeping these men in prison or doing nothing to help them. This threw me into a despondent mood. I had learned to expect that kind of attitude from the rich and powerful and those who fawned upon them, but to find the foremost local leaders of Labor either acting or thinking with them was more than I could calmly bear. I remember writing my thoughts to Clarence Darrow when they were at their darkest. I will quote his reply:

"Of course, my dear Older, I feel as hopeless as you do about things; but of course we had no right to expect that a man was anything but a man, or could ever be anything else. His status, capacities, feelings are all as fixed as the monkey's. He has never been different, never will be, and never can be. But I presume you and I will go on dreaming to the end."

It was at this time I began eagerly reading all the books I could find on psychology, or human behavior. Among them, I remember, were Trotter's "Instincts of the Herd," Dr. Berman's "Glands Regulating Personality," and John Dewey's "Human Nature and Conduct." There were many others, but these three made the greatest impression upon my mind and seemed more nearly to corroborate my feelings as to the hopelessness of trying to change human nature.

Dewey, probably the most profound American psychologist now living, has not much hope. He says:

"Up to the present time we have depended upon the clash of war, the strain of revolution, the emergence of heroic individuals, the impact of migrations generated by war and famine, the incoming of barbarians to change established institutions. . . .

"We cannot breed in men the desire to get something for as nearly nothing as possible and in the end not pay the price."

He thinks something might be done by more enlightened education of the young, but he is not very hopeful, probably less so than he permits any one to know.

Dr. Berman thinks our conduct is regulated by our ductless glands, and if our conduct is bad it is because the thyroid, the pituitary or some other gland is out of order. If he is right, then no one is to be blamed for anything.

Absorbing the thoughts of these men has had a calming influence upon me, which fits in nicely with my advancing years. Losing my faith in the ability of man to change much has not made me cynical. His helplessness and his inability to do any better than he does incline me toward a greater pity and compassion for all mankind. From being a savage fighter against wrong and injustice as I saw them in the old days, I have gone clear over to the point where I do not blame any one for anything. I believe at all times man does the best he is capable of at the moment. It may be a very bad best, but it is HIS best. If I continue to progress along these lines, and live long enough, I may yet be able to pass what I consider the supreme test—TOLERANCE FOR THE INTOLERANT.